# KINGS, QUEENS, BONES AND BASTARDS

❧ ❧

Who's Who in the English Monarchy
from Egbert to Elizabeth II

# KINGS, QUEENS, BONES AND BASTARDS

Who's Who in the English Monarchy
from Egbert to Elizabeth II

DAVID HILLIAM

SUTTON PUBLISHING

First published in 1998 by
Sutton Publishing Limited · Phoenix Mill
Thrupp · Stroud · Gloucestershire · GL5 2BU

Paperback edition first published 1999
Reprinted in 2000 (twice), 2001 (third reprint), 2002, 2003

This new revised paperback edition first published in 2004
Reprinted 2006

British Library Cataloguing in Publication Data
A catalogue record for this book is available from the British Library

ISBN 0 7509 3553 7

Typeset in 10/14pt Sabon.
Typesetting and origination by
Sutton Publishing Limited.
Printed and bound in Great Britain by
J.H. Haynes & Co. Ltd, Sparkford.

# CONTENTS

# PREFACE

This is an account of all the reigning kings and queens of England, including the 'Protectors', Oliver Cromwell and his son Richard, from Saxon times to the present day. Many history books begin with the reign of William the Conqueror, but this chronicle starts with the Saxon King Egbert, who reigned from AD 802 to 839 and is considered to be the first 'King of the English' (*Rex Anglorum*). Indeed, although some of the details about these early kings are difficult to verify, even so the line of the English monarchy can be traced back with some certainty over more than 1,200 years to King Egbert (see Appendix, pp. 239–41).

The famous and not so famous strengths and successes of each of these monarchs are recounted, as well as their flaws and indiscretions, most of which are far more well known than any of their achievements. It picks over skeletons that have already been displayed for all the world to see, as well as unearthing a few that had been stashed at the back of the royal closet.

Also included is a chapter dedicated to queens and consorts, who are usually completely ignored unless they happen to have been beheaded, or have met with some other unseemly demise. The collection of short biographies shows that they deserve much more attention, for they were often remarkable personalities in their own right.

Bones and burial places hold a curious if macabre fascination. They remind us that even the greatest monarch will eventually crumble to dust and lose his power for ever. Here is an account of what has happened to the mortal remains of the men and women who once shaped the course of English history. Their bones have been venerated, lost, broken up, stolen, even boiled and a fair few flung into rivers and bogs. Fate has not always been kind to them.

Fate was also usually unkind, if not downright unpleasant, to the not so proper companions and offspring of kings. Most kings have had mistresses. And most mistresses have produced bastards. The extra-marital exploits of English kings (and some queens) provide an astonishing sub-plot to the more predictable history of battles and torture and death. Very few of our kings have been faithful to their wives; many have had illegitimate children; some have been homosexual; some have been almost compulsively promiscuous. One took a vow of chastity. In the final chapter here at least some of the facts are revealed.

# THE DISTANT PAST: ROMANS TO SAXONS

## JUST AFTER THE ROMANS LEFT BRITAIN

The history of Britain immediately after the Romans departed is rather shadowy and confusing. When the last Roman ship left these shores about AD 410 there was an awkward power-vacuum. Total chaos prevailed, and various petty chieftains squabbled among themselves for tiny kingdoms. About forty years later one of these rulers, Vortigern, was so desperate to beat off some northern tribesmen who were troubling him that he imported allies from the continent to help. This was the beginning, for not only did they come but they stayed – boatload after boatload of eager immigrants: Angles, Saxons, Jutes, Frisians, Franks. The Anglo-Saxon invasion had begun.

The native Britons, or Celts, were pushed further and further into the fringes of the British Isles – into Cornwall, Wales, Scotland. Meanwhile there was a frantic free-for-all as the marauding Saxons seized whatever bits of land they could. Naturally, there was opposition from the Celts, and the almost legendary King Arthur was one of those who led them in trying to beat off the advancing Saxons. However, nothing could stop them arriving and settling.

After a century or so, in about AD 550, there were probably as many as a thousand little Saxon 'kingdoms', some only a few square miles in area. There's very little to see nowadays as a reminder of those years, but we do have some clues about the local chieftains of that time in the place-names which still survive.

## INGS BEFORE KINGS

Look on a map of England and see what a large number of towns and villages have names ending in –ING, or –INGHAM, or –INGTON. The word *ingas* meant 'family' or 'followers', so a chief's name (say, Tota, Wocca, Haefer, or Padda) would be perpetuated in the name of the spot

1

where his boat landed or where he carved out his little kingdom, and this would be followed by –ING to show that Tota's family or Wocca's followers had settled there with him. Tooting, Woking, Havering and Paddington are typical examples.

A *ham* meant 'home' or 'homestead', and a *tun* was 'enclosure' and later came to mean 'village' or 'town'. So a village with a name such as Washington would suggest that it was the 'town where Wassa's people live'. Old Wassa would have been amazed if he had known how world famous his name would become many centuries later!

Gradually, these tiny settlements grouped into larger units and eventually, in the sixth century, seven major Anglo-Saxon kingdoms emerged. And then, in the year 825, these seven kingdoms at last became united under the dominant King Egbert of Wessex, who is therefore regarded as the very first king of a more or less united England. But first, let's look at those seven Saxon kingdoms.

## THE SEVEN SAXON KINGDOMS

The seven Saxon kingdoms each lasted for about three hundred years, until finally King Egbert of Wessex was hailed as 'Bretwalda' or 'sole ruler of Britain' round about the year AD 825. For this reason, Egbert is generally recognised as the first English king, and it is possible to trace a line of descent from him right down to our present Queen Elizabeth II. The seven Saxon kingdoms were: Kent, East Anglia, Essex, Sussex, Mercia, Northumberland and Wessex. The 'sex' part of these names is simply a shortened form of 'Saxon', so that 'Essex' means 'East Saxons', 'Sussex' means 'South Saxons', and 'Wessex', of course, means 'West Saxons'.

KENT is considered to have been the first Saxon kingdom, founded shortly after Vortigern's invitation to the continental communities to come to his aid. The first Kentish kings were the brothers Hengist and Horsa. Unfortunately Horsa was killed in battle, but Hengist ruled Kent from about AD 455 to 488. Thereafter, a line of seventeen Kentish kings ruled this part of England until it acknowledged King Egbert in 825.

EAST ANGLIA had a series of sixteen kings, called 'Wuffings', after their first king, Wuffa. The last king of East Anglia was St Edmund, after whom the city of Bury St Edmunds is named.

ESSEX had a line of fifteen kings before acknowledging Egbert in 825.

SUSSEX had a line of nine kings, but the records are incomplete.

MERCIA's line of kings is also incomplete, but fifteen kings are recorded before Egbert was acknowledged. One of the Mercian kings was the famous and influential King Offa, who constructed a 120-mile long earthwork to protect his kingdom from the Welsh.

NORTHUMBRIA had a line of twenty-five kings until its King Eanred did homage to Egbert in 827.

Finally, WESSEX had its own line of nineteen kings, the last of whom was Egbert himself, who can therefore be seen as the nineteenth king of Wessex as well as the first king of England. Relatively little is known about some of these kings of Wessex, but some of them were great men, who ruled valiantly in difficult times. For your interest, and for the sake of completeness, here is the line of Wessex kings, stretching from the first, Cerdic, to Egbert. ('His' refers to the immediate predecessor.)

## THE KINGS OF WESSEX WERE:

| Monarch | Reigned |
| --- | --- |
| Cerdic (first king of Wessex) | 519–534 |
| Cynric (his son) | 534–560 |
| Ceawlin (his son) | 560–591 |
| Ceol | 591–597 |
| Ceolwulf (his brother) | 597–611 |
| Cynegils | 611–643 |
| Cenwalh (his son) | 643–672 |
| Seaxburgh (his wife) | c. 672–674 |
| Cenfus (grandson of Ceolwulf) | 674 |
| Aescwine (his son) | 674–676 |
| Centwine (brother of Cenwalh) | 676–685 |
| Cadwalla (desc. from Ceawlin) | 685–688 |
| Ine | 688–726 |
| Ethelheard | 726–740 |
| Cuthred | 740–756 |
| Sigeberht | 756–757 |
| Cynewulf | 757–786 |
| Beohrtric | 786–802 |
| Egbert | 802–839 |

Including these early Wessex rulers, then, the line of succession of English monarchs stretches from Cerdic to the House of Windsor. This is a time-span of almost fifteen centuries.

# NINE DYNASTIES OF ENGLISH MONARCHY

⫷⫸ ⫷⫸

To get an overall picture of the long line of English kings and queens, perhaps it's convenient to think in terms of nine dynasties. Each has its own special quality. The word 'dynasty' itself is rarely used today, but a visitor to Britain will surely come across references to the following names of royal families. To begin with, then, we'll list the dynasties and their monarchs, and this will give you a useful basic check-list of British royalty. The dates given are the years during which the monarchs actually reigned. ('His' and 'her' refer back to the immediate predecessor.)

## 1. SAXON KINGS OF ENGLAND

As has been explained, King Egbert was the first king to be considered as the ruler of all England. Including Egbert, there were seventeen Saxon kings of England before William the Conqueror. After fifteen of these, the line was temporarily broken by four Danish kings. Then the Saxon kings were restored. Strictly speaking, these Saxon kings do not constitute a 'dynasty' as they did not always follow as a hereditary blood-relationship. However, they do constitute an easily understood line of rulers.

### THE SAXON KINGS WERE:

| Monarch | Reigned |
| --- | --- |
| Egbert | 802–839 |
| Ethelwulf (his son) | 839–858 |
| Ethelbald (his son) | 858–860 |
| Ethelbert (his brother) | 860–865 |
| Ethelred I (his brother) | 866–871 |
| Alfred the Great (his brother) | 871–899 |

| Monarch | Reigned |
|---|---|
| Edward the Elder (his son) | 899–924 |
| Athelstan (his son) | 924–939 |
| Edmund I (his half-brother) | 939–946 |
| Edred (his brother) | 946–955 |
| Edwy (his nephew) | 955–959 |
| Edgar (his brother) | 959–975 |
| Edward (Martyr and Saint; his son) | 975–978 |
| Ethelred II (the Unready; his half-brother) | 978–1016 |
| Edmund II (Ironside; his son) | 1016 |

## 2. DANISH KINGS OF ENGLAND

The Vikings (Danes and Norwegians) had begun their raids into England in the eighth century, and had conquered and settled in the north and east. At the end of the ninth century they renewed their pressure, and after Ethelred II had fled, Sweyn Forkbeard was acknowledged as king in 1013. He reigned for only a few weeks, and his son, Canute, seized power in 1016 and was crowned in 1018.

### THE DANISH KINGS WERE:

| Monarch | Reigned |
|---|---|
| Sweyn Forkbeard | 1013–1014 |
| Canute (nowadays often spelt Cnut) | 1016–1035 |
| Harold I (Harefoot; his son) | 1035–1040 |
| Hardecanute (his half-brother) | 1040–1042 |

## (1.) SAXON KINGS OF ENGLAND RESTORED

On the death of Hardecanute, his half-brother Edward (the Confessor) returned from his exile in Normandy, and so the Saxon line was restored.

| Edward the Confessor (Saint) | 1042–1066 |
|---|---|
| Harold II (killed at the Battle of Hastings) | 1066 |

## 3. NORMAN KINGS OF ENGLAND

The Battle of Hastings, on 14 October 1066, was the most important single event in the history of England. On that day Harold, the last Saxon king, was killed and William of Normandy seized power. It is generally believed that William had been promised the throne by his uncle, Edward the Confessor. Harold II had also promised to support William's claim, having been tricked and pressurised to do so when he had been shipwrecked in Normandy a few years earlier. Thus William the Conqueror felt that he had a right to the kingdom, as well as proving his authority by overwhelming might. (Note that, at the end of the line, Matilda reigned for a few months in 1141, during her civil war with Stephen.)

### THE NORMAN KINGS WERE:

| Monarch | Reigned |
| --- | --- |
| William I (the Conqueror) | 1066–1087 |
| William II (Rufus; his son) | 1087–1100 |
| Henry I (his brother) | 1100–1135 |
| Stephen (his nephew) | 1135–1154 |
| Matilda; daughter of Henry I | 1141 |

## 4. PLANTAGENET KINGS OF ENGLAND

The Plantagenet dynasty was the longest line in English history, lasting 341 years with fourteen kings. It began with Henry II, who was the son of Count Geoffrey V of Anjou and his wife Matilda, daughter of Henry I and granddaughter of William the Conqueror.

The throne had been promised originally to Matilda, Henry I's daughter, but when Henry died, Matilda's cousin Stephen seized power. Matilda fought fiercely and lengthily to claim what she knew was rightfully hers. For a few months she was actually declared to be 'Lady of the English', but luck was against her, and she reluctantly gave up the struggle. However, a compromise was reached when Stephen's own son died: the crown was to pass to her son, Henry. Accordingly, when Stephen died in 1154, a new dynasty was begun – the Plantagenets. The name 'Plantagenet' comes from the fact that Count Geoffrey used to wear a sprig of yellow broom flower on his helmet as an identifying emblem. The Latin name for broom is *planta genista*.

The Plantagenet family finally lost control of the throne at the Battle of Bosworth in 1485, when the Welshman Henry Tudor overthrew the 'hunchback' Richard III.

## THE PLANTAGENET KINGS WERE:

| Monarch | Reigned |
|---|---|
| Henry II (son of Matilda) | 1154–1189 |
| Richard I (Lion-Heart; his son) | 1189–1199 |
| John (his brother) | 1199–1216 |
| Henry III (his son) | 1216–1272 |
| Edward I (his son) | 1272–1307 |
| Edward II (his son) | 1307–1327 |
| Edward III (his son) | 1327–1377 |
| Richard II (his grandson and son of the Black Prince) | 1377–1399 |
| Henry IV (grandson of Edward III) | 1399–1413 |
| Henry V (his son) | 1413–1422 |
| Henry VI (his son) | 1422–1461 and 1470–1471 |
| Edward IV (his distant cousin) | 1461–1470 and 1471–1483 |
| Edward V (his son; never crowned; king briefly in 1483) | |
| Richard III (his uncle; brother of Edward IV) | 1483–1485 |

# 5. TUDOR MONARCHS OF ENGLAND

The reign of the Tudor monarchs coincided with the conclusion of the Middle Ages and the beginning of the modern world. Theirs was the age of discovering new lands, the age of new thinking, the Reformation and the Renaissance. The setting-up of the printing press in England by Caxton came only just a few years before Henry Tudor's triumph at the Battle of Bosworth in 1485.

Richard III became increasingly unpopular. He had been 'Protector' or regent of England at the death of his brother, Edward IV, as the latter's rightful heir, Edward V, was only thirteen years of age at the time. However, Richard quickly had himself crowned king, and the boy-king

Edward and his younger brother mysteriously 'disappeared' in the Tower of London, almost certainly murdered on the orders of Richard.

Henry Tudor, Earl of Richmond, spearheaded the nobles' dissatisfaction with Richard's rule. He had no real claim to the throne, although his grandmother had been Queen Catherine, widow of King Henry V. However, he ruled wisely and brought much-needed peace and order to the country.

Included in the Tudor monarchy is the nine-day reign of Lady Jane Grey. Never really a queen, for she was not crowned, Lady Jane was wrongly pushed into prominence in 1553 by her father-in-law, the Duke of Northumberland.

## THE TUDOR MONARCHS WERE:

| Monarch | Reigned |
| --- | --- |
| Henry VII | 1485–1509 |
| Henry VIII (his son) | 1509–1547 |
| Edward VI (his son) | 1547–1553 |
| Lady Jane Grey | 1553 |
| Mary I (Edward's half-sister) | 1553–1558 |
| Elizabeth I (her half-sister) | 1558–1603 |

# 6. STUART MONARCHS OF ENGLAND

Elizabeth I died a virgin. It was not until she was lying on her deathbed that she whispered, almost incoherently, whom she wished to succeed her. It was to be King James VI of Scotland. He was the son of Queen Elizabeth's Catholic cousin, Mary, Queen of Scots. Accordingly, James VI of Scotland was crowned James I of England in 1603, and he was king of both countries.

The Stuarts were perhaps the unluckiest dynasty, and Charles I was driven from power by the Parliamentarians in the Civil War. Ultimately, he was beheaded, and the country was ruled by Parliament and the 'Protector', Oliver Cromwell, who was succeeded by his son, Richard Cromwell, in 1658. Richard Cromwell was not strong enough to cope with the task, and the intolerable chaotic situation called for the 'Restoration' of the monarchy.

## THE STUART MONARCHS WERE:

| Monarch | Reigned |
|---|---|
| James I | 1603–1625 |
| Charles I (his son; executed in 1649) | 1625–1649 |
| Parliament | 1649–1653 |
| (Oliver Cromwell | 1653–1658) |
| (Richard Cromwell (his son) | 1658–1659) |
| Charles II (son of Charles I) | 1660–1685 |
| James II (his brother) | 1685–1689 |
| William III and Mary II (jointly) (Mary was James II's daughter) | 1689–1694 |
| William (alone, after Mary's death) | 1694–1702 |
| Anne (Mary's sister) | 1702–1714 |

# 7. HANOVERIAN MONARCHS OF ENGLAND

Queen Anne, the last Stuart monarch, tried desperately to produce an heir, but all of her eighteen children were either stillborn or died shortly afterwards. When Queen Anne herself died there was no immediately obvious successor. An Act of Parliament prevented (and still prevents) any Catholic or even anyone married to a Catholic from becoming sovereign of England. Strictly speaking, from the hereditary point of view, the throne should have been offered to the Catholic descendants of James II, but the fact that they were Catholics made this impossible.

The nearest Protestant claimant, therefore, was found to be George, son of Sophia, wife of the Elector of Hanover and granddaughter of James I. Accordingly, George was invited to come to England in 1714 to become its king.

## THE HANOVERIAN MONARCHS WERE:

| Monarch | Reigned |
|---|---|
| George I (great-grandson of James I) | 1714–1727 |
| George II (his son) | 1727–1760 |
| George III (his grandson) | 1760–1820 |
| George IV (his son) | 1820–1830 |
| William IV (his brother) | 1830–1837 |
| Victoria (his niece and granddaughter of George III) | 1837–1901 |

Queen Victoria married Prince Albert of Saxe-Coburg-Gotha, so the next two kings briefly constituted a new line.

## 8. SAXE-COBURG-GOTHA MONARCHS OF ENGLAND

| Monarch | Reigned |
|---|---|
| Edward VII (Victoria's son) | 1901–1910 |
| George V (his son) | 1910–1936 |

## 9. THE HOUSE OF WINDSOR

During the First World War the dislike of all things connected with Germany became so intense in England that George V felt it was necessary to abandon all his German titles. Queen Victoria's husband, Prince Albert, had given his family name, Saxe-Coburg-Gotha, to the royal house, but this was no longer regarded as appropriate for an English king. Therefore, in July 1917 King George V announced that henceforth he and his family would adopt 'House of Windsor' as their new dynastic name. It is acknowledged that it was the king's private secretary, Lord Stamfordham, who first suggested 'Windsor' as a royal surname.

### MONARCHS OF THE HOUSE OF WINDSOR:

| Monarch | Reigned |
|---|---|
| George V (adopting a new name in 1917) | 1910–1936 |
| Edward VIII (his son; not crowned but reigned Jan.–Dec. 1936) | |
| George VI (his brother) | 1936–1952 |
| Elizabeth II (his daughter) | 1952– |

# KINGS AND REIGNING QUEENS OF ENGLAND

❧ ❧

The early kings are remembered for their deeds and battles, but hardly for their personalities. Many were crowned at Kingston upon Thames, where today the stone upon which this crowning ceremony took place can still be seen in the centre of the town. It is an intriguing link with the earliest emergence of the royal succession.

## EGBERT

### *c.* 770–839   REIGNED 802–839

### *Son of Ealhmund of Kent*

Egbert was king of the West Saxons who gradually forced his dominance over the other Saxon kingdoms. He defeated the Mercians at the Battle of Ellandune (near Swindon) in 825 and was acknowledged as 'Bretwalda' or 'King of Britain' by the other Saxon kingdoms south of the Humber at that important date. Various kings of some of these Saxon kingdoms continued to exist, so the dominance was not entirely clear-cut; nevertheless, Egbert is considered to be the first overall king of the English. His bones lie in a chest near the altar in Winchester Cathedral.

## ETHELWULF

### *c.* 800–858   REIGNED 839–858

### *Son of Egbert and Redburga*

Crowned at Kingston upon Thames, Ethelwulf had been 'sub-king' of Kent and was Bishop of Winchester for a while. He fought successfully against the Danes, winning a victory at Oakley in Surrey; he also won another battle at sea. He took his son, the future Alfred the Great, on a pilgrimage to Rome and on the way back, aged about fifty-six himself, he married the Emperor Charlemagne's thirteen-year-old granddaughter Judith (his second marriage; his first was to Osburga, daughter of Oslac of Hampshire). When he got back to England he found his son Ethelbald in open revolt, and under pressure he found himself obliged to share the throne with him. He lived for only a further two years.

# ETHELBALD

## c. 834–860    REIGNED 858–860

### Son of Ethelwulf and Osburga

Like his father, Ethelbald was crowned at Kingston upon Thames. He married his father's widow Judith (she was still only fifteen), which shocked his contemporaries, who regarded the marriage as incestuous. His reign and marriage lasted only two and a half years before he died. Ethelbald was buried at Sherborne Abbey in Dorset.

# ETHELBERT

## c. 836–865    REIGNED 860–865

### Son of Ethelwulf and Osburga

Ethelbald's younger brother and sub-king of Kent and Essex, Ethelbert was crowned at Kingston upon Thames. During his reign the Danes were creating havoc in the south-east and destroyed Winchester in 860. Like his predecessor brother, he died young and was buried at Sherborne Abbey.

# ETHELRED I

## c. 840–871    REIGNED 865–871

### Son of Ethelwulf and Osburga

Ethelbert's younger brother was crowned at Kingston upon Thames. Although the name of his wife is not recorded, Ethelred had two children – Ethelhelm and Ethelward. He fought no fewer than eight battles against the Danes, and died of wounds after the Battle of Merton in Oxfordshire.

Perhaps surprisingly, Ethelred I was venerated as a saint, and was held in great esteem because of his piety. The story is told that before the crucial Battle of Ashdown, despite the urgency of the situation he refused to rise from his knees or leave his tent until he had completed hearing the Mass. He said he would not serve man before God.

Ethelred is buried in Wimborne Minster, Dorset, where a Purbeck marble slab is believed to be a part of that which originally covered his grave. Such was his fame that a memorial brass was put in Wimborne Abbey in 1440, six hundred years after his birth – the only memorial brass effigy of an English king.

## ALFRED THE GREAT
### *c.* 849–899    REIGNED 871–899
### *Son of Ethelwulf and Osburga*

The only appropriate title for Alfred is 'the Great'. He was an outstanding Saxon king, and would have made a brilliant monarch in any age. He married Elswitha, and they had two sons and three daughters.

Alfred was born in Wantage, Berkshire. As a boy he travelled twice to Rome and had been an honoured guest of Pope Leo IV, who confirmed him, so he had a broader vision of European culture than most of his predecessors. He was the youngest of the family. Three of his brothers had been Saxon kings before him, then, after helping his brother King Ethelred to fight eight battles against the Danes, he had the sadness of seeing him die of wounds after the Battle of Merton. He was elected king over Ethelred's sons.

The first years of his reign were desperate. The Danes were moving further and further into the west of England. In January 878 they made a surprise attack and gained even more territory, so that Alfred had to go into hiding in marshy land near Athelney, in Somerset. This is where the episode of 'Alfred and the cakes' is supposed to have taken place. (Disguised as an ordinary traveller, he stayed for a while in a swineherd's cottage, and after letting some cakes burn, which he had been asked to look after, he earned a sharp rebuke from the swineherd's wife, who of course did not know who he was.) Ironically, the cake story, which is probably invention, is remembered more than many of his real achievements.

Patiently and with great courage and tenacity, Alfred gathered his army together again and fought one of the most important battles in English history, the Battle of Edington, near Westbury in Wiltshire, in May 878. It was ferocious fighting with swords and axes, lasting for many hours. However, the Danes were decisively defeated, and the threat to Wessex was halted. But the most interesting thing about this victory was the way in which Alfred dealt with the defeated Danish leader Guthrum and the remains of his army. Alfred pursued them back to their camp at Wedmore, near Bath, and surrounded them. He had them completely in his power and could have starved or slaughtered every one of them. They begged for mercy and said he could take as many hostages as he liked if only Alfred would let them go. Quite astonishingly, Alfred insisted that Guthrum became baptised as a Christian and stood godfather to him; then he entertained the whole Danish army for twelve days and gave them gifts. After this he let them go and enjoyed peace for fourteen years.

In 886 Alfred captured London and in the subsequent peace treaty allowed the Danes to stay in East Anglia, but Wessex and the south were left to Alfred. In the following years Alfred showed himself to be an imaginative and innovative peacetime ruler; in fact, it has been said that if he had never fought a battle he would still have been one of Britain's greatest kings.

He reorganised the defences of Wessex and set up a rota-system for military service, so that he could always have a standing army and yet men could also get on with their farming or other jobs in peace. He restored fortresses throughout Wessex and caused new ones to be built, thus founding dozens of new towns. These were 'boroughs' (the Saxon word *burh* meant 'fortress'). The largest of these in Wessex was his capital, Winchester.

Realising that the Danes would still attempt further invasions, he built large speedy ships, and successfully fought several sea battles. He is generally regarded as being the 'father of the English navy'.

In addition to all this, Alfred revised the laws of the land; introduced many new ones; invited foreign scholars to his court; encouraged learning and the arts; set in motion the writing of the great *Anglo-Saxon Chronicle*; learnt Latin himself and translated books by Boethius, Bede, Gregory the Great, Orosius and St Augustine; invented a clock made with candles; and started the 'Book of Winchester', which was a survey of the counties, parishes and hundreds into which he divided his kingdom.

Alfred was only fifty when he died in Winchester in 899. A thousand years later his great reign was celebrated by the erection of a magnificent statue in Winchester, his capital city.

His presence is felt there still.

It is sad to record that Alfred's remains have been lost. In the eighteenth century some bones were found in a stone coffin on the site of Hyde Abbey in Winchester. They were tipped out and reburied. A century later they were dug up again, exhibited in London, and then returned to Winchester. They now rest outside the east end of St Bartholomew's Church in that city. . . . But no one will ever know if these are really Alfred's.

# EDWARD THE ELDER
## 870–924   REIGNED 899–924
### *Son of Alfred the Great and Elswitha*

As his predecessors before him, Edward the Elder was crowned at Kingston upon Thames. Like his father, he fought successfully against the Danes, capturing the Danish Five Boroughs of Leicester, Stamford, Nottingham, Derby and Lincoln. He also fortified many other towns. He completely annexed Mercia after the death of his sister Ethelfleda, who had been its ruler.

Edward the Elder probably holds the paternity record among English kings for legitimate children, fathering two sons and a daughter by Egwina; ten children by Elfleda; and five more (including two future kings, Edmund I and Edred) by Edgifu. Edward the Elder is also believed to have had a bastard son, Gregory, who later became Abbot of Einsiedlen in Germany.

He died in Farndon-on-Dee, Cheshire, and was buried in Winchester. He was succeeded by his eldest son, Athelstan.

# ATHELSTAN
## *c.* 895–939   REIGNED 924–939
### *Son of Edward the Elder and Egwina*

Crowned at Kingston upon Thames, Athelstan was the first undisputed king of all England; the Welsh and Scottish kings also paid him homage.

He arranged politically advantageous marriages for his sisters: one of them to the Holy Roman Emperor Otto the Great; another to Hugh Capet of France; and another to King Charles of the West Franks. He was a great king, giving hospitality to other kings, passing humane laws, introducing a national coinage, and administering the unified country with skill.

Athelstan died on 27 October 939 and was buried at Malmesbury, north Wiltshire. He was unmarried and was succeeded by his half-brother, Edmund.

## EDMUND I (THE ELDER)

### *c.* 921–946   REIGNED 939–946

*Son of Edward the Elder and Edgifu*

Edmund I was only eighteen when he was crowned at Kingston upon Thames, and he was only twenty-five when he was involved in a brawl and stabbed to death by Leofa, an outlawed thief. His reign, though brief, was nevertheless full of incident and he had fought successfully against the Vikings in the Midlands and Northumbria.

He married twice: firstly, (Saint) Elgifu, by whom he had two sons, Edwy and Edgar; and secondly, Ethelfled of Damerham. His premature death occurred in Pucklechurch, Gloucestershire, on 26 May 946, and he was buried at Glastonbury in Somerset. His brother, Edred, succeeded him.

## EDRED

### 923–955   REIGNED 946–955

*Son of Edward the Elder and Edgifu*

Crowned at Kingston upon Thames, Edred's relatively short reign saw much fighting, especially in the north, where he fought the Dane Eric Bloodaxe. He managed to establish dominance in Northumbria when Eric Bloodaxe was killed in battle in 954.

Edred was advised by St Dunstan, Abbot of Glastonbury, to help establish monastic centres of learning. Unmarried, Edred reigned for only nine-and-a-half years. He died on 23 November 955 in Frome, Somerset, and was buried in Winchester. He was succeeded by his nephew Edwy.

## EDWY THE FAIR

### *c.* 940–959   REIGNED 955–959

*Son of Edmund I (the Elder) and Elgifu*

Edwy was only fifteen when he came to the throne, crowned at Kingston upon Thames, and nineteen when he was probably murdered. He was a weak and incompetent youth who would probably have plunged England into chaos if he had lived, but his reign was mercifully brief.

He is notorious for having left the table at his coronation banquet in order to make love to his mistress (another Elgifu, his stepmother's daughter), and had to be brought back and listen to rebukes from

Archbishop Odo. He married the mistress, but then had to banish her because he was related to her, thus making the marriage illegal.

He exiled the famous church leader Dunstan; lost control of Mercia and Northumbria; and was finally forced to give up his throne to his younger brother Edgar. He died at Gloucester on 1 October 959.

# EDGAR THE PEACEFUL
## *c. 944–975*   REIGNED 959–975
### *Son of Edmund I (the Elder) and Elgifu*

Edgar was successful in many ways and brought stability and prosperity to the country. He was fortunate in having good advisers; St Dunstan, whom he brought back from exile to become Archbishop of Canterbury; St Oswald, Archbishop of York; and St Aethelwold, the Bishop of Winchester.

Edgar made a point of strengthening the Church, and founded forty religious houses, encouraging learning and culture. He deliberately delayed his coronation until 973 and then held a magnificent ceremony in Bath. This coronation service, devised by St Dunstan, was the first to include the practice of anointing the monarch, with the Biblical words, *Zadok the priest and Nathan the prophet anointed Solomon king* being said or sung. This same service has been used by every English monarch since Edgar's coronation in 973. Later that year the famous incident took place when he was rowed in state on the River Dee by seven Welsh and Scottish kings (Malcolm of Strathclyde, Kenneth II of Scotland, Maccus of the Isle of Man, and various Welsh kings). This publicity stunt was a memorable public relations exercise which has been depicted again and again over the centuries.

Edgar ruled over a peaceful and united country, dying on 8 July 975. He was buried at Glastonbury Abbey, Somerset, and was succeeded by Edward the Martyr, his only son by his first wife, Ethelfled. Edgar also had a daughter, Edith, by Wulfryth, although it is unclear whether she was a mistress or his second wife. His third wife, Elfrida, bore him two sons, Edmund Aetheling and Ethelred, who became Ethelred II (the Unready).

# EDWARD THE MARTYR

## *c. 963–978   REIGNED 975–978*

### *Son of Edgar I (the Peaceful) and Ethelfled*

Edward was about twelve when his father Edgar died and was king for less than three years. He too was crowned at Kingston upon Thames. He was murdered, on 18 March 978, probably on the orders of his stepmother, Elfrida, when he went to visit her at Corfe Castle. Her motive was that she wanted to place her own son Ethelred on the throne.

The murder was a bloody affair, and shortly afterwards miracles were reported to have happened at his tomb, which led to his becoming known as Saint and Martyr. He was buried first at Wareham without any royal honours, and then, when the miracles began to occur, it was decided to remove his body for reburial near the high altar in Shaftesbury Abbey.

The solemn transfer from Wareham to Shaftesbury was the occasion of what was probably the greatest religious procession ever to take place in Dorset. The slow cortège took seven full days to cover the 25-mile journey, and further miracles were said to have occurred during that time.

Although King Edward, Saint and Martyr, was of very little importance during his lifetime, his influence continues even today as pilgrims come to visit his modern shrine in Brookwood Cemetery near Woking, Surrey. If Edward's death had been plotted by Elfrida, then the plan worked; his younger half-brother Ethelred (the Unready) was ready enough to succeed him.

# ETHELRED II (THE UNREADY)

## *c. 968–1016   REIGNED 978–1016*

### *Son of Edgar I (the Peaceful) and Elfrida*

Ethelred II was crowned at Kingston upon Thames at the age of about ten. The title or nickname 'The Unready' means that he was *unraed*, which is Saxon for 'ill-advised' or 'lacking advice'. Certainly, he was ill-advised to try to buy off the Danes and Vikings. He spent enormous sums in protection money; then he tried massacring the Danish settlers; finally he had to flee the country when the Danish King Sweyn invaded England.

Sweyn ruled briefly as uncrowned king but soon died. Ethelred was brought back, but then he too died, on 23 April 1016, and was buried in

Old St Paul's in London; the throne passed to his son, Edmund Ironside. Edmund was one of about thirteen children by Ethelred's first wife, Elfled of Northumbria. He had three other children by his second wife, Emma of Normandy, including Edward, later known as Edward the Confessor.

# EDMUND II (IRONSIDE)
### *c*. 992–1016   REIGNED APRIL–NOV. 1016
### *Son of Ethelred (the Unready) and Elfled*

Edmund II was crowned at Old St Paul's Cathedral, London. Struggling against the Danes, he fought four battles, won three, but then was let down by the Mercians and had to partition the country, sharing it with the Danish King Canute, son of Sweyn Forkbeard. Edmund died soon after, on 30 November 1016, probably murdered; he was buried in Glastonbury Abbey. So the throne was left entirely to the Danes, led by King Canute. Edmund's two sons, by his wife Eadgyth, were but infants and were banished.

# SWEYN FORKBEARD
### REIGNED BRIEFLY 1013–1014

Forkbeard was constantly attacking England from about 994 onwards. In 1013 he invaded in earnest, driving Ethelred II temporarily from the throne. He reigned uncrowned for a few weeks only, being killed after falling from his horse. Edmund returned, but Forkbeard's incursions had paved the way for his son, Canute.

# CANUTE
### *c*. 992–1035   REIGNED 1016–1035
### *Son of Sweyn Forkbeard and Gunhild of Poland*

Canute was a great king. Although arguably he was a 'foreign invader', he brought peace and stability to the country and ruled wisely and well. He had fought Edmund Ironside and had forced him to partition the country, but then when Edmund died he was sole ruler for almost twenty years. This rule was supported by the Saxon *Witan* or parliament, and he was crowned in St Paul's in London. He was also King of Norway and Denmark, but spent most of his time in England, living in Winchester, the old capital.

He was a strong believer in Christianity and made a pilgrimage to Rome. The story of 'Canute and the waves', in which he is reputed to have shown his flattering courtiers that even he could not control the tides, is probably the only thing that many people remember about him. In Winchester it is told how, after this episode with the waves, he rode his horse up the aisle of the old Saxon cathedral and placed his golden crown on the high altar, in token that only God was powerful enough to rule the elements.

Canute's first consort was Elfgifu of Northampton. It is unclear whether he married her, but she bore him two sons, including Harold I (Harold Harefoot). A master-stroke was to marry Emma, the widow of Ethelred the Unready, as his second wife, by whom he had Hardecanute and two daughters, Gunhild, and a little unnamed daughter who died, possibly drowned, aged only eight. Her remains lie in Holy Trinity Church, Bosham, Sussex, where her grave is marked by a striking engraving of the black raven – symbol of the ferocious, warlike Danes.

Canute was strong, popular, and maintained good trade relations with the continent. He and Emma lived happily together for seventeen years.

Canute died on 12 November 1035, and his bones still lie in the cathedral at Winchester. After his death the throne passed to his son Harold I ('Harefoot').

# HAROLD I (HAROLD HAREFOOT)
## 1016–1040   REIGNED 1035–1040
### Son of Canute and Elfgifu of Northampton

Harold was crowned at Oxford. His was a short and brutal reign. He exiled his stepmother Emma to Bruges, and is generally believed to have blinded and murdered Ethelred's son Alfred, who was a possible rival to the throne. It was no great loss to the country when he died, aged about twenty-four. He was succeeded by his half-brother, Hardecanute.

# HARDECANUTE
## c. 1018–1042   REIGNED 1040–1042
### Son of Canute and Emma of Normandy

Hardecanute was crowned at Canterbury. Arguably, he should have succeeded his father instead of Harold I, so he showed what he thought of

Harold by digging up his body and throwing it into a bog. He murdered Earl Edwulf of Northumbria; burned the city of Worcester; plundered and taxed his subjects to excess. His name literally meant 'Deadly Cnut': in fact, he was thoroughly hated. He died from a fit while drinking at a wedding feast and was buried at Winchester.

Emma's son, Edward the Confessor, who had been brought up in Normandy, was now invited to become the next king, thus restoring the Saxon line.

# EDWARD THE CONFESSOR
## c. 1004–1066   REIGNED 1042–1066
### Son of Ethelred II (the Unready) and Emma of Normandy

**Perhaps considered slightly eccentric by some, Edward the Confessor has left an indelible mark on English history and was regarded as the Patron Saint of England for many centuries.**

For most people the Saxon kings are only vague, shadowy figures. But Edward, the last of them (if you don't count Harold), has immense importance in English history. Not only was he the founder of Westminster Abbey, the focal point of all our royal coronations, but also he established Westminster Palace, our present seat of government. Today, the Houses of Parliament meet in what is still known as the 'Palace of Westminster' on the very same spot that Edward chose for his London home.

Edward was the child of mixed cultures: his father, Ethelred, was Saxon, but his mother, Emma, was Norman. Ethelred died, and Emma remarried, this time to the fierce Dane, King Canute. Perhaps being tactful, Emma kept young Edward well out of sight, and had him brought up among her own relations in Normandy. Therefore, though Edward was Saxon, his upbringing was essentially Norman, and it was inevitable that he should bring his Norman friends and advisers with him to England when he became king. Duke William of Normandy, soon to become William the Conqueror, was Edward's great-nephew and friend, and it seems that Edward had promised to make William his heir. In fact, this was William's main reason for invading England: to claim what he believed to be his rightful inheritance.

So, what sort of person was Edward? Well, he seems to have been something of an oddity. Some say that he was an albino, because he had an exceptionally red face and snow-white skin, hair and beard. Certainly he seems to have been rather unworldly and more fitted for the life of a monk than of a king. The very name that people gave him, 'Confessor', suggests that he was regarded more as a priest than as a king. Early on in life he had taken a vow of chastity, and was believed to have refused to consummate his marriage to Edith, daughter of Godwin, Earl of Wessex. Not surprisingly, he had no heir. An early writer tells how he loved talking with monks and abbots, and particularly 'used to stand with lamb-like meekness and tranquil mind at the holy masses'. Perhaps surprisingly to modern minds, he was also a fervent huntsman, 'delighted by the baying and scrambling of the hounds'.

At any rate, Edward enjoyed rather a relaxed lifestyle, leaving the business of governing and keeping order very largely to others while he occupied himself with his new abbey and palace near London. Interestingly, the very name 'Westminster' means the 'monastery in the west', and that is how Londoners of his time regarded it, as it was well outside the city walls. Edward lived to see the completion of the abbey, but he was far too ill to attend its opening ceremony on 28 December 1065. He died only a few days later, early in the fateful year 1066.

During his lifetime Edward acquired an awesome reputation for holiness and for being able to heal people by laying his hands on them. He began the royal custom of touching people suffering from a skin disease known as 'the King's Evil'. There is a description of this in Shakespeare's *Macbeth*, and the custom lasted, off and on, right into the eighteenth century. Queen Anne was the last monarch to practise this.

In 1163, almost a century after his death, Edward was formally proclaimed a saint, and in 1269 his bones were laid in Westminster Abbey in what was then the most sumptuously decorated shrine in the western world. He was England's patron saint for over four centuries, and every year thousands of pilgrims visited his shrine, kneeling each side of it and reaching up to get as close as possible to the body of the saint. Sick pilgrims used to stay overnight near the shrine in the hope of being cured. His cult died out only with the destruction of the monasteries at the time of the Reformation.

Edward the Confessor's bones are still there today, raised high up in the shrine just behind the high altar of Westminster Abbey. In a sense, those bones represent a meeting-point in English history, for Edward was not only great-great-great-grandson of the Saxon king Alfred the Great, but also stepson of the Danish King Canute, and great-uncle of the first Norman king, William the Conqueror.

# HAROLD II

## *c.* 1020–1066    REIGNED JAN.–OCT. 1066

### *Son of Godwin, Earl of Wessex, and Gytha*

**Harold II had no real claim to the throne, but was brother-in-law of Edward the Confessor. He is described as tall, handsome, brave, forceful and strong, with a bold, attractive personality.**

Edward the Confessor died on 5 January 1066 and was buried the following day in his recently completed Westminster Abbey. Immediately after the funeral and with astonishing – arguably unseemly – haste, Harold had himself elected king. Literally within hours he was crowned in the abbey that had just witnessed Edward's burial.

In fact, Harold had no real claim to the throne, except that he was the Confessor's brother-in-law: there were at least three other claimants. There was Edgar the Atheling, for example, descendant of Ethelred the Unready; but then, he was only a boy and an easy push-over. Also claiming the throne was Hardrada, King of Norway; but he was miles away, and though he was likely to cause trouble, Harold guessed that it would be at least a month or two before Hardrada could press his claim. And finally, of course, there was Duke William of Normandy.

William's claim was rather more embarrassing, for it was generally believed that Edward the Confessor had made some sort of promise to his nephew William to make him his heir. But there was another promise that was even more difficult to forget: it was well known that Harold himself had personally and publicly promised William that he would support his claim to the English throne. And a promise is a promise. The occasion when Harold made that promise is depicted for all to see on the Bayeux Tapestry. The Normans naturally wanted to give it as much publicity as possible, for it legitimised their conquest.

What had happened was that Harold, high-born and in command of the Saxon armies under the 'lamb-like' Edward the Confessor, had been unfortunate enough to be shipwrecked on the shores of Normandy. It was inevitable that Harold should be given hospitality by William, but both men knew they were rivals, and Harold was in William's power. It was a tense situation. After maintaining civilities for a few days, William demanded a public oath of loyalty from Harold. Obviously, in the circumstances Harold simply had to comply.

No one who was present at that oath-ceremony was likely to forget it.

William sat on his throne as Duke, while all around him stood his barons, knights, churchmen and priests. In the centre of the room was a holy book, a missal, resting on an old chest which was covered by a rich piece of cloth. Watched by everybody, Harold moved forward, put his hand on the chest and swore a solemn oath of loyalty to William as heir to the throne of England. 'So help me God,' he declared. It was William who then moved forward and with a fine sense of drama pulled away the concealing cloth to reveal a precious casket filled with holy relics of Norman saints – a spine-chilling collection of sacred bones, a skull, a grisly dried finger. Instantly, Harold realised how he had been tricked, for his oath had been made in the holiest and most binding circumstances possible. He would be a traitor before God if ever he went back on his solemn words. William let Harold go. Within weeks King Edward the Confessor had died and the throne of England was vacant. And, despite his oath, Harold moved with unholy speed to have himself elected and crowned king. This then, was the situation at the beginning of the year 1066.

Of course, it is possible to excuse Harold for breaking his promise because he gave it under duress. And as for taking the throne, it was clearly as the result of a free election among his Saxon peers. After all, Harold was well respected, he had been in charge of the army for thirteen years and had performed excellent service. He was officially known as 'Subregulus' or 'Under-king'. Nevertheless, the speed with which he was crowned and the solemn oath he had sworn before God gave considerable cause for alarm.

When Easter came Harold wore his crown in public. What would God do? Surely some sign of the Almighty's anger would be seen. An oath had been made in His name. People waited anxiously. . . . And they did not wait in vain. Just a few weeks afterwards a horrible portent appeared: a huge streak of fire resembling a flaming sword hung in the clear night skies. Seven nights it showed itself. God had spoken. Not realising that it was one of the periodic visits of Halley's comet, priests hastened to their churches and offered special prayers for safety, and monks and prophets foretold doom and disaster.

It was in this context that Harold began to receive news that both William in the south and Hardrada in the north were plotting independently to invade England and defeat him. Even worse, his own younger brother, Tostig, was planning to join forces with Hardrada. The problem was acute: who would strike first – William or Hardrada?

In the event, it was Hardrada. Quickly, Harold assembled his army and force-marched them northwards at speed. It took him just a few days to reach York on a hot September day, where he learned that Tostig and Hardrada had assembled their men about 8 miles to the east, at Stamford

Bridge. Before dawn on Wednesday 25 September, Harold moved out of York to join battle with his enemies. Briefly, Harold met his brother just before the fighting began, and offered him a third of his kingdom if he would desert Hardrada. 'And what will you give to Hardrada?' asked Tostig. Harold's reply is memorable: 'I'll give him six feet of English earth,' he said, 'or as he's taller than most, I'll give him seven feet, for his grave.' The brothers parted, and on 25 September the bloody Battle of Stamford Bridge was fought. Hardrada and Tostig were both killed, and their whole army was butchered to death, or else taken prisoner and then burnt.

It was while Harold was celebrating his victory back in York that he heard the devastating news that William of Normandy had already landed on the south coast. Remember, Harold had just marched 200 miles from London to fight and win a battle. Now he had to march the same distance back again, and he did it in just four days. Having arrived, and after making this supreme physical effort, he had to organise his troops quickly for yet another march, a mere 60 miles further, down to the coast to meet William.

The Battle of Hastings, a few days later, was the turning-point in English history, and everyone knows its outcome. It is pictured in graphic detail in the Bayeux Tapestry. The artist did not forget to add the fatal comet either. Harold died fighting. Not only was he struck in the eye by an arrow, but he was also run through by two lances and struck on the head by a sword. A group of Norman knights surrounded him and one of them, Ivo of Ponthieu, tried his best to hack off his leg – a needless mutilation. When he heard of it, William ordered Ivo to be stripped of his knighthood.

William was now indeed the Conqueror. In his eyes Harold had been merely a usurper, so did not deserve a royal burial. He was simply placed under a cairn of stones on the cliff-top near the spot where he fell. Thus ended the Saxon kings.

# WILLIAM I (THE CONQUEROR)
## 1027/8–1087   REIGNED 1066–1087
### Son of Robert the Devil and Arlette, a tanner's daughter

**Founder of the Norman civilisation in England, William I (or William the Conqueror) was powerful, dominant, pious and ruthless in imposing law and order. He became obese in his later years.**

William the Conqueror was a bastard – more precisely, he was the illegitimate son of Robert the Devil, Duke of Normandy, and Arlette, the teenage daughter of a local tanner from the little French town of Falaise, where they lived. One day, Robert saw Arlette washing in the river near his castle. She was revealing much of her teenage charms. Robert was only seventeen himself, and he simply couldn't resist her. . . . There was no marriage, but, as the old chronicler wrote, 'in the fulness of time she bore him a son'. William had arrived.

It was left to Arlette to bring up young William, and it must have been a tough upbringing. His father was always away, picking quarrels, fighting off enemies. One day Robert went off on a pilgrimage never to return, so William became Duke of Normandy at the tender age of seven or eight. Three of his guardians were murdered so William had to grow up quickly and learn how to rule Normandy for himself. Almost against the odds he survived, thanks to his sheer physical strength and powerful character.

After a somewhat tempestuous courtship William married his cousin Matilda of Flanders, and they had four sons and six daughters. And unusually for those days he was quite faithful to her. When she died in 1083 aged fifty-one William was so grieved that as a gesture he swore to give up his favourite occupation, hunting, and he kept his vow.

No one will ever know when William conceived his bold plan to invade England, but quite likely his ambition was first aroused when he visited his great-uncle, King Edward the Confessor, fifteen years before the momentous Battle of Hastings. On that visit Edward is supposed to have told William that he would make him his heir. Then there was that memorable occasion when Harold, shipwrecked in Normandy and in William's power, had been 'persuaded' to make a solemn promise to support his claim to the English throne. William must therefore have felt doubly justified in making his invasion plans with the promise made to him by Edward the Confessor, and the solemn oath made to him by Harold. England was his by right. There was no doubt either, after that decisive battle at Hastings, that England belonged to him by force. On Christmas Day 1066 William was crowned in the same new abbey that had already seen the funeral of Edward and the coronation of Harold. Finally, England was his by indisputable law and the ancient ritual of anointment.

The year 1066 is engraved on the minds of many as the date when English history began. And indeed it marks a turning-point in our whole way of life. The Saxon world of Alfred the Great and his successors gave way to the Norman world of William, who brought with him a new language and a new administration of ferocious efficiency. He immediately began a building programme of castles and cathedrals of unparalleled

## THE TOWER OF LONDON

The Tower of London is, in fact, a complex of twenty towers, nineteen of which are built in a huge circle around the main fortress in the middle, which is called the White Tower, because at one time it was coated with whitewash. The White Tower stands on the site of William the Conqueror's first wooden fort, quickly constructed immediately after he had settled here. In 1078 he ordered the building of the present massive stone fortress, which stands 90 feet high and has walls 15 feet thick at the base. No one has ever captured the Tower of London!

The whole collection of towers is permeated with royal associations. The main White Tower served as the royal residence for all medieval kings, but of course became less used as other palaces were built. Other recent towers with special royal memories are the Wakefield Tower, in which Henry VI was murdered; the Bloody Tower, in which the young princes were most probably murdered on orders of Richard III; and the Beauchamp Tower was the prison of Lord Guilford Dudley, who perhaps scratched the name 'Jane' twice on the wall here.

On Tower Green Anne Boleyn, Catherine Howard and Lady Jane Grey were beheaded, and they are buried in the nearby chapel of St Peter ad Vincula. 'Traitors' Gate' was the entrance through which prisoners were brought from the Thames. It was through this waterside gate that the future Queen Elizabeth I was forced to come, weeping and protesting, as her half-sister Queen Mary I ordered her detainment.

In its time the Tower has acted as fortress, palace, storehouse, arsenal, treasury, mint, prison, and even zoo. Henry III kept leopards, a polar bear, an elephant and lions here. In fact, animals were here until 1834, when they were sent to the new zoo in Regent's Park.

magnificence throughout the land. The story of the conquest after 1066 is one also of ruthless force. Local revolts were fiercely suppressed, especially the opposition in East Anglia led by Hereward the Wake. William pushed relentlessly into Wales, into Scotland, and in about six or seven years Norman rule was virtually complete. The 'feudal system' was established.

In order to get a clear idea of what he owned, William ordered a complete inventory of all lands and buildings throughout the kingdom, later to be known as the Domesday Book. It is a remarkable document, a fascinating account of the land which William now held tightly in his conqueror's fist. Then, in 1086 he summoned all landholders to the bleak hill-top fortress of Old Sarum, the old city of Salisbury, to swear allegiance to him in a ceremony we now call the Oath of Salisbury. Oaths were important to William. And to make sure that he had no opposition from the Church, he sacked the old Saxon Archbishop, Stigand, and put Lanfranc in his place, the monk who had negotiated with the Pope about William's marriage to his cousin. Lanfranc quickly transformed the Church along Norman lines.

The Normans were the greatest builders of their time. William's most famous personal contribution is the Tower of London – that is, the massive foursquare building known as the White Tower. And at the same time he also began to build that other great royal residence Windsor Castle, choosing the site himself. Winchester was still the capital of the country, and to make sure that everyone knew that he was king, William had himself re-crowned there almost every Easter, in the Old Minster. Meanwhile, he ordered a vast new cathedral to be built, just alongside the Saxon Old Minster, so that people should recognise that the Old Minster simply wasn't good enough and would be demolished just as soon as the new cathedral was ready. And for his personal pleasure he ordered a large tract of forest near Winchester to be cleared of unnecessary farms and villages. A 'New Forest' would be the king's own hunting-ground. Deer still graze there today.

You might well suppose that William enjoyed a happy and successful reign, but towards the end of his life the reverse is true. His later years were clouded by the rebellions of his eldest son, Robert. What was worse, Matilda, his faithful wife, actually supported Robert against her husband. There were reconciliations, but family atmosphere must have been soured. After a final flaming row, Robert rode off with William roaring curses after him. Matilda retired to Normandy, where she died. And with battles, revolts, family feuds and the death of his wife, the last four years of his life must have been lonely and melancholy for William. He was King of England, but as well as this he was still Duke of Normandy, and his territories were enormous. He must have been forever on horseback.

One day, quarrelling with King Philip of France, who had taunted him for being so fat, and whose soldiers were continually plundering his Norman lands, William's final battle came. Marching on Paris, he had just devastated the little town of Mantes, beside the River Seine. The whole town was in flames and William's successful soldiers were busy pillaging and looting. Then, just as he rode through the ashes in triumph, his horse trod on a burning cinder, reared up and plunged, throwing the corpulent sixty-year-old king forward on to the iron horn of his saddle. He received mortal internal injuries. After six weeks of agony the Conqueror died, still in his native Normandy, in the priory of St Gervais just outside Rouen. His body was taken for burial in the abbey which he himself had built at Caen, where it still remains today.

William had been a ruthless and quick-tempered king, but he had a passion for law and order, so that when he died people spoke of 'the good peace he made in this land so that a man might go the length and breadth of the kingdom with his pockets full of gold . . . and no man durst slay another'. It was a fitting tribute to the unprecedented firmness of rule which William the Conqueror had brought to England.

# WILLIAM II (RUFUS)
## 1056–1100   REIGNED 1087–1100
### Son of William the Conqueror and Matilda of Flanders

**William II, William Rufus, was the third son of the Conqueror. Although described as sadistic, homosexual, ruthless, and an atheist, he was William's favourite son. He got his nickname, Rufus, because of his flaming ginger hair and his ruddy complexion.**

William II was lucky to become king, but it was according to the Conqueror's dying wishes. The eldest son, Robert, received the Dukedom of Normandy; Richard, the second son, had been killed in a hunting accident; Rufus was given the throne of England; and the youngest son, Henry (later to become Henry I), was fobbed off with just £5,000 in silver.

The story of Rufus's reign is a sordid account of rebellions, skirmishes, deceit, broken promises and savage violence. Mutilations were common and horrific. Once, when a nobleman was accused of treason, Rufus had his eyes pulled out and his testicles cut off. No one has spoken well of Rufus, either during his lifetime or since. He sneered at Christianity. When Church posts fell vacant he simply refused to fill them, seizing the money for himself. The Archbishop of Canterbury, the saintly Anselm, preached fiercely against Rufus's homosexual lifestyle, but Rufus was openly contemptuous and made the Archbishop's life so difficult that the poor old man fled to live in Rome. Rufus simply grabbed his property.

One positive and valuable legacy from Rufus, however, is Westminster Hall, for he was directly and personally responsible for this historic building. The great hall, almost 240 feet long and 68 feet wide, was built in 1097–9, and has witnessed countless scenes of royal splendour. The last king to lie in state there was George VI, father of Queen Elizabeth II. Winston Churchill lay in state there when he died in 1965, as did Queen Elizabeth the Queen Mother when she died in 2002. In a famous boast Rufus said that this huge hall was 'a mere bed-chamber' compared with the palace he intended to build beside it. But fate intervened and he was dead before he could even start his new palace.

The death of William Rufus, killed by an arrow in the New Forest, will always remain a mystery. Was it an accident, or was it murder? Certainly, a charcoal-burner called Purkiss found his corpse in a leafy glade, and all the king's hunting-companions had fled. (The man under most suspicion, Sir Walter Tyrell, never returned to England, dying later in the Holy Land.) Purkiss covered the king's body, which still had the arrow sticking out, and trundled it by cart to Winchester. The monks in the cathedral there were terrified to see the king's corpse. They quickly buried it under one of the towers without any of the proper rites of the Church. And when the tower fell down a few years later, everyone was convinced that it was a judgement of God, showing displeasure that such a wicked man as Rufus should have been buried there.

As for Purkiss the charcoal-burner, he was rewarded with an acre or two of land in the New Forest and his descendants lived there well into the nineteenth century. A Purkiss of the eighteenth century is said to have still possessed the axle, made of yew, of the original cart. And there are Purkisses in the area still, claiming lineal descent from the old charcoal-burner who chanced to find the dead king. The place where Rufus is supposed to have been found is marked in the New Forest by a memorial called the Rufus Stone, easily marked for motorists about half a mile off the A34 from Bournemouth to Winchester.

No one mourned Rufus.

# HENRY I

### 1068–1135   REIGNED 1100–1135

*Son of William the Conqueror and Matilda of Flanders*

An excellent administrator, Henry I was nicknamed 'Beauclerc', meaning
that he was well educated, and also 'Lion of Justice', which suggests a love
of law and order. He is described as energetic, opportunistic, determined
and ruthless; and he holds the royal record for illegitimate children.

Henry was the youngest and cleverest of the Conqueror's sons. He ruled England with firmness and skill for thirty-five years, but strictly speaking he had no right to be king at all. When Rufus lay dead in that New Forest clearing, the throne should have passed, by right, to his elder brother, Robert Curthose, and Henry himself must have been acutely aware of this.

However, Henry was a supreme opportunist. He too was in the New Forest on that fatal day, and when he heard of Rufus's death he didn't waste a moment. He galloped as fast as he could first to the royal palace at Winchester, where he demanded the keys to the treasury. Friends of Robert tried in vain to stop him. A crowd gathered, but Henry brandished his sword and swore that he was the rightful heir. Luckily for him he was popular with the majority, and the castle and all its treasure were handed over to him. Then he made the 60-mile dash to London, and in just three days he had himself crowned king. He was aged thirty-one and still unmarried.

Where was Robert Curthose, the rightful claimant to the throne? Well, he was, of course, Duke of Normandy, and it so happened that at this time he was away on a crusade. Robert had been absent for four years and had been an extremely successful crusader. The Christian leaders had even offered to make him King of Jerusalem, but this he had turned down. Instead, he had decided to return home to his Dukedom of Normandy and was actually on his way back just as his young brother Henry was having himself crowned King of England.

Henry knew that he would inevitably have to face a showdown with Robert, so he did everything possible to settle himself firmly on the throne before Robert could turn up. Within just three months he married Princess Matilda of Scotland, who was descended from Alfred the Great. This was a brilliantly clever political marriage, as it pleased both the Scots and the Saxon English. He re-established the laws of the Conqueror; repealed the unpopular laws of Rufus; got rid of undesirable nobles; and recalled Anselm, Archbishop of Canterbury, back from France, where he had been hiding from Rufus.

Robert finally arrived in England the following year, landing at Portsmouth with his invading army and then marching purposefully inland to meet Henry and his defending army at Alton in Hampshire. There was a tense moment when the opposing armies formed a huge circle and the two brothers walked towards each other in the middle. It speaks much for Henry's very considerable negotiating skills that within minutes he and Robert were hugging each other in an astonishing display of reconciliation.

Sadly, the friendship did not last. A few years later Robert was making such a nuisance of himself that Henry invaded Normandy to settle his brother once

## WHAT HAPPENED TO ROBERT CURTHOSE?

It seems only right to spare a thought for the pathetic figure of Robert Curthose. (The name means 'short trousers' – apparently he had stocky little legs.) Robert, who might easily have been King Robert I of England if only Henry had not been so ruthless and determined, was captured at the Battle of Tinchebray in 1106. It is astonishing to remember that after this battle Henry kept his elder brother captive for the rest of his life, holding him in a succession of castles: in Wareham, Dorset; Bristol; and finally Cardiff. Robert survived the Battle of Tinchebray by almost twenty-eight years and died in 1134, aged eighty, only a few months before Henry himself. Robert is buried in Gloucester Cathedral, where there is a fine wooden effigy of him in crusader's armour.

How sad it is to think that this once-powerful warrior, eldest son of the Conqueror and once the wealthy Duke of Normandy who actually turned down the honour of becoming King of Jerusalem, should have spent his long final years trying to learn Welsh in Cardiff Castle. Passing the tedious days there he wrote a gentle little poem in Welsh about a tree which he could just see from the draughty window of his cell. Visitors to Cardiff Castle can go into the old castle keep where Robert was imprisoned, and a small picture of him is painted among the fanciful nineteenth-century decorations of the rebuilt banqueting hall.

One of the fascinating 'ifs' of history is the question of how the English monarchy would have developed after Rufus, if only Robert had taken over.

and for all. In a resounding victory at Tinchebray, about 40 miles east of Avranches, Henry captured Robert and established himself as Duke of Normandy. History had come full circle, for Henry was now both King of England and Duke of Normandy, just as his father the Conqueror had been.

After this, Henry's long reign in England was a model of firm rule. He enjoyed life to the full, with a wife, three healthy legitimate children, many mistresses and about twenty-five bastards. He still holds the paternity record among English kings. And he was a good parent to them all. However, his final years were shattered by disappointment and grief when his two legitimate sons, William and Richard, were drowned off the coast of Normandy. The two youngsters were aboard a brand-new boat called *The White Ship* and were sailing back to England separately from their father. A large quantity of wine was aboard and by the time the boat set sail the princes, the passengers and sailors were in a rip-roaring mood, jeering and mocking the priests who had come to bless the ship with holy water. On its maiden voyage, *The White Ship*, sailing from Barfleur, struck a rock and sank like a stone; out of the 300 men and women on board only one man lived to tell the tale, Berold, a butcher of Rouen.

Henry was devastated. Tradition says that 'he never smiled again'. His wife, the Scottish Matilda, had already died, so, within months, desperate for another male heir, Henry married again, to Adela of Louvain. He was fifty-three: she was eighteen. No heir came. Eventually, despairing of ever having another son, he made plans to hand over the throne, on his death, to his daughter, another Matilda.

Henry lived on for another fifteen years, dying, memorably, of ptomaine poisoning. He was buried in Reading Abbey, which he himself had founded.

# STEPHEN

### *c.* 1097–1154   REIGNED 1135–1154

*Son of Stephen and Adela, daughter of William the Conqueror*

**By general agreement, Stephen is regarded as one of the worst kings the nation has ever had. His reign was a complete disaster, although as a person he seems to have been kindly and easy-going; he is described as amiable, courageous and generous, although a usurper and quite out of his depth as a king.**

As a young man Stephen had been well liked by his uncle, Henry I, who gave him so much land and property each side of the Channel that he became one of the richest and most powerful of all the Norman nobles. However, the moment Henry was dead, Stephen wasted no time in claiming the throne for himself, despite having sworn an oath to support Henry's daughter Matilda as successor. On the whole, he received plenty of support from the Norman barons, even though they too had sworn allegiance to Matilda. Probably the very idea of a woman coming to the throne was more than they could take. For a while things went reasonably well, but as soon as Stephen's incompetence revealed itself and Matilda could muster her supporters, all hell broke loose. Virtually the whole history of Stephen's reign is a confused tangle of civil conflict, with sieges, battles, imprisonments and supporters switching sides.

The worst months for Stephen were in 1141, when he was captured during a skirmish just outside Lincoln. After this, Matilda became 'Domina', or 'Lady of the English' for a few months. No one ever called her 'Queen', as she never quite managed to get herself crowned.

It must have been an amazing scene when Stephen was seized. Against all advice he left an advantageous position, got off his horse and fought with spectacular courage. When his massive sword broke he snatched a huge Danish axe and swirled it about him like a madman, scattering or killing his foes. Then the axe broke and someone felled him with a stone. A knight called William of Cahagnes rushed in and grabbed him by the helmet and yelled 'Come here everyone! I've got the king!' They quickly clapped him in chains and took him first to Gloucester, where Matilda could gloat over him, and then to Bristol, where he was flung into a dungeon. Later, Stephen was released in exchange for Matilda's half-brother, Robert of Gloucester, taken prisoner near Winchester. And then it was Matilda's turn to be besieged, this time in Oxford, but she staged a dramatic night-time escape.

Eventually even the iron-willed Matilda became tired of the constant struggle, and when Stephen's sons died a sort of compromise was worked out between the two opposing factions. Stephen was to keep the throne for his lifetime, but Matilda's son Henry would succeed him when he died. A ruptured appendix led to Stephen's death in 1154 and ended nineteen years of chaos. His reign had been so awful that people said that it was a time when 'Christ and his saints slept'.

# MATILDA

## 1102–1167   'REIGNED' FEB.–NOV. 1141

### Daughter of Henry I and Matilda of Scotland

Although courageous and determined, and the perpetrator of several great escapes, Matilda is remembered as a haughty, self-willed, arrogant, tactless 'queen'. Known as the Empress Matilda because of her first marriage to the Holy Roman Emperor, Henry V, she was the mother of the long-reigning Plantagenet dynasty.

After *The White Ship* disaster, Matilda had been promised the throne. Imagine, therefore, her fury and frustration when her cousin Stephen moved in smartly and had himself crowned instead. For virtually all of Stephen's reign Matilda struggled to assert her rights and for eight months or so in the year 1141 she was to all intents and purposes the Queen of England, being given the title 'Domina' or 'Lady of the English'. However, she was never crowned, and was so domineering and arrogant that she lost much of the goodwill she might have otherwise had. Eventually, after a lengthy, hectic and unsuccessful campaign, she left England for good, presumably in despair and disgust.

Winchester, in particular, suffered badly from Matilda's actions. Its powerful bishop, Henry of Blois, was Stephen's younger brother, and generally supported him. However, after a while he switched allegiance to Matilda and it was Bishop Henry who proclaimed her to be 'Domina'. But when Matilda showed herself to be so unpopular, demanding huge taxes, Bishop Henry switched his allegiance back to Stephen, and when Matilda returned to Winchester and set up quarters there he systematically set fire to the town from his Wolvesey Castle, on the outskirts, hoping to drive her out. For six weeks the whole of the city of Winchester was in flames. Dwellings, churches, monasteries, and even the royal palaces were utterly destroyed.

Eventually, when a relief army from London arrived to support the Bishop, all Matilda's barons and knights fled in panic, stripping themselves of armour and even giving false names to the local peasants who challenged them. Matilda managed to escape, but her faithful half-brother Robert was captured at Stockbridge, about 10 miles away. As if part of some game, Stephen and Robert, both now prisoners, were exchanged one for another, and on 1 November 1141 King Stephen regained his kingdom after being held captive since 2 February. These were the effective dates when Matilda could claim to have 'ruled' England.

One of the most dramatic incidents of the war took place in the bitterly cold December of the following year. By that time Stephen had besieged Matilda for three months in Oxford Castle. She must have been getting desperate, so one night she lowered herself by rope from St George's Tower, which still exists, crossed the icy river wearing white clothes as camouflage in the snow, and made her way across country to Wallingford Castle, 13 miles away. This was not her only dramatic escape, for in the previous year she had managed to escape from Devizes, disguised as a corpse, dressed in a shroud, and bound fast to a bier.

All in all Matilda had an astonishingly eventful life. She had been born in London and when she was only twelve she was married to the Holy Roman Emperor Henry V. She learned German and went to live in Germany. Because of this marriage she is often referred to as 'the Empress Matilda'. Her Emperor husband had died in 1125, and she married again, this time to Geoffrey IV ('The Handsome'), Count of Anjou, by whom she had three sons, the most important of whom was to become Henry II of England.

The final thing to say about Matilda is that although she was unpopular herself, and never managed to become queen as her father had intended, nevertheless she was the mother of the Plantagenets, a dynasty that remained in power for 350 years, ending only with the Tudor victory at the Battle of

Bosworth. Matilda is buried in Fontevrault Abbey in France, having lived to see the first thirteen years of the reign of her Plantagenet son, King Henry II.

# HENRY II

## 1133–1189   REIGNED 1154–1189

### Son of Geoffrey IV, Count of Anjou and Matilda

**Powerful, resolute and bursting with energy, Henry II was also known to be lecherous and quick-tempered. Perhaps he is best remembered for his unfortunate role in the murder of Thomas Becket.**

With his strength and organisational skills, Henry II was just what England needed after the disastrous King Stephen. He had already inherited the rich lands of Anjou from his father and acquired the French province of Aquitaine from his wife, so when he came to the English throne, aged twenty-one, he possessed the largest empire in Europe.

Henry was constantly and frenetically on the move to keep a watchful eye over his vast territories. He spent only 13 years of his 34-year reign in England, but he insisted that horses were always kept ready for his use in abbeys all over the country. No one knew when he would make his sudden appearances. He seemed to be everywhere at once. Remorselessly he forced law and order upon the kingdom. He strengthened the legal system, imposed taxes, and curbed the unruly barons by pulling down their castles. All in all, Henry was an outstanding king, but in a monumental row with the Church he met his match in Thomas Becket, Archbishop of Canterbury.

Henry declared that the Church was subject to the law of the land, but with superb arrogance Becket told him that the Church was above it. It was a collision course, and everyone knows the dramatic outcome. Henry's short temper blazed out: 'Isn't there anyone who'll get rid of this wretched priest?' And instantly four of his knights, dutifully taking the hint, galloped off to Canterbury, cracked open Becket's skull and prised out his brains on to the cold cathedral floor. The effect on Europe was electrifying.

Henry realised that Becket, dead though he was, had triumphed. A martyr. A saint. A victim of monstrous sacrilege in his own cathedral. A gigantic gesture of penitence was necessary, so Henry walked barefoot into Canterbury, wearing nothing but a shirt. He knelt at the cathedral porch. Then, with bleeding feet, he made his way to the spot where the murder had taken place and kissed the stone where the archbishop had fallen. After a ceremony of penitence and absolution he submitted to being beaten: three strokes from each of the eighty

## WINDSOR CASTLE

Situated in Berkshire, Windsor Castle was founded by William the Conqueror, and has grown over the centuries. Henry II began the very distinctive Round Tower. Here the future Edward III was born, and later, when he became king, he founded the Order of the Garter here in 1344. The future Henry VI was born here too, against the express wishes of his father, Henry V, who had conceived the notion that to be born here would prove unlucky. Perhaps he was right!

Royal associations with Windsor Castle are so numerous that it would be impossible to list them. George III, in his madness, died here. So did William IV and Prince Albert. But on the whole the castle has remained very much a place of royal residence, away from London and yet near enough to be convenient to return there quickly.

Much of the splendour of the interior was the inspiration of George IV, who personally supervised an extensive rebuilding programme in the 1820s. It was then that the Round Tower was raised.

After the disastrous fire of 1992, Windsor Castle has been skilfully and beautifully restored. It was reopened exactly five years afterwards, on 20 November 1997, coincidentally marking the fiftieth wedding anniversary of Queen Elizabeth II and Philip, Duke of Edinburgh.

monks, and five strokes from each of the various bishops and abbots. Still muddy and unwashed, he then spent the whole of the next night in the dark cathedral crypt, fasting and praying, and nearly catching his death of cold.

Although Henry is known for pulling down castles he disapproved of, he was equally energetic in building and enlarging castles he enjoyed living in. The lower half of the famous Round Tower in Windsor is his. He enlarged the fortifications at Gloucester and Guildford, refounded Waltham Abbey as a penance for Becket's murder, and converted the hunting lodge at Woodstock in Oxfordshire into a palace where he lived with his mistress, Rosamund Clifford, the 'Fair Rosamund'. 'Fair Rosamund's Well', where his famous concubine is said to have bathed, is still to be seen in the grounds of Blenheim Palace, but no trace remains of the 'bower' or labyrinth that Henry is said to have built for her.

Only two of Henry's sons survived him – Richard and John. His first-born, William, who was born four months after his wedding to Eleanor of

Aquitaine, died as a toddler, but the next son, Henry, born in 1155, was actually crowned in Westminster Abbey when he was fifteen, while his father was still alive. It was a French custom to crown the heir, to ensure a smooth succession. The young Henry was known as 'The Young King', so for thirteen years it was possible to say that England had *two* kings. The Young King continually annoyed his father by demanding and expecting more power and authority than Henry was prepared to give him, and there was much friction between them. However, the Young King died of dysentery when he was twenty-eight, so never succeeded to the throne.

Henry's other sons conspired against him towards the end of his life, helped and encouraged by Eleanor his wife, who became estranged from him when 'Fair Rosamund' made her appearance. Henry put Eleanor under house arrest in Winchester for sixteen years. It wasn't until his death in 1189 that she regained her freedom and power.

Henry's reign was an odd mixture of success and failure. He was enraged at the disloyalty of his sons, who joined the King of France to defeat him in battle. His dying words, after he suffered a stroke, show how deeply and bitterly he regarded himself as a failure: 'Shame, shame on a conquered King!' Arguably, however, his constructive and firm rule had been of immeasurable benefit to England.

# RICHARD I (THE LIONHEART)
## 1157–1199   REIGNED 1189–1199
### Son of Henry II and Eleanor of Aquitaine

**Impetuous, romantic, homosexual, poetic; Richard I was a brilliant soldier but a hopeless king. Most people remember him as 'Coeur de Lion' – the Lionheart: the great crusader, superb in battle against Saladin; cruelly captured and imprisoned by somebody somewhere until his faithful minstrel Blondel sang beneath his window and discovered him; hero of Robin Hood and his merry men as they valiantly campaigned against the evil Sheriff of Nottingham and Richard's wicked brother, John.**

The images commonly presented of Richard I are perpetuated by the romantic and idealised statue of him on horseback that stands just outside the Houses of Parliament. But is this a true picture? Sadly, it has to be said that Richard was one of our worst kings. He simply hadn't the slightest interest in being king. He was in England for only a few months of his ten-year reign, and he openly admitted that he would have sold the whole of

London if he could have found a rich enough buyer. And, of course, if he had sold it he would have rushed off at once on one of his interminable wars.

For Richard, life was just one long series of military adventures. Indeed, it must be admitted that he was a brilliant soldier. From his earliest boyhood he was constantly practising the arts of war in tournaments and knightly games. He was only sixteen when he first campaigned with his brothers against his father, Henry II, in France. Encouraged by his mother, Eleanor, he continued to battle frequently against his father, allying himself with King Philip of France. Eventually, Richard and Philip forced the ageing King Henry to surrender. The anguish of defeat almost certainly killed the old king, who died of cerebral haemorrhage.

After his coronation, Richard immediately made plans for a crusade to free the Holy Land from the Turks under Saladin. Off he went, with his gay friend Philip of France, hoping for the glory and spoils of war. However, when they got to Sicily the two kings quarrelled, partly because Richard refused to marry Philip's sister, Alys. Just then, his indefatigable mother turned up with an alternative bride, Berengaria of Navarre, whom she had personally escorted from Spain, having negotiated the marriage herself. Philip left Sicily in a rage.

Then began a series of wildly improbable adventures for Richard. He sent his mother back home to England and pushed on to the Holy Land, still unmarried, but taking Berengaria with him. Berengaria's ship was nearly seized by the Greek ruler of Cyprus, providing Richard with a perfect excuse for invading and capturing the whole island. So it was in Limassol in Cyprus that Richard and Berengaria got married: surely the most unlikely place for the wedding of an English king. Berengaria was actually crowned Queen of England and Cyprus.

Although brides were not much use on a crusade, Richard took Berengaria to the Holy Land: he pressed on to win victories at Acre and Jaffa; just failed to capture Jerusalem; and negotiated a valuable truce with Saladin, to make it possible for Christians to gain access to Jerusalem. Richard then left Berengaria to sail alone to England, while he himself started to make the journey by land to Europe. On the way back he was captured by the Duke of Austria, who sold him to Emperor Henry VI for 150,000 marks. Back in England it took a quarter of every man's income for a whole year to raise the necessary ransom money. Pigs were killed, sheep shorn, church plate sold. It was an expensive business rescuing Richard.

When eventually he got back home, Richard gave himself a second coronation, in Winchester Cathedral. However, England still meant nothing to him, and he spent virtually the rest of his life in France, trying to recapture the lands and castles that his former friend King Philip had seized from him during his absence. Queen Berengaria didn't meet Richard again for years. Although a sort of reconciliation was made, no children came. It must have been a miserable marriage.

It was almost inevitable that Richard should be killed in some skirmish or other, as fighting was his perpetual lifestyle. One day, as he was besieging an insignificant little castle at Châlus in France, an archer shot him in the shoulder. The arrow was hacked out, but gangrene set in. Richard, with romantic generosity, ordered the archer, whose name was Bertram, to come to his deathbed. He pardoned him, gave him a hundred shillings and set him free. Then he died.

Richard the Lionheart, finest crusader of all time, died without a legitimate heir, and in agony, aged forty-one, leaving his neglected throne to his younger brother, John. Berengaria, his equally neglected queen, spent the rest of her life in a French nunnery.

As for Bertram the archer, despite the king's pardon he was flayed alive and hanged.

# JOHN

## 1167–1216   REIGNED 1199–1216

### *Son of Henry II and Eleanor of Aquitaine*

**The younger brother of Richard I, John is reputed to have been treacherous, cruel, untrustworthy, greedy, lustful, unlucky – and probably much maligned. He is perhaps most remembered for his signing of the Magna Carta.**

For centuries all historians agreed that King John was bad. Not just incompetent, but spectacularly awful as a human being as well as a king. His upbringing didn't help. His mother, Eleanor of Aquitaine, was forty-five when she had him – the last of her eight children. He cannot have been particularly welcome, and his parents became more than estranged shortly after his birth, his mother being virtually under house arrest. His older brothers treated him with contempt.

There was no territory left to give John, so he gained the curious nickname 'Lackland'. In fact, the only way he could gain any wealth was by making a shamelessly loveless marriage to a rich heiress. Later on, when he was king, he fell desperately in love with a twelve-year-old, Isabella of Angoulême, and ditched his first wife without a qualm. Isabella gave him six children. He also had twelve bastards by various other women. (He sent a poisoned egg to one woman who turned him down.)

Richard I, his brother, was almost always out of England during his reign, so in his absence John was constantly interfering and helping himself to whatever he could. However, when Richard was dying he made John his successor, despite the fact that a young nephew, Arthur, was closer in line to the throne. John seized the first opportunity he could to imprison the sixteen-year-old Arthur. It was alleged that he murdered him personally, tying a stone to his body and throwing the corpse into the River Seine. Whatever the details were, Arthur certainly disappeared in sinister circumstances. One nobleman's wife was starved to death in Windsor Castle's dungeon for daring to suggest that John was responsible.

Wars with France lost John much of his territory in France: Normandy, Anjou, Poitou, Maine, Touraine. It was the beginning of the inevitable separation of the two countries. At the same time, quarrels with the Church led the Pope to excommunicate John. For more than five years from March 1208 to July 1213, all church services in England and Wales were banned. No weddings, no funerals, no bells, just a religious silence. The Pope 'gave' England to the King of France, and when the French forces landed to collect 'their' kingdom, John abjectly surrendered his kingdom to the Pope, agreeing to hold England as his vassal.

Drastic times call forth drastic measures. The best thing to come out of John's difficult reign was the formulation of a kind of bill of rights, the first of its kind: the famous Magna Carta. In June 1215 a large gathering of dignitaries assembled in a Surrey meadow called Runnymede and forced John to sign this important document, which in essence gave the Church its independence, prevented arbitrary taxes and made it impossible to be punished without trial. The law was to be upheld, even by kings. John was furious, and although within weeks he got the Pope to annul the Charter, his days were numbered.

By now the country was in chaos. The barons, in despair, invited Louis Capet, son of King Philip II of France, to come and take over as king. Louis arrived with an army and settled into London and Winchester. In essence there was civil war, aggravated by an invasion by the Scots deep into England. John did have a kind of grudging backing from the bishops, because of the Pope's support. However, he could find nobody to fight for him and had to import foreign mercenaries.

Travelling with all his treasure, not trusting to leave it anywhere out of sight, John's luck finally ran out. He happened to be moving his wagon-train of bullion and jewellery too near the sea in Norfolk, and when the tide came in quickly he lost wagon-load upon wagon-load of valuables in the soggy marshes. He lost not only the crown of Edward the Confessor, the Empress Matilda's crown, the orb and sceptre, and all the jewellery of his mother, who had been the richest woman in the world, but also gold cups, chalices, crosses, unset jewels – all the wealth that effectively enabled him to pay those foreign mercenary soldiers. The loss of this treasure meant that he was rendered powerless.

Within days John was dead, probably poisoned. The corpse was taken to Worcester Cathedral and buried before the high altar, on John's own wishes, so that he could be near his favourite saint, St Wulfstan.

Such is the story of John. But nowadays it is recognised that he has always had an extremely bad press, perhaps unfairly so. The early historians were monks who were still rankled by his differences with the Church. In fact, nowadays we can appreciate that John did at least try to grapple with the many problems that beset the country, unlike Stephen or his older brother, Richard I, who simply ignored them. Looking afresh at his reign, we can realise that he built up England's navy and sea defences; he was an able administrator; he travelled incessantly to supervise the performance of his officials; and he tried to ensure a healthy economy. Possibly the most important thing he lacked was luck. Modern historians are far less condemning of John than those of former centuries. But it will be a long time before he loses his image of the archetypal Bad King.

# HENRY III

## 1207–1272   REIGNED 1216–1272

### Son of John and Isabella of Angoulême

**Although weak, extravagant and incompetent, Henry III was a great builder and supporter of the arts. He was a civilised and thoroughly nice human being – with no idea how to fight. As he came to the throne so young, Henry III's reign was one of the longest – fifty-six years.**

In many respects Henry III was quite untypical of kings in those years, and had no interest or skill in making war. In fact, he was the first peaceful and arts-loving king since Edward the Confessor. He recognised this similarity himself, and spent much of his time enlarging and beautifying Westminster Abbey in order to give greater honour to the Confessor. Henry was nine when he was crowned, and so obviously there had to be guardians and regents. It's probably true to say that he never did quite learn to take control of things. He was far too interested in his building projects, and also far too generous to his many French relations. His wife, Eleanor of Provence, certainly brought culture to England, but she also brought a huge retinue of foreign friends and relations. Also, Henry's mother, Isabella, had returned to France, remarried and had many children, and Henry invited many of his half-brothers across and placed them in high positions.

Henry was kind. Too kind. He gave away so much and spent so much on his artistic projects that eventually the barons rebelled at the costly way he was ruling. When Henry asked for yet more money, he was forced to sign a set of guide-lines called the Provisions of Oxford, in which, basically, he had to submit to a form of Parliament, summoned by a capable ring-leader among the barons, Simon de Montfort, Earl of Leicester.

Two things emerged from Henry's reign: the beginnings of Parliament, and the beautifully rebuilt Westminster Abbey. In a way, they represented two very positive marks of progress. Many cathedrals were built or rebuilt in his time, with his encouragement: Wells, Lincoln, Peterborough. Salisbury Cathedral is perhaps the finest example. The Great Hall in Winchester, where visitors today can see 'King Arthur's Table', was built by Henry. He loved Winchester, for it was his birth-place, and he even referred to himself as 'Henry of Winchester'.

Franciscan and Dominican friars came to England during his reign, and the universities of Oxford and Cambridge were beginning to establish themselves. Bit by bit, England was gradually becoming civilised.

Henry was lucky to have an exceptionally able and loving son, Edward, named, of course, after his patron saint. In the course of his long conflict with Simon de Montfort and the barons, Henry and Edward had fought and lost the Battle of Lewes in 1264 and each had been taken prisoner. They were held in separate places but Edward managed to escape and turned the tables on Simon at the Battle of Evesham the following year. Thanks to Edward, Simon was killed and Henry was restored.

Henry returned to his church-building, and Edward, his war-loving son, went off on a crusade, together with his wife, Eleanor. It was while they were still away that three messengers arrived. The first told them that their elder boy was dead; the second told them that their second boy was dead; the third announced that Edward's father Henry was dead. Everyone who witnessed Edward's reaction to these sad tidings was somewhat surprised. He accepted the deaths of his babies with calm resignation; but he was overwhelmed with grief to hear of his father's death. When asked why, he replied: 'A man may have more sons – but never another father.' It was a sincere tribute from son to father, and tells us more about Henry than volumes of history ever can.

Henry is buried, appropriately, near his beloved Edward the Confessor in the enlarged Westminster Abbey, which is his greatest memorial.

# EDWARD I
## 1239–1307   REIGNED 1272–1307
### *Son of Henry III and Eleanor of Provence*

**Strong, capable and energetic, the 'Hammer of the Scots' and inventor of the title 'Prince of Wales' was a great administrator and legal innovator. Edward I was a king who made many improvements to his realm.**

What a pity it is that we have no effigy, no picture, no visual record of this great king! Even his tomb in Westminster Abbey is a vast ugly lump, hidden in the shadows, with its famous inscription 'Hammer of the Scots' scrawled in a messy way on the side – just a bit of seventeenth-century graffiti on a fourteenth-century stone coffin. The result is that many people hardly know or remember one of England's greatest kings.

Like so many successful monarchs, Edward I possessed intense energy, ferocious fighting skills, and supreme determination. However, to these qualities he added the essential virtue of a good ruler – he genuinely wanted to bring law, order and prosperity to the land. He saw what was needed, took good advice, and recognised that his first duty was to his country rather than to himself.

We owe our Parliament to Edward. He organised what was called the Model Parliament in 1295, laying down the system of representative government which we have developed over the centuries. In this, his ideas were centuries ahead of the time in which he lived. Also, we owe much of our legal system to his inspiration: the great common law courts took shape under his active encouragement.

He tried harder than any king before him to create a United Kingdom, and almost succeeded. Wales was crushed; Edward chopped up the body of his Welsh opponent Llewellyn ap Gruffyd and stuck his head on a high pole in London. Then, to restore goodwill, he presented his young son, also Edward, born in his new castle at Caernarvon, to the countrymen of Wales as a kind of peace-offering, entitling him 'Prince of Wales' – the very first of the long line which has continued until this day.

With Scotland, however, Edward failed. At least, every time Edward turned his back, his attempts to annex that country were systematically undone. Certainly, he made his mark there, and brought the famous 'Coronation Stone', the Stone of Scone, to London as part of his booty. Every English monarch since then has been crowned while sitting over it, and the Coronation Chair that contained it for seven centuries is yet another of Edward's legacies to us, for he ordered it to be made.

In the first of his three major attempts to capture Scotland he defeated John Balliol. In his second attempt he defeated William Wallace, chopping him up in the same way as Llewellyn. However, a third expedition became necessary when Robert the Bruce had himself crowned king, taking Wallace's place. By now Edward was getting on for seventy, but still in the saddle, still determined to press on with what he saw as an essential unifying task. He got as far as Burgh-on-Sands, near Carlisle, and then fell ill. On his deathbed he ordered his corpse to be boiled down to remove all the flesh, so that his bones could go forward into battle leading his army into a final victory against the Scots. (As it happened, neither the boiling nor the victory took place.)

Edward's life was immensely varied, but basically consisted of battles and legislation. In his early youth he had defended his father, Henry III, and had restored him to his throne with a military victory over Simon de Montfort at Evesham. As a young man before becoming king he enjoyed an adventurous time in the Holy Land, travelling with his vivacious Spanish wife, who nursed him back to health after an assassin's attack. Edward and Eleanor of Castile formed a great partnership. His imaginative memorials to her – the twelve beautiful 'Eleanor Crosses' – are as much a comment on Edward himself as they are on his wife. And although we cannot quite visualise this great king, at least we can linger beside Eleanor's elegant effigy in Westminster Abbey and reflect upon one of the greatest reigns in our history.

# EDWARD II
## 1284–1327   REIGNED 1307–1327
### *Son of Edward I and Eleanor of Castile*

**Appallingly tactless, self-centred, homosexual and incompetent, it has been said that Edward II was his father's greatest failure.**

Edward II was only twenty-three when he succeeded Edward I, and a greater contrast could hardly be imagined between the two sovereigns, father and son.

It was plain to his wife, Princess Isabella of France, and to everyone else, that his sexual appetites were centred on the insufferably vain and grasping Piers Gaveston. As soon as she arrived in England, aged twelve, to marry Edward, Isabella noticed that Gaveston was wearing rings and jewels which her own father had just given to Edward. Edward and his gay companion were publicly kissing and embracing.

Isabella wrote home in her misery, describing herself as the most wretched wife in the world. Nevertheless, for many years she acted as a loyal and supportive consort, bore Edward four children, and helped him even on his admittedly unsuccessful military campaigns.

The barons, finally, could put up with Gaveston no longer. They trapped him, ran him through with swords and decapitated him. Edward then turned his affections on the Despensers, father and son, and it was at this point that Isabella's patience gave way. She took a lover herself, Roger Mortimer, and did all she could to thwart Edward and wreck the lives of his newest favourites. The elder Despenser was mangled to death: hanged, drawn and quartered. The younger Despenser suffered likewise, a month later.

For a while Isabella, whose nickname had now become 'The She-Wolf of France', and her lover ruled the kingdom. Edward was forced to abdicate, and then suffered the cruellest fate to befall any English monarch: he was murdered by having a red-hot poker thrust up his anus.

During this disastrous reign Scotland finally asserted its independence by inflicting a resounding defeat upon Edward at the Battle of Bannockburn in 1314. It wasn't until nearly four hundred years later (1707) that a peaceful Act of Union was to bind the two countries together.

It was left to Edward's son, another Edward – the Third – to re-establish law, order and authority. It could be said that Edward III was Edward II's greatest success.

# EDWARD III
## 1312–1377   REIGNED 1327–1377
### Son of Edward II and Isabella of France

**Edward III was a strong monarch, ambitious to restore influence in France. He was active and energetic as a young ruler; majestic and powerful in middle age; and rather sad and senile at the end.**

Like many monarchs who rule for a long time – and Edward's reign lasted for over fifty years – we can see many changes. The vigorous fourteen-year-old who boldly seized the throne was certainly not the same man who slipped into a rather feeble old age, mocked by his greedy mistress, half a century later.

The beginning of Edward's reign was awe-inspiring. Although only fourteen when he became king, he swiftly seized real power, personally capturing his mother and her lover Mortimer as they shared a bedroom in Nottingham Castle. After a show trial, Mortimer was executed, and Isabella, though pardoned, was put under virtual house arrest for the rest of her life at Castle Rising in Norfolk. Then, with supreme self-confidence, Edward began a reign of magnificent success.

Edward was the archetypal medieval kingly king: tall, handsome, magnificently generous, filled with noble ideas of grandeur. He entertained on a lavish scale. He won resounding victories over the French both on sea (Battle of Sluys) and land (Battle of Crécy); gained huge tracts of territory; treated captured kings (David of Scotland and John of France) as honoured guests. His son and heir, the Black Prince, also won a tremendous victory over the French at Poitiers. He built a splendid shrine in Gloucester Cathedral in memory of his dead father. It seemed that whatever he did was effected with honour, success and more than a touch of royal glamour.

Inspired by the legends of King Arthur and the Knights of the Round Table, Edward deliberately tried to recreate the courtly life of Camelot, and in pursuit of this ideal he founded England's noblest order of chivalry – the Order of the Garter – which still remains the highest honour which can be conferred.

It was at a Round Table tournament held at Windsor in 1334 that Edward swore to establish a new order of Arthurian knights, and then, four years later, at a ball to celebrate the capture of Calais, the garter of one of the court ladies fell to the floor. With a dramatic royal gesture, Edward immediately picked it up and tied it round his own leg. His famous remark as he did so, '*Honi soit qui mal y pense*' ('Evil be to him who evil thinks'), is still the proud motto of the Garter Knights, for this was the occasion when he fulfilled his vow to create his company of noble knights. The Garter Chapel at Windsor continues to give a thrill of historical greatness even today, and we must remember that it is to Edward III that we are indebted for this unique feature of English history.

It would be nice to record that Edward III's reign continued to be an unqualified success, but sadly everything went wrong towards the end. The French gradually regained much of the land he had taken; the Black Death brought economic disasters; the heir to the throne, the famous Black Prince, died in mid-life; and Edward himself became prematurely senile and a victim of his harpy of a mistress, Alice Perrers, who stripped him of his jewels even as he lay on his deathbed.

Despite the important events in his life, it is not easy to know Edward as a person. His marriage to Philippa of Hainault was fruitful: eight sons and five daughters. However, his magnificent effigy in Westminster Abbey seems almost too perfect, aloof and God-like. He must have known that his death would be followed by a period of serious difficulties for the monarchy.

# RICHARD II
## 1367–1400   REIGNED 1377–1399
### Son of the Black Prince and Joan of Kent

**The grandson of Edward III, Richard was far too young and immature when he succeeded to the throne. He was artistic, rather effeminate, and insensitive in wielding his authority.**

When a child comes to the throne it is almost always a recipe for disaster. And Richard was only ten when he was crowned. Naturally enough, there were plenty of ambitious uncles and nobles to tell him what to do, as well as his mother, the 'Fair Maid of Kent', who as Dowager Princess of Wales must have been disappointed not to become queen.

Richard was simply not the king his father would have been. England needed a firm warrior king, wielding powerful and tactful authority. However, Richard was still an immature young teenager, far more interested in books, literature, clothes and fashion. He was the inventor of the handkerchief.

True, he showed extraordinary courage in defusing an ugly situation during the Peasants' Revolt in 1381, in a demonstration against the Poll Tax. A menacing mob had gathered at Smithfield in London, and the Mayor of London had just stabbed and killed their leader, Wat Tyler. Richard, a boy of only fourteen at the time, boldly rode up to them, alone, and called out 'Sirs, would you kill your king? I am your king. I am your captain and your leader.' The astonished mob were persuaded to disperse. It was Richard's finest moment. But alas, this flair for leadership and bold gesture never came to him again, and it is easy to see the rest of his life as one prolonged failure. However, this is perhaps a little unfair.

Artistically, Richard's reign was flamboyant and extravagant, and he and his first wife, Anne of Bohemia, kept a magnificent, opulent court. Both he and Anne wore quite extraordinary clothes; they entertained on a huge scale, with exotic cooking which led him to be called 'the best . . . vyander of all Christian Kings'. His lasting achievement was the rebuilding of Westminster Hall with its magnificent hammer-beam roof; and he also gave generously towards York Minster, Canterbury Cathedral, Eltham and Sheen.

A rather macabre act – but one which we must be grateful for – was that he ordered his own tomb in Westminster Abbey to be made before he died. (And remember, he was only thirty-three when he was murdered.) It was a double-effigy, and originally, before mutilation, it showed him holding hands with his first queen, Anne of Bohemia. He must have seen this on many occasions, for Anne died early, aged only twenty-eight, and sadly, childless. Some people have come to think that Richard became a changed man after Anne died. Certainly, he was grief-stricken. He ordered the palace of Sheen, where she died, to be completely razed to the ground and demolished.

The country needed an heir, so Richard married again, a little seven-year-old French princess, Isabella. It was an extraordinary choice, even if it was for political reasons.

Richard's rule became more and more arbitrary. As a young teenager he had necessarily been forced to accept the authority of a kind of regency council; but when he reached manhood he quickly asserted his own will, and tried to rule single-handedly. However, parliamentary power was too well established by then, and when he became manifestly unfair and capricious, this was the signal for his cousin, Henry Bolingbroke, to lead open rebellion.

Henry Bolingbroke became King Henry IV in 1399. Richard was forced to abdicate, and after a few months' imprisonment in Pontefract Castle in Yorkshire, somehow he died. Murdered? Self-starvation? No one will ever really know. Certainly, his corpse was put on public show to 'prove' that he hadn't been killed. But rumours of dirty work have circulated ever since, given huge publicity by no less a writer than William Shakespeare.

# HENRY IV

## 1367–1413   REIGNED 1399–1413

### *Son of John of Gaunt and Blanche of Lancaster*

**Henry IV usurped the throne, deposing his cousin, Richard II. He was a guilt-ridden, uneasy, superstitious, not to mention itchy man.**

Henry Bolingbroke was only a few months older than his cousin, Richard II, and there was no love lost between them. Henry's father was John of Gaunt, who had acted as uncle-regent to Richard II in his early years as king. Richard chafed under this, and was particularly frustrated when a council of five noblemen was set up to rule over him. Henry Bolingbroke – the future King Henry IV – had been one of these five 'Lords Appellant' as they were called.

As soon as he could, Richard disbanded the Lords Appellant. Two of them he arrested and beheaded; a third he flung into life imprisonment; and as for the other two, one was Bolingbroke and the other was the Duke of Norfolk. When these two fell out with one another, Richard acted in an extraordinary way. First of all, a spectacular pageant was arranged at which Henry Bolingbroke and the Duke of Norfolk were to fight a duel. Then, at the very last moment, Richard stepped in and publicly forbade it. Then, again publicly, he banished both the would-be contestants: Norfolk for life, and Henry Bolingbroke for ten years.

Henry Bolingbroke dutifully disappeared for a while, but when his father, John of Gaunt, died and Richard seized all Henry's rightful inheritance, quite naturally he was filled with anger and vengeance. It was inevitable that Henry would return and claim back what Richard had taken from him. Well, return he did, and Henry's revenge took the form of seizing Richard and then the throne. He set himself up as King Henry IV, murdered Richard and then tried to prove that he had a legal right to the succession.

Such a state of affairs – 'a scrambling and unquiet time' as Shakespeare called it – led to a constant succession of rebellions. For the whole of his time as king Henry was forced to beat off rivals and rebels. Troubles of one sort or another worried him till he died: arguments in parliament, fighting along the Welsh and Scottish borders; plots and skirmishes. Executions were constantly necessary, simply to keep himself in power. Henry even executed the Archbishop of York, who had supported one of the rebellions.

The strain of events seriously undermined his health. He contracted a troublesome skin disease, eczema or perhaps leprosy. Rumour had it that this illness was the revenge of God, and that it had been inflicted upon him on the day that the Archbishop was executed. Poor Henry itched until he died.

But Henry's conscience hurt him even more than his eczema. He knew he had blood on his hands. He knew his claim to the throne was pretty thin. He knew, too, that his son was waiting impatiently for him to die. Hope flickered in his mind that if he went on a crusade he might be forgiven, and a soothsayer had predicted that he would die in Jerusalem. However, Henry was to be cheated of his dream. He collapsed in a kind of fit while praying in Westminster Abbey and was taken to a nearby room. He recovered just enough to ask where he was. When told that it was called the 'Jerusalem Chamber' he knew his end had come: 'Praise be to the Father of Heaven, for now I know I shall die in this chamber, according to the prophecy of me beforesaid that I should die in Jerusalem.'

Shakespeare, as always, provides the perfect quotation. He gives the dying Henry a line which perhaps sums up the very nature of monarchy: 'Uneasy lies the head that wears a crown.'

Tourists to Westminster Abbey today might like to know that the 'Jerusalem Chamber' is situated just alongside the present bookshop, to the right of the main door of the Abbey, as you enter.

According to his own wish, Henry was buried in Canterbury Cathedral, near the shrine of Thomas Becket. His life-like effigy is worth studying. It is not the image of a happy man.

# HENRY V

## 1387–1422   REIGNED 1413–1422

### Son of Henry IV and Mary de Bohun

**Tall, handsome, young and vigorous, Henry V was a charismatic leader, if a little impetuous with it.**

Thanks to Shakespeare we probably feel we know Henry V better than any other king. Lawrence Olivier and Kenneth Branagh have given us unforgettable portraits of this dashing young ne'er-do-well turned warrior-king.

According to Shakespeare, young Prince Hal, as Henry was called while still in his teens, enjoyed a wild lifestyle with an old reprobate of a companion, Sir John Falstaff, and a motley collection of other rogues and thieves. The Boar's Head tavern (what a marvellous spoonerism of a name!) saw him as a regular tippler.

Then, on reaching the throne, Henry surprised everyone by throwing off this image, disowning Falstaff and the others, and turning into a model medieval king. We see him lay claim to France, become the idol of his serving soldiers, lead his army to a brilliant victory at Agincourt, and finally marry the French Princess Catherine of Valois, in a suitably masculine and non-French-speaking manner. . . . Some of this is true.

What stands out supremely is that Henry V was a superb soldier and leader of men. His outstanding victory at Agincourt seized the imagination of the country. His army of 8,000 men suffered negligible losses, yet the opposing French army of 50,000 was totally crushed, with thousands of men killed or taken prisoner.

There can hardly have been anything before or since to match the welcome which Henry and his army received from the rapturous crowds back home. When he reached Dover the throng plunged into the sea and carried him shoulder high to the shore. As they marched to London they were greeted by villagers and townsfolk who turned out in their thousands, and when Henry and his men finally reached Blackheath on the outskirts of London they were met by archbishops, bishops, abbots, nobles, the Lord Mayor, sheriffs, aldermen and a vast multitude of cheering citizens. London was a scene of utter delirium. Quite literally, wine ran from public fountains.

Henry's marriage to Catherine was both political and romantic. He not only gained a couple of million French crowns as dowry, becoming heir to the French throne and Regent to the mad King Charles VI, but he also gained a loving and beautiful young wife. He was thirty-three, and she was nineteen.

This was the pinnacle of Henry's brief reign.

But the war with France never ceased. He was constantly trying to gain more and more territory, conquering or avenging. Just two years after his marriage, still with his army, he caught dysentery and died. His little son and heir, another Henry, was just nine months old.

# HENRY VI

## 1421–1471   REIGNED 1422–1461 AND 1470–1471
### Son of Henry V and Catherine of Valois

**Henry VI was temperamentally not suited to be king. He was gentle, scholarly, intensely religious, kind and generous – he would much rather have been a monk.**

It was the misfortune of Henry VI to succeed to the throne when he was only nine months old. Naturally, there were plenty of nobles around who were only too anxious to take over power, and throughout his reign he was for all practical purposes regarded as a puppet. The Yorkist and Lancastrian rivals in the Wars of the Roses battled away over his head. Sometimes he was king. Sometimes he wasn't.

The situation was made even worse by the fact that twice in his life he suffered complete mental breakdown. The first lasted for about eighteen months, and when he recovered he was 'as a man who wakes after a long dream'. He had to be introduced to his own baby son, Edward, who had been born shortly after he had lapsed into his period of mental paralysis. History books naturally regard him as weak and ineffectual. Eventually, he was deposed for good, and quietly murdered in the Tower of London, on the orders of good King Edward IV. Despite this inefficiency, Henry was regarded as a saint. Throughout his life, he had been exceptionally pious. He was a natural scholar, quiet, sensitive, gentle and unworldly. He even became a 'Confrater' of the Benedictine Order – in other words, a kind of associate monk.

After his murder he was buried by the authorities deliberately in a rather out-of-the-way place, Chertsey Abbey, in Surrey. Such was his popular esteem that it was claimed that no fewer than 174 miracles took place at his tomb, 23 of which were accepted by the Church as proven. Richard III had his body transferred and reburied in St George's Chapel, Windsor, and to this spot came large numbers of pilgrims. His tomb is still there, and near it is a fascinating old octagonal iron alms-box bearing the royal initial H, where people would place their offerings in his memory.

Henry VII was determined to support the move to make Henry VI a saint. Negotiations were well advanced with the Pope, and the whole purpose of the construction of the elaborately carved King Henry VII's Chapel in Westminster Abbey was to provide a suitable setting for Henry VI's shrine when he became a saint. Alas, Henry VII died before this could be accomplished, and Henry VIII's break with Rome finally destroyed the negotiation procedure which would have led to the canonisation of Henry VI.

Visitors to the Tower of London can see a plaque on a floor in the Wakefield Tower, marking the spot where Henry was murdered; visitors to Windsor can see his tomb – for he never was moved to Westminster. But Henry's greatest monuments are the two outstandingly beautiful educational foundations, Eton and King's College, Cambridge. Henry's main passions in life were religion and education, and in these two buildings he united those interests. He immersed himself in establishing both these colleges; at Eton for schoolboys, and at Cambridge for their continuing studies at university.

Despite a reputation for weakness and failure as a king, Henry is still venerated as a patron of education and the arts. Even today members of the 'Henry VI Society' are continuing to press forward the claim to make him a saint. They may yet succeed.

# EDWARD IV

## 1442–1483    REIGNED 1461–1470 AND 1471–1483

### Son of Richard, Duke of York, and Cecily Neville

**A distant cousin of Henry VI, Edward was allegedly the most handsome of all the English kings. Nevertheless, he was also unscrupulous and quick to turn events to his own advantage.**

The Wars of the Roses are guaranteed to confuse anybody. Even if you manage, momentarily, to grasp the details, you're sure to forget them after a good night's sleep. To understand the background, you must remember that Edward III, who died in 1377, had many sons, and the squabbles of the next century were all down to the rivalries of the descendants of these sons.

The three sons whose families fought each other until the Tudors swept them away were: (1) The Black Prince, whose son became Richard II; (2) John of Gaunt, whose son, Henry Bolingbroke, seized the throne from Richard and became Henry IV; and (3) Edmund, Duke of York, whose great-grandson, Edward (IV), decided that he would make a much better king than Henry VI and therefore seized the throne from him.

John of Gaunt was Duke of Lancaster, so his descendants – Henry IV, Henry V and Henry VI – and all their supporters are known as 'Lancastrians', with a red rose as their emblem. On the other side, Edward IV and his brother Richard III, being descendants of Edmund, Duke of York, were known as 'Yorkists', with the emblem of a white rose. Everyone agrees that Henry VI was by no means a warrior king. In gentler times he would have been looked after with care, and his better qualities would have been valued. However, the first problem was that he came to the throne as a nine-month-old baby, and so regal power was up for grabs for many years. Regents were the order of the day. Secondly, Henry was temperamentally a monk rather than a king. And thirdly, his mental instability, leading to periods of total incapacity, meant that he was never fully in command of the throne.

It was into this power vacuum that Edward strode. Massively tall, remarkably handsome, firm of will, ferocious in temper, glib of tongue, and a lecherous *bon viveur*. The queen he chose for himself was Elizabeth Woodville, a strikingly beautiful young widow (her married name was Grey), with long blonde hair. He kept this marriage a total secret, even from parliament, and there was an embarrassing moment when, being publicly asked to consider marriage, he had to confess that he was already hitched. What made it worse, in some people's eyes, was that Elizabeth was not only of relatively low birth, but also of Lancastrian stock. (Incidentally, a later member of the Grey family, Lady Jane Grey, was to become pitifully famous in the next century.)

The battles of the Yorkists and Lancastrians make tedious reading. It was not a struggle of ideas, such as Protestant against Catholic or royalist against parliamentarian. It was simply a set of struggles to grab or keep hold of power.

Although the Lancastrians managed to gain victories at Wakefield (1460) and St Albans (1461), the Yorkists were generally much better organised, and Edward gained the throne at the bloodiest battle in English history, fought in snow just outside the Yorkshire town of Towton, in 1461. There were many other skirmishes and battles. Henry VI's queen, Margaret of Anjou, did most of the organisation on the Lancastrian side, on behalf of her weak husband. An unscrupulous manipulator, a nobleman usually referred to as Warwick the Kingmaker, switched allegiance halfway through the struggle. The whole period was a mess. But on the whole the ordinary people of England just went about their business without being too much affected.

Henry VI had two periods of kingship, and so did Edward IV, but in the end, after the decisive Battle of Tewkesbury (1471) Edward finally won, murdered Henry and remained king until his death twelve years later, in 1483.

Generally speaking, Edward IV was an energetic, ruthless opportunist. After a life of battles to gain the English throne, he then invaded France. With huge success at the Treaty of Picquigny in 1475 he managed to squeeze 75,000 crowns out of the French King Louis XI, plus annual payments of 20,000 if only he would leave France for good. It was virtually a protection racket. Nevertheless, it did mean that Edward was able to live comfortably on his earnings. After all, he'd also confiscated plenty of wealth from the defeated Lancastrian estates. He died, fairly unexpectedly, aged only forty-one, probably of sheer self-indulgence and pneumonia. He had several mistresses, and it is said of him that: 'In food and drink he was most immoderate: . . . it was his habit to take an emetic for the delight of gorging his stomach one more . . . he was grown fat in his loins.'

Today we can enjoy two permanent memorials of Edward's reign. Firstly, he was the king who encouraged the new invention of printing in England. His patronage supported William Caxton, who set up his printing presses in Westminster. Secondly, as he was somewhat jealous to see Henry VI's beautiful Eton College every time he looked out of his windows at Windsor Castle, he decided that he, too, would build something worth remembering. The result of this is one of our greatest architectural glories – St George's Chapel, Windsor. The present building is largely his inspiration.

Edward, probably the most powerfully-built of all our monarchs, was buried in St George's Chapel in 1483 – the first English king to be buried there. His monument, however, with its huge and ugly lettering, is of eighteenth-century workmanship.

## WAS EDWARD IV A BASTARD?

In 2004, a fascinatingly seditious TV programme, *Britain's Real Monarch*, was presented by Tony Robinson and researched by Michael K. Jones. Its argument was that Edward IV was illegitimate. Cecily Neville, his mother, couldn't have conceived him in wedlock, as her husband was away at the appropriate time. Indeed, Edward was physically very unlike his father.

Cecily was so furious with Edward over his secret marriage to Elizabeth Woodville that she repeatedly declared him to be a bastard, even at the loss of her own reputation. This explains why Edward's brother, Richard III, was so ready to assume the throne, disregarding Edward's sons – who had no claim to it if their father was illegitimate.

Recently-discovered documents point conclusively to Edward's bastardy. Following this, the TV programme traced the 'true' lineage of the royal line. It led to a somewhat bemused family in the Australian outback …

# EDWARD V

## 1470–1483   'REIGNED' 9 APRIL–25 JUNE 1483

### *Son of Edward IV and Elizabeth Woodville*

**One of the 'Princes in the Tower', Edward V was a poor little boy, murdered, probably by his Uncle Dick (King Richard III), a few weeks before his thirteenth birthday.**

The fate of the 'Princes in the Tower' is virtually a part of English folklore, but few people can remember exactly who these 'Princes' were. The facts are that one of them was King Edward V, aged twelve, who was never crowned; and the other was Richard, Duke of York, his brother, aged nine and heir to the throne. Anyone else who wanted to become king, therefore, would have to do away with both of these boys. The finger of history points accusingly at their uncle, Richard, Duke of Gloucester, who proclaimed himself king. As for the royal children, prisoners in the Tower of London, they simply disappeared.

Quite properly, young Edward was regarded as king from the moment his father, Edward IV, suddenly and unexpectedly died of pneumonia. The boy king was living in Ludlow Castle at the time, so preparations were made for him to travel down to London. His mother, Queen Elizabeth Woodville, begged that he should be accompanied by an army to protect him. Her fears were laughed at, but she was quickly proved right. Almost immediately, Edward's Uncle Richard, Duke of Gloucester, arrested the young king's Woodville relations and bundled the lad into the Tower of London.

Meanwhile, his mother fled into sanctuary in Westminster Abbey with all her other children, some of them hardly more than toddlers: Anne and Catherine, Bridget and Elizabeth, Cicely and Richard. She must have been at her wits' end. Eye-witnesses describe her sitting weeping and helpless on the rushes covering the floor. The ruthless Duke of Gloucester then insisted that Richard, her nine-year-old younger son, should be taken away from her and sent to join his brother in the Tower. Within three weeks the ambitious duke had had himself crowned, calling himself King Richard III.

Elizabeth must have been cruelly threatened to let her younger boy go. 'Farewell, my sweete sonne,' she said. 'Let me kiss you ere you go – for God knows if we shall ever kiss again.' She fainted, and when she regained consciousness she filled the building with the sound of her frantic sobbings. She never saw her boys again. They were last seen in the Tower grounds playing with bows and arrows, quite oblivious of what was to happen. . . .

Some human bones were discovered in the Tower about two centuries later, and Charles II ordered them to be interred in Westminster Abbey.

# RICHARD III

## 1452–1485   REIGNED 1483–1485

### *Son of Richard, Duke of York, and Cecily Neville*

**The brother of Edward IV and uncle of Edward V; was he really a murderous villain, or just another monarch with a bad public image? Did he really deserve a 'winter of discontent'?**

Shakespeare has given us an unforgettable picture of Richard III as a villainous hunchback. But then, Shakespeare lived in the reign of Good Queen Bess, whose grandfather, Henry VII, had won the Battle of Bosworth, witnessed the death of Richard and seized his crown. It would hardly have been tactful to have portrayed Richard as anything other than a wicked monster.

In fact, virtually all Tudor writers elaborated Richard's ugliness and evil character. It was given out that he had spent two years in his mother's womb, and after a difficult birth he had emerged with hair down to his shoulders, and a full set of teeth: 'To signify thou cam'st to bite the world . . .'.

The one deed that Richard will always be accused of is the murder of the two princes in the Tower. No proof exists – even of the fact that they *were* murdered. The two boys simply disappeared. No one ever discovered what became of them. The fact remains, however, that Richard, their uncle, who was their guardian accountable for their welfare, suddenly claimed the crown, and no one dared ask awkward questions.

Well, one nobleman, Lord Hastings, did express some misgivings about the way things were being handled, so Richard simply arrested him at a Council meeting and had him beheaded on the spot. After that, silence about the princes was understandable.

In the face of all the bad press given to him by the Tudors, it is extremely difficult to arrive at the truth. An active society exists to redeem his good name. And reading some of the voluminous pamphlets produced in his favour, you begin to believe he was a paragon of virtue. Who will ever know?

It is certainly known that during his brother's reign Richard had been a tower of strength to him, maintaining peace and governing wisely and well in the north of England. He was based in York, where he became greatly respected and loved. He never lost his good reputation in the north. However, when he became king he hardly had time to do much, in a short reign of only twenty-six months. Like all usurpers he had many enemies, and he had to deal with a rebellion led by the Duke of Buckingham, his former friend and ally. Buckingham was immediately beheaded, in Salisbury market place, and Richard knew from then on that his enemies were looking towards Henry Tudor, Earl of Richmond, as a new leader. Henry was biding his time, in Brittany.

Eventually, as everyone knows, Henry Tudor spearheaded the revolt against Richard. He landed at Milford Haven, hoping to recruit Welshmen for his cause. Then he marched towards Leicester, where the decisive Battle of Bosworth brought the long succession of Plantagenets to an end. Some of the legends about the battle are questionable, but it is nice to remember them. Certainly, the Earl of Stanley swayed the course of history by suddenly making up his mind to support Henry rather than Richard. Certainly, Richard fought bravely to defend himself. But whether the crown was really found in a hawthorn bush, and whether Stanley really did crown Henry on the spot will never be proved.

Richard's naked carcass was slung over his horse and taken back to Leicester for a crude burial. Later his bones were flung into a river and lost. The Tudors had taken over.

# HENRY VII

## 1457–1509   REIGNED 1485–1509

### Son of Edmund Tudor and Margaret Beaufort

**Henry VII can be described as prudent, tight-fisted, thoughtful and cultured. Although never popular, nevertheless he gave England a much-needed period of peace and stability.**

In his later years Henry became something of a recluse, presiding over a gloomy court, and counting his money. He personally went through the nation's accounts. However, as a young man he was bold, energetic and determined. A contemporary writer describes him as 'remarkably attractive and his face was cheerful, especially when speaking'.

Why did he emerge as leader of the opposition to Richard III? Well, his background is interesting. On his father's side, his grandfather had been that Owen Tudor who had been Henry V's personal attendant, and who had fallen in love with Henry's queen, Catherine of Valois, after Henry V had died, marrying her in great secrecy and fathering no fewer than five children before their secret came out.

As for Henry's mother, Margaret Beaufort, she was aged only thirteen when she gave birth to him, but she was already a widow. Her husband, Henry's father, had died as a prisoner of the Yorkists. Margaret Beaufort was descended from John of Gaunt, Duke of Lancaster and son of Edward III. She was the latter's great-great-granddaughter. The future Henry VII, then, never knew his father. What he did know was that when Henry VI was murdered in 1471, he, Henry Tudor, aged sixteen, immediately became the head of the House of Lancaster. As such, any enemy of the Yorkists would naturally look to him as leader of the opposition.

The teenage Henry had royal blood in his veins, and had no reason to love the Yorkists who had killed his father. And being who he was, he had to be constantly on guard to avoid capture by the Yorkists. For fourteen years he lived in exile in Brittany. Clearly, he was a king in waiting.

The story of the Battle of Bosworth needs no retelling. It was, of course, one of the great turning-points of history, though perhaps at the time it may have seemed just another of those interminable skirmishes between Yorkists and Lancastrians.

In hindsight, however, we can see that Henry Tudor's sheer mastery of statecraft helped to steer England back into peace and prosperity. He may perhaps appear somewhat dull as a king, but he had had excitement enough as a boy, and he was wise enough to realise that kingship was a skill which needed hard and patient work.

He had to cope with two possible threats from people pretending to have claims to the throne. The first was Lambert Simnel, whose supporters actually crowned him 'Edward VI' in Ireland. Henry was merciful, and when eventually Simnel was defeated and captured Henry simply put him to work as a turn-spit in his kitchens. Far better than making a martyr out of him!

Then there was Perkin Warbeck, who claimed to be the younger of the two 'Princes in the Tower', calling himself 'Richard IV'. But he too was treated leniently, until he became too much of a nuisance.

Perhaps Henry's master-stroke was his marriage to Edward IV's daughter, Elizabeth of York. As far back as 1483, even before Bosworth and while he was still in exile, Henry had taken a solemn oath, on Christmas Day, in Rennes Cathedral that when he became King of England he would marry the Princess Elizabeth, heiress of the House of York. On the face of it, this union looks like a cool premeditated marriage of convenience, and certainly it did serve, very successfully, to unite the warring factions of York and Lancaster. The red and white 'Tudor Rose' was a logo which everybody could understand: unity at last.

However, Henry and Elizabeth became a devoted couple. Almost uniquely among English kings, Henry was totally faithful to his young wife, ten years his junior. Together they took immense pride in their growing family. Henry made special arrangements for Elizabeth to give birth to her first child at Winchester. It was a boy, and the nation rejoiced as they christened him Arthur, a name which recaptured the past legendary glory of Britain.

But alas, Arthur died aged fifteen, and his parents were distracted with grief. It was left for the younger boy, the future Henry VIII, to become heir and marry Arthur's young widow, Catherine of Aragon.

And then, a year later, Elizabeth herself died in childbirth. Henry was again distraught. For the rest of his life he withdrew more and more into his own private busy world of keeping England solvent.

We owe much to Henry VII. He gave England peace and prosperity, which it desperately needed; he founded the remarkable Tudor dynasty; he started England off on its course of exploration and foreign trade in the newly discovered world, encouraging the Cabots in their voyages to North America.

Finally, we must thank him for one of the most beautiful pieces of architecture in the world – his chapel in Westminster Abbey. Originally, he had wanted to rehabilitate his ancestor Henry VI, pressing the Pope to declare his predecessor a saint. The arrangements were never completed, but the chapel now contains his own tomb, a magnificent memorial with a life-like effigy by the Italian sculptor Torrigiano.

It is a great pity that Henry VII's other architectural masterpiece, Richmond Palace, has not survived. This was another extraordinarily beautiful building; it had fourteen turrets and a great tower. It was his favourite place of residence, and was also greatly enjoyed by Henry VIII and Elizabeth I, who eventually died there. It was built on the site of Sheen Palace, which had been destroyed by fire. Henry renamed it Richmond in reference to his own former earldom. Although the palace has gone, the name remains.

Henry VII's personal bereavements aged him prematurely, and he died at the age of fifty-two, leaving the throne to his boundlessly energetic second son, Henry VIII.

# HENRY VIII
## 1491–1547   REIGNED 1509–1547
### Son of Henry VII and Elizabeth of York

**Henry VIII began life as a hugely talented, attractive and intelligent man, but he became increasingly cruel, savagely ruthless, and a bloated monster. The curious thing is that he was astonishingly popular throughout his reign, and even today the cocksure figure of 'Bluff King Hal' has a quaint and comforting charm about it.**

Henry VIII was not quite eighteen when he came to the throne, and just a few days before his coronation he had married a Spanish princess, Catherine of Aragon. She was twenty-three at the time, and had previously been the wife of Henry's older brother, Arthur, the heir to the throne. Arthur had died suddenly in 1502, so Henry was unexpectedly pitchforked into being the next king. Until that time it had been planned that he would become Archbishop of Canterbury. Nevertheless, kings had to have wives and Catherine was available. It seemed a sensible arrangement.

The troubles of the Wars of the Roses were only a generation away, and the Tudors were still considered upstarts by many of the old Plantagenet supporters. Therefore it was vital that Henry should have a son and heir. A nightmare of chaos was likely unless there was a clear succession. As the

## HAMPTON COURT PALACE

Situated in what is now Greater London, about 3 miles from Kingston upon Thames, Hampton Court Palace was built between 1514 and 1520 for Cardinal Wolsey, and was then given by him to Henry VIII in a vain attempt to win back royal favour. Over the next two and a quarter centuries all Britain's kings and queens lived here and many additions have been made to the original Tudor palace.

Upon taking possession, Henry VIII added the Great Hall, a new kitchen, a tilt-yard and the real-tennis court. It was here that he fêted Anne Boleyn; here that Jane Seymour gave birth to the future Edward VI and shortly afterwards died; here that Henry lived briefly with Anne of Cleves; here that he adored Catherine Howard until he heard of her infidelities; here that he married Catherine Parr, his sixth and final wife.

Mary I and her husband Philip of Spain lived here, as did Elizabeth I, James I, Charles I, and Oliver Cromwell, governing England as Lord Protector. Charles II brought his mistresses here. It was the favourite residence of William and Mary, who redecorated it, and it was while riding to Hampton Court from Kensington that William fell and received his fatal injuries. Queen Anne gave birth to her longest-living son, the Duke of Gloucester, at Hampton Court.

George I and George II both lived here, but one day George II lost his temper with his grandson, the future George III, and boxed his ears. Perhaps the effect of this was to make George III dislike Hampton Court, for after he became king in 1760 he never even visited the place again, nor has any sovereign lived there since that time.

A part of Hampton Court Palace was damaged by fire in 1986 but it has now been fully restored. There is so much to see here that half a day is hardly enough. There are six separate routes to take: Henry VIII's State Apartments; the Queen's Apartments; the Georgian Rooms; the King's Apartments; the Wolsey Rooms and Renaissance Picture Gallery; and the Tudor Kitchens. There are 60 acres of Palace Gardens to see – Tudor, Baroque and Victorian – laid out by generations of royal gardeners; a greenhouse containing the largest and oldest vine in the world, planted in 1768; and you can always get lost in the Maze, set out by the gardeners of William III's reign in the 1690s.

years went on, Catherine of Aragon seemed less and less likely to produce the necessary son. True, they had a daughter, Mary, but that wasn't quite enough. Thus began the long and tragic succession of marriage disasters that marked Henry's reign.

After more than twenty years with Catherine, Henry fell in love with the 'concubine', Anne Boleyn. She held out for marriage with him, and so he did everything he could to get a divorce. The only excuse he could find was the rather specious one that Catherine had been his sister-in-law, and it was against Church law to marry your brother's wife. In vain did poor Catherine plead that she and Arthur had both been only fifteen when they married; that the marriage had only lasted four months and had never been consummated. Henry stripped her of her title and privileges, placed her under house arrest, and declared their only daughter to be a bastard.

Anne Boleyn enjoyed a brief three-year marriage, but was beheaded for alleged infidelity. Her fate was not helped by the fact that she too did not produce a son. Their only daughter, Elizabeth, was also declared a bastard.

Henry's next wife, Jane Seymour was more successful. She did produce a son, Edward, but she died just twelve days after giving birth.

Thomas Cromwell, Henry's chief adviser at the time, suggested Anne of Cleves as the next wife, for political reasons. Although Holbein produced a favourable picture of her, Henry was disgusted by Anne's looks when he met her. He went through the marriage ceremony, but then abandoned her and gave her the official status of 'sister'. Cromwell was beheaded.

Meanwhile, Henry had genuinely fallen in love again, this time with Catherine Howard. She was only eighteen when they married, and he enjoyed a lively time with her for well over a year. But she was too lively, and after eighteen months he had her beheaded for adultery.

By this time Henry was sick, fat, and in agony with an ulcerous leg. It seems astonishing that he should actually marry again. However, his eye finally fell on Catherine Parr. She had twice been widowed, but she was still only thirty-one. She gave him some comfort in tending his leg, but even she almost lost her head for voicing her religious opinions too freely. Luckily for her, Henry died three years later.

Henry's marriages make fascinating reading, and they are what most people remember. However, his real contribution to England's history lies in the gigantic religious and social changes he made.

Breaking with the Pope over his divorce with Catherine of Aragon, he declared himself head of the Church in England. Then, in order to destroy the power of catholicism in England, and incidentally acquire massive riches for himself, he 'dissolved' all the 823 abbeys and monasteries throughout the kingdom. This was the most far-reaching sudden change ever made in the lifestyle of the country. Thomas Cromwell pushed through this 'Dissolution of the Monasteries' with incredible ruthlessness. Within a few years hundreds of beautiful buildings were broken up and all the monks were forced to abandon their monastic ways. It's probably true to say that no other monarch could have done such deeds and survived.

More positively, Henry personally supervised the completion of the magnificent extension to Westminster Abbey known as Henry VII's Chapel; he also added to the great palace of Hampton Court, given to him by Cardinal Wolsey; and he founded Trinity College, Cambridge.

But the most memorable building associated with Henry VIII is King's College Chapel, Cambridge. This chapel had been started by Henry VI and the shell of the building is his. However, the interior decorations are pure Tudor, with the Tudor Rose and other Tudor emblems everywhere. The wooden screen leading to the choir was carved in those brief few months when Henry doted on Anne Boleyn, so that the initials of Henry and Anne can be seen there.

Henry VIII's was an immensely energetic reign. He strengthened the English navy; he incorporated Wales into England; made Ireland a kingdom; waged wars in France and Scotland; and involved himself deeply in the religious controversies of the time. Above all, he tolerated no opposition. He executed at least fifty people who crossed his will, including two of his most trusted chief advisers: Sir Thomas More and Thomas Cromwell. Cardinal Wolsey only just escaped execution by diplomatically dying first. Henry VIII enjoyed absolute power.

# EDWARD VI

## 1537–1553   REIGNED 1547–1553

### Son of Henry VIII and Jane Seymour

**A precocious and rather cold child, Edward was only nine years old when he came to the throne and only fifteen when he died. Nevertheless, he made his mark.**

Family life cannot have been easy for Edward VI. His mother, Jane Seymour, died a fortnight after his birth; his first stepmother, Anne of Cleves, was divorced from his father before he was three; his second stepmother, Catherine Howard, was beheaded for adultery when he was four; and his syphilitic father died when he was nine.

In the early years of his reign, Edward was guided by his mother's brother, Edward Seymour, Duke of Somerset, who took the title of Lord Protector. But when he was twelve there was a power struggle and the role of Protector was taken over by John Dudley, Duke of Northumberland. Somerset was executed. There is something chilling about the calm way Edward recorded his uncle's execution. In his diary he noted: 'Somerset had his head cut off.'

Edward was highly intelligent, taking a keen interest in all the religious controversies of the age. He was a fanatical supporter of the new Protestantism. He liked nothing better than to argue theological issues with bishops; among his Court Preachers were John Knox, Ridley, Cranmer, Latimer and Hooper.

In medieval England people left sums of money to have masses said for them after their death. In large churches and cathedrals there are beautiful 'Chantries' where these masses used to be said. As Protestants no longer believed in saying prayers for the dead, a special Act of Parliament, the 'Dissolution of the Chantries Act', put a final stop to this ancient custom. Many of the chantry priests had been useful in providing local education, so when education seemed to suffer as a result of this Act, Edward was personally concerned to establish new grammar schools to make up this loss. To this day there are a number of 'King Edward VI' schools in England, dating from this time.

Poor Edward. He suffered with pulmonary tuberculosis and spent many months dying. Plans to marry him off to all sorts of people had to be abandoned. His 'Protector', the wicked Duke of Northumberland, did not publicly declare Edward's death for several days, so that he could make schemes for the succession. There were even rumours of poison.

Edward would have been horrified if he knew that his Catholic half-sister Mary would succeed him. His last words were: 'O my Lord God, defend this realm from papistry.' He is buried in Westminster Abbey.

# LADY JANE GREY
## 1537–1554   REIGNED IN JULY 1553
### Daughter of Henry Grey and Lady Frances Brandon

The 'Nine Days Queen'. A clever teenager, petite, fair-haired and freckled, Lady Jane was cruelly manipulated into being declared queen on the death of King Edward VI, her second cousin. Her reign lasted only nine days.

There is no figure more tragic or more pathetic in the whole line of British kings and queens than Lady Jane Grey, who was only fifteen when she became queen, and sixteen when they chopped off her head.

Lady Jane spent her life among royalty, being a great-granddaughter of King Henry VII. If only King Edward VI had lived, she might easily have married him. Indeed, at one time there had been talk of this. After all, she was exactly the same age as the king, so she must have been almost the only young companion he had ever known. Henry VIII's widowed queen, Catherine Parr, helped in her education and upbringing, and the two future queens, Mary and Elizabeth, cousins of her mother, were kind to her, treating her like a younger sister. Elizabeth was only five years older than Jane. Brilliantly intelligent, Jane genuinely preferred reading Plato in the original Greek rather than hunting on her father's magnificent estate at Bradgate Park, near Leicester.

It would never have remotely occurred to Jane that she might possibly be offered the crown. Her great-uncle, Henry VIII, had made the line of succession perfectly clear; the throne would go first to his son Edward, and then, if events proved necessary, successively to his daughters Mary and Elizabeth. Some people were very worried that Mary, a fervent Catholic, might reverse all the Protestant reforms if ever she became queen, but on the whole the people of England had an affection for her as they thought that she and her mother, Catherine of Aragon, had been badly treated.

The villain in the story of Lady Jane Grey was the unscrupulous arch-schemer, Robert Dudley, Duke of Northumberland, who was virtually dictator of England during the reign of the boy-king, Edward VI. When it became clear that Edward was dying, the Duke of Northumberland first persuaded Jane's parents to marry Jane to his own son, Guilford Dudley. Then, playing on the king's Protestant faith, the Duke persuaded Edward to 'devise' the throne to Jane, as she was also a staunch Protestant. By this means he not only hoped to prevent Mary from re-introducing the Catholic faith into England, but also hoped that it would make his son the king consort, and thus his own power would be perpetuated.

At every stage in the plot the fifteen-year-old Jane was bullied into submission. She knew her situation with perfect clarity, and was absolutely horrified when she was told she was to be made queen. 'The crown is not my right,' she said, 'and pleaseth me not. The Lady Mary is the rightful heir.'

Mary, of course, quickly claimed the throne, with overwhelming popular support. The ordinary people hardly knew Jane, and they hated the Duke of Northumberland. The conspiracy crumbled, and the Duke was executed immediately. Poor Jane was kept prisoner in the Tower of London for six months before Mary finally decided to have her executed too. From her room in the Tower Lady Jane saw the decapitated body of her teenage husband Guilford Dudley wheeled past her apartments in a hand-cart, knowing that within minutes it would be her turn to lay her head on the block.

As she stood on Tower Green that cold February morning she made a brave speech, saying 'I do wash my hands in innocency before God'. But the axeman was ready: 'So perish all the Queen's enemies!' he declared, as he dutifully held up a hideous dripping object. 'Behold the head of a traitor!'

# MARY I

## 1516–1558   REIGNED 1553–1558

### *Daughter of Henry VIII and Catherine of Aragon*

**An intensely Catholic soul, Mary suffered greatly as a child and young woman under her father's very Protestant reign. She became quite pathetic in her unrequited love for Philip of Spain.**

'Bloody Mary!' For many people this sums up the woman and her reign. However, one has to feel sorry for her. Mary endured a terrible childhood. Her mother, Catherine of Aragon, was rejected and banished from court; she herself was publicly declared a bastard; she saw her father marry and then behead his concubine Anne Boleyn. As a fervent Catholic she watched as her father dismantled the whole structure of Catholicism in England. She witnessed the death of a second stepmother after childbirth, the ill-treatment of a third stepmother, and then saw a fourth stepmother beheaded. Perhaps to her relief her fifth stepmother, Catherine Parr, was actually kind and sympathetic.

Nevertheless, at her father's death Mary found her precocious little half-brother, Edward, twenty-one years younger than herself, positively menacing in his insistence that she should abandon her Catholic religion and follow his own fanatically held Protestantism. Even when Edward died, she found her way to the throne barred by a crude and clumsy plot to oust her from her rightful inheritance. Poor Mary! Almost nothing in the thirty-seven years leading up to her coronation prepared her for handling the situation. Instead, she was ruthlessly determined to restore the Catholic faith to England, come what may.

## 'BLOODY MARY' AND THE VICTIMS OF RELIGIOUS PERSECUTION

Statistics are notoriously unreliable, but according to one account the number of people burnt during the reign of Mary amounted to 288, and many more perished in prison, starved or maltreated. The burnings are well authenticated, and left terrible memories of her reign.

An edition of *Foxe's Book of Martyrs*, giving details, records: 'There were burnt 5 bishops, 21 divines, 8 gentlemen, 84 artificers, 100 husbandmen, servants and labourers, 26 wives, 9 virgins, 2 boys, and 2 infants. 64 more were persecuted for their religion, whereof 7 were whipped, 16 perished in prison and 12 were buried in dunghills.'

The deaths took place all over the country, in the four years from 1555 to 1558. The first recorded was John Rogers, a priest, who was burnt at Smithfield in London on 4 February 1555, and the last were John Corneford, Christopher Browne, John Herst, Alice Snoth and Catherine Tynley, all of whom were burnt at Canterbury on 10 November 1558, just a week before Mary herself died.

It is only when we remember the scale of this terror that we can understand the desperate reluctance to bring back another Catholic monarch to the throne. Shouts of 'No Popery' were heard even in the twentieth century.

And then what a disastrous marriage! She had actually been betrothed, as a child and political pawn, to the Holy Roman Emperor, Charles V. Now, in her late thirties, she persuaded herself that her best choice would be his son, Philip. Accordingly, Philip arrived in England and they were married in sumptuous state in Winchester Cathedral. Today in that cathedral we can still see the elegant chair given to her by the Pope, and in which she sat on that occasion, probably the happiest day of her life.

But then everything went sour. Philip could barely conceal his distaste for her and flirted with her ladies-in-waiting, showing much more interest in Mary's half-sister, Elizabeth. He left England as soon as he decently could, and returned only once, staying for only a few weeks. Pathetically, Mary thought she was pregnant, but her swollen stomach turned out to be the symptom of some dreadful illness. She was heartbroken to find out that she had deluded herself by imagining a pregnancy.

Meanwhile, determined as ever to rid the realm of Protestants, she literally and physically burnt hundreds of people all over the country who still clung to their Protestant faith. They ranged from bishops and even an archbishop to ordinary humble folk, weavers, shoemakers, wheelwrights. Even cripples and blind youngsters were pushed into the flames. Such actions were neither forgotten nor forgiven. Even while she was alive she was called 'Bloody Mary', and great was the rejoicing when she died.

Perhaps the most fundamental result of Mary's reign was the generation of an intense hatred and fear of Catholic extremism. The cry 'No Popery' has been heard ever since. Over a century later, this fear was enough to force another monarch, James II, from the throne and to prompt the passing of a law preventing any Catholic from ever becoming king, or a ruling monarch from marrying a Catholic. This law still binds the monarchy today.

At Mary's death, her half-sister, Elizabeth, was ready and waiting to take the throne.

# ELIZABETH I

## 1533–1603  REIGNED 1558–1603

### *Daughter of Henry VIII and Anne Boleyn*

**Elizabeth I was, without a doubt, one of the world's greatest monarchs. She dominated England for almost half a century, and, wily, manipulative, imperious and theatrical, she has fascinated historians ever since.**

The secret of Elizabeth's brilliant skill in statecraft probably lies in the terrible events she experienced during those dangerous twenty-five years before she became queen. Just imagine: she was only two-and-a-half when her mother, Queen Anne Boleyn, was savagely beheaded. She lived to see four stepmothers disappear: one dying after childbirth, the next divorced, the next beheaded, and the final one, Catherine Parr, dying in childbirth having remarried almost immediately after the death of Henry VIII. She was publicly declared a bastard, and knew what it was to be poor, unloved, and virtually under constant house arrest.

During the reigns of her half-brother and her half-sister, Elizabeth was occasionally in favour but mostly in semi-banishment from the court. People around her were constantly being imprisoned and beheaded, sometimes for their deeds, sometimes for their religion, sometimes simply for being who they were, as in the case of her young cousin, Lady Jane Grey.

Perhaps Elizabeth's worst moment was during the reign of Mary, when she was taken, aged twenty, as a prisoner to the Tower of London, suspected of treason. Life must have seemed absolutely hopeless, and Elizabeth simply refused to enter the Tower by 'Traitors' Gate'. She sat on a stone by the muddy river-bank. 'I am come in no traitor,' she sobbed, 'but as true a woman to the Queen's Majesty as any now living.' But they forced her in and she remained a prisoner for two months.

Elizabeth wrote to Mary begging for freedom. But although she was later transferred to Woodstock, conditions were still claustrophobic; sixty soldiers were sent there to guard her and prevent her from escaping. Miserably she scratched a sad little rhyme on her window-pane with a diamond: 'Much suspected, "of me/Nothing proved can be" Quoth Elizabeth, prisoner'.

All through these desperate years she learned many lessons. She learned how to survive. She learned how to be diplomatic. And, seeing the mistakes of others, she learned how to be queen. So when Mary died, Elizabeth took to her duties with consummate artistry. No one has ever practised royal skills so successfully.

To begin with, she dressed for the part with spectacular finery. Just consider the many elaborate paintings of Elizabeth. Who else could have worn those gorgeous dresses, those fantastic jewels, those awe-inspiring collars?

Then, she delighted in moving about the country, staying with loyal and enthusiastic subjects. Once she stayed three whole weeks at Kenilworth Castle. The entertainments put on nightly for her pleasure were among the wonders of the century. The people loved her, and she flattered them as no other monarch has ever done, before or since, by telling them how much she loved them. 'You may well have a greater prince,' she said, 'but you shall never have a more loving prince.' She meant it, boasting that she was wholly English ('Mere English') as opposed to her half-sister, who was, of course, half-Spanish.

One notable feature of her reign was the abatement of religious fanaticism. Feelings were still high after the intolerance of the previous reign. But Elizabeth's Protestantism was less ferocious. Nevertheless, possible threats against the throne were another matter. Elizabeth felt she simply had to order the execution of her Catholic cousin, Mary, Queen of Scots. But it took her months to bring herself to sign the death-warrant.

All through her reign she used her virginity to tease and intrigue. Marriage was a trump-card which she constantly had in her hand, but which she resolutely refused to play. Who *would* she marry? Philip of Spain? the Duke of Alençon? The Archduke of Austria? No one could tell. Her heart probably belonged to Robert Dudley, Earl of Leicester, but somehow the years slipped by and to the end she remained the Virgin Queen. She was pleased when Sir Walter Raleigh proposed calling his new American settlement Virginia after her. It's probably the only territory ever named after spinsterhood!

Her long reign was remarkable for the great men and great events it inspired: Shakespeare, Francis Drake, Walter Raleigh, Philip Sidney. She remained at the centre of events and caught the spirit of the age.

Let us give her the last word. Here is Elizabeth's magnificent speech at Tilbury, when she talked directly to her troops, inspiring courage in the face of threatened invasion. Who could resist these words?

> Let tyrants fear . . . I have placed my chiefest strength and goodwill in the loyal hearts and goodwill of my subjects . . . I know I have but the body of a weak and feeble woman: but I have the heart and stomach of a king – and a king of England too – and think it foul scorn that Parma or Spain or any Prince of Europe should dare to invade the borders of my realm.

Surely this remains the greatest speech ever made by an English monarch.

Her magnificent tomb in Westminster Abbey shows her in old age. It does not flatter: even today we can sense the awe she must have inspired.

# JAMES I
## 1566–1625
### REIGNED 1567–1625 AS JAMES VI OF SCOTLAND
### REIGNED 1603–1625 AS JAMES I OF ENGLAND

*Son of Henry Stuart, Lord Darnley, and Mary, Queen of Scots*

**Regarded as 'the wisest fool in Christendom', James I was deeply learned but totally eccentric.**

Admittedly, Elizabeth's reign was a hard act to follow. Nevertheless, everyone must have thought James a real oddity. With a tongue too big for his mouth James slobbered and drooled. He never washed, so that his black hands felt like satin. He wore padded clothes as a protection against

73

assassins. He delighted in plunging his legs bloodily into the bowels of the animals he hunted and killed. Although married, he was quite openly homosexual, publicly slavering kisses upon his favourites. Despite this, he was intelligent, shrewd and well experienced in kingship. After all, in Scotland he had been king since babyhood, and he was thirty-seven when he moved from his modest Edinburgh court to the elaborate sophistication of London.

It's easy to laugh at James, but it has been said that he seemed to be made up of two men: a nervous, drivelling idiot, and a witty, well-read scholar. Certainly he enjoyed writing and arguing. He published collections of verse as well as books on the paranormal, political theory, and the health hazards of smoking. He personally supervised the team of scholars and bishops who produced the Authorised Version of the Bible in 1611, one of the greatest glories of the English language. It was dedicated to James as 'principal mover and author of the work'.

Every time we use the term 'Great Britain' we should remember that it was James I who invented it. He introduced it so as to recognise the fact that England, Wales and Scotland had at last become united, after a fashion, under his kingship.

He introduced two sports into England: 'horse-running' (he started Epsom Races), and the Scottish game of golf.

The early years of James's reign happily coincided with the greatest period of Shakespeare's writing. James enthusiastically supported all forms of theatrical entertainment and honoured Shakespeare's company with the title of 'The King's Players'. And in compliment to the new king and his interest in witchcraft, Shakespeare produced his Scottish tragedy, *Macbeth*. Ben Jonson and Inigo Jones developed elaborate court masques for him, virtually a new art-form under James's active encouragement.

Nevertheless, it has to be admitted that on the whole James was a weak and foolish king. Discontent grew more and more as he insisted quite obsessively on his 'Divine Right' to rule without any need to take advice from Parliament. And then there was his embarrassing homosexuality, which didn't exactly increase his reputation or popularity.

James became increasingly senile, deteriorating mentally and physically. Finally, he suffered a stroke, which left him without any control of himself, and from which he died. It was a pathetic end to a very mixed-up reign.

# CHARLES I

## 1600–1649   REIGNED 1625–1649

### Son of James I and Anne of Denmark

'Charles the Martyr' was cultured but proud, filled with a sense of Divine Righteousness. He was the only English king to be put on trial, sentenced, and executed.

The life of Charles I unfolds like some remorseless Greek tragedy. Poor Charles! Melancholy, lonely, proud – he haunts us with his death. Even now, wreaths appear round his statue in Whitehall on the anniversary of that dismal snowy day in January when his head was severed from his body in one savage blow.

Charles was never born to be king. If only his elder brother hadn't gone swimming in the Thames and caught that fatal chill we might well have had a strong and purposeful King Henry the Ninth. . . . But that was not to be.

Charles was only three when his father left Scotland to become King of England. It must have been an exciting change. But he never lost his Scottish accent. Probably he had a happy childhood, but when he was twelve the sad death of his brother Henry pushed him into the alarming certainty of being future king.

Perhaps the jolliest time of his life was when he and James's favourite, Steenie, travelled incognito to Spain, to woo the Spanish Princess Anna. They wore false beards and called themselves John and Thomas Smith. Charles even fell in love with Anna. But it was a madcap scheme which came to nothing. On his return to England Charles was quickly pushed into a political betrothal to Henrietta Maria, the fifteen-year-old sister of King Louis XIII of France.

Within a few months, James died and Charles, aged twenty-four, succeeded to the throne. And what a muddled, exasperating reign it was to be! He was desperately shy, yet insufferably arrogant. His deeply held conviction that he ruled by 'Divine Right' coloured everything he did. He believed quite literally that he had God's authority to do whatever he wished. Three times he dissolved Parliament, and for eleven whole years he tried to rule the country by himself.

He relied for advice on his friend Steenie, the Duke of Buckingham. Then, when Steenie was stabbed to death in Portsmouth, he turned more and more to his wife Henrietta Maria and also to Tom Wentworth, whom he created Earl of Strafford. It wasn't long before Parliament came up with an excuse to have 'Black Tom' executed for treason, after which it publicly rebuked King Charles for his poor kingship in its now famous 'Grand Remonstrance'.

The whole situation became ever more unbearable and inevitably boiled over into civil war in 1642. Battles, skirmishes, sieges, imprisonments, foiled attempts to escape: the next few years remain a confused tale of kingly incompetence and parliamentary determination. Oliver Cromwell, MP for Huntingdon, increasingly found himself taking charge over the country. Eventually it seemed to everybody that the only way of getting rid of this embarrassment was to send Charles to the execution block.

The death of Charles is indelibly imprinted on the nation's memory. It was a kind of ritual sacrifice. Having been imprisoned for months in various strongholds, Charles was eventually tried and sentenced in Westminster Hall. It was solemnly proclaimed that:

> Charles Stuart, for levying war against the present Parliament and people therein represented, should be put to death by beheading as a tyrant, traitor, murderer and public enemy of the good people of this land.

So, on 30 January 1649, the hapless king walked with superb dignity with his captors from St James's Palace to the Palace of Whitehall. He had the forethought to wear two shirts, to keep himself warm on that bitter cold day. It was not for extra comfort: he simply didn't want to be seen to shiver and seem afraid. 'I would have no such imputation,' he declared. 'I bless my God I am prepared.'

It was an awesome end. He stepped on to the wooden scaffold which had been constructed outside the Banqueting House, and he spoke with unforgettable courage to the crowds that had assembled: 'I go from a corruptible to an incorruptible crown, where no disturbances can be,' he declared.

And an eyewitness described how 'there was such a groan by the thousands present as I never heard before, and desire I may never hear again'.

Charles was buried, rather surreptitiously, in St George's Chapel, Windsor.

# OLIVER CROMWELL
## 1599–1658 LORD PROTECTOR 1653–1658
### Son of Sir Henry Cromwell

**Firm, God-fearing, capable and honest, Oliver Cromwell was ruthless to those who opposed him.**

Strictly speaking, Oliver Cromwell should not appear in these pages, as he was never king. All the same, he was offered the crown, and had all the power and dignity of a king during the brief period when he was 'Lord Protector'.

Cromwell was born at Huntingdon in 1599, son of Sir Henry Cromwell of Hinchinbrook. His grandfather had been a Welshman called Richard Williams, a nephew and protégé of Henry VIII's notorious minister, Thomas Cromwell, responsible for organising the Dissolution of the Monasteries, and for arranging the embarrassing unwanted marriage between Henry VIII and Anne of Cleves. Oliver Cromwell owes his name to the fact that this grandfather changed his name from Williams to Cromwell as a compliment to Thomas Cromwell. Thus even at this time the family must have been proud of helping to shape the course of English history.

Oliver was MP for Huntingdon, like the former Conservative Prime Minister John Major. He quickly became well known for his passionate speeches against the king. During the Civil War he showed outstanding military capacity and after Charles had been beheaded he became Chairman of the Council of State. On 16 December 1653 he was declared 'Lord Protector' and thus virtually became a dictator, ruling by decree.

Cromwell's installation as Lord Protector took place at a magnificent ceremony in Westminster Hall. The streets were lined with troops, and Cromwell himself used the King's State Coach of crimson and gold, drawn by six white horses. He was conducted in state to a throne, in front of which was a table covered with velvet fringed with gold, on which was a Bible, a sword and a sceptre. And when he had taken the oath a flourish of trumpets announced to all the crowds inside and outside the hall, that 'England had a Vice-roy' – for this was what the royalists first called him.

As 'Protector' then, Cromwell is inseparable from the line of kings, and foreign ambassadors reported admiringly of his dignity and authority. He preferred to live at Hampton Court, and resided there as a monarch, receiving guests and foreign visitors with ceremony. The French Ambassador wrote to his government after one such visit:

You would scarcely notice any change, except that in the place of the King, the throne is occupied by Mr Cromwell, arrayed in purple velvet edged and lined with ermine. He sits on a golden chair, raised three steps above his attendants; but unlike the late Court, the ladies of the Protector's family are rarely seen and take little part in official life.

All the same, Mrs Cromwell did her part in entertaining ambassadors and their wives and kept a book of useful recipes for such occasions.

Cromwell allowed no licentiousness of any kind. He flatly refused to receive Christina, Queen of Sweden, because he didn't approve of her private life. Dances and plays were forbidden. But he loved music, and his Secretary, none other than the great poet John Milton, author of 'Paradise Lost', used to play the organ at Hampton Court for his entertainment.

Parliamentarian soldiers ruined many beautiful cathedrals and churches with their pillaging and crude destruction of statues. Perhaps Cromwell himself was not personally to blame, but he has never been forgotten or forgiven by the Irish for his ruthless massacres at Wexford and Drogheda during the Civil War. The point to remember is that Cromwell, like any rising dictator, simply did not tolerate opposition. Once he became Protector, he became much more flexible. In a letter to the French minister Cardinal Mazarin he wrote these words: 'I desire from my heart, I have prayed for it, I have waited for the day to see union and right understanding between godly people, Scots, English, Jews, Gentiles, Presbyterians, Independents, Anabaptists, and all.' He is known to have deplored the persecution of Catholics.

Proof of Oliver's tolerance was that he allowed Jews back into England; they had been banished from our shores by Edward I almost four centuries before. Manasseh Ben Israel travelled to England to beg Cromwell to allow Jewish people to return. Some of the first to arrive settled in Petticoat Lane in London, adding great vivacity to the area. The Jews were so delighted with this new freedom and with Cromwell's part in it that one Rabbi actually went to Huntingdonshire to study Cromwell's genealogical tree, hoping to prove that Cromwell was descended from the royal line of Judah. He wasn't.

Oliver didn't live long as Protector. He died on his 'fortunate day' – 3 September, the date of two of his most successful battles (Dunbar in 1650, and Worcester in 1651). The night of his passing, in 1658, was marked by one of the most terrifying storms London has ever seen,

# THE CIVIL WAR, 1642–6 AND 1648–51

The Civil War was a turning-point in English history. After Charles I was defied, defeated and executed, the monarchy was never the same again. The Parliamentarian 'Roundheads' and the Royalist 'Cavaliers' first clashed at Hull in April 1642, when Charles was refused access to an arsenal for use against the Parliamentarians. A few weeks later, on 22 August, Charles raised his own standard in Nottingham.

All told, there were about 600 battles, skirmishes and sieges, and many places throughout the country bear witness to the bitter struggles between the Roundheads and the Cavaliers. The main battles in the First Civil War (1642–6) were: Edgehill (Warks.), 23 Oct. 1642; Newbury (Berks.), 20 Sept. 1643 and again 27 Oct. 1644; Marston Moor (near York), 2 July 1644; and Naseby (Northants.), 14 June 1645. Fighting continued until May 1646, when Charles surrendered. He was put on trial and executed on 30 January 1649.

Meanwhile, Royalist forces fought back, helped by the Scots. However, they were again defeated at Preston (Lancs.), 20 Aug. 1648; Dunbar (Lothian), 4 Sept. 1650; and the final and decisive battle at Worcester, 3 Sept. 1651. After this, Charles's son, the future Charles II, had to hide in an oak tree to escape capture, eventually making his way to France, where he lived in exile until Cromwell's death and the collapse of the Commonwealth.

Cromwell's role began when he raised a troop of cavalry, which he led in the Battle of Edgehill. His cavalry charge won the day at Marston Moor, and under the supreme command of Thomas Fairfax he led the victory at Naseby. His victories in the Second Civil War (1648–51) include Preston, Dunbar and Worcester, and he stamped out opposition in Ireland by massacring garrisons at Drogheda and Wexford. Cromwell became Chairman of the Council of State after Charles's execution, and in December 1653 he was proclaimed 'Lord Protector'.

causing the Thames to overflow its banks, church steeples to be blown down, and hundreds of houses to lose their roofs. Superstitious folk remembered it.

Someone who saw Cromwell's interment in Westminster Abbey described it as 'the joyfullest funeral he ever saw'. But his corpse was not to stay there long. Less than a year after the restoration of the monarchy, Oliver Cromwell's body was dug up, hanged, and chopped into pieces.

# RICHARD CROMWELL
## 1626–1712   LORD PROTECTOR SEPT. 1658–MAY 1659
### Son of Oliver and Elizabeth Cromwell

**After his father, Richard Cromwell was out of his depth. He simply couldn't cope with the job he inherited. On the difference between Oliver Cromwell and his son, someone living at the time remarked: 'The vulture died, and out of his ashes rose a tit-mouse.'**

Richard's two elder brothers had died, so after his father's death, rather reluctantly he found himself landed with the job of running the country. Although Oliver Cromwell had refused the crown in 1657, he did accept the right to nominate Richard as his successor. The principle of hereditary succession appears somewhat odd in these circumstances. Nevertheless, they were strange times, and a clearly defined succession is always a necessity. Accordingly, when Oliver died, Richard found himself the centre-piece of a magnificent installation ceremony in Westminster Hall, becoming Lord Protector II.

Immediately, Richard found himself struggling with a multitude of conflicting factions. He dissolved Parliament, and then in desperation recalled the Rump Parliament which had existed in 1653. Eventually, he had to admit defeat, and abdicated of his own accord in May 1659, just before Charles II returned. After the Restoration of the monarchy, Richard Cromwell was treated appallingly by Parliament and found it necessary to flee the country.

In fact, Parliament owed Richard £29,000, and set up a committee to look into the matter and to put things right. It was decided to sell off some plate and furniture to settle the debt, but this was never done, and the unfortunate Richard was obliged to live abroad, fleeing from arrest as a debtor. His poor wife Dorothy waited fifteen years for his return, but died without ever seeing him again. Meanwhile, he lived first in France and then in Geneva, under the assumed name of 'John Clarke'. Eventually, in 1680, he returned to England, still as John Clarke, and lived part of his time at Cheshunt, where he died on 12 July 1712, aged eighty-six, and part of his time with his daughter at Hursley, near Winchester, Hampshire.

A story is told that at a court ceremonial in 1709, presided over by Queen Anne, amid the throng of onlookers was an old man of eighty-three, dressed as a poor countryman. 'Have you ever seen such a sight before?' asked someone, rather patronisingly. 'Never since I sat in her chair,' came the surprising reply. . . . It was 'Idle Dick' himself.

# CHARLES II

## 1630–1685   REIGNED 1660–1685

### *Son of Charles I and Henrietta Maria*

**Charles II succeeded to the throne in 1649, on the death of his father, but effectively he reigned from 1660 to 1685. A witty and urbane seducer, a charming and ruthless opportunist and a lying deceiver, Charles was a complex and fascinating human being.**

If you had to choose just one monarch to be your companion on a desert island, the choice would have to be Charles II. As a human being, he was utterly kind and charming, full of fun and laughter, brave, resourceful. Perhaps rather self-indulgent, nevertheless he knew what it was to suffer hardship and yet remain cheerful.

His childhood was eventful. He grew up in the difficult years when his father Charles I was losing respect, losing battles, and eventually losing his head. Charles II himself, as a lad of twelve, was present at the Battle of Edgehill. He was involved in later battles, but as the royalist situation worsened, his father sent him to join his mother Henrietta Maria in Paris. He was only nineteen when he learned of his father's execution. He burst into tears as the messengers bringing the bad news called him 'Your Majesty'. Naturally, he wanted to claim his kingdom. But how? This was the question which he had to face for the next eleven years.

His first idea was to try to gain a foothold in Scotland. After all, he was King of Scotland as well as King of England, so it was an obvious starting-point. Accordingly, he landed in Scotland, where he was crowned king in the parish church of Scone on 1 January 1651. Then, as soon as he could, later that year, aged twenty-one, he crossed the border, marching south with an army of almost 17,000 soldiers, mainly Scottish. Cromwell marched north to meet him and the two armies met at Worcester.

The Battle of Worcester took place on 3 September and from the top of Worcester Cathedral tower Charles sadly watched the defeat of his Scottish army. It was Cromwell's 'lucky day', for it was coincidentally exactly a year beforehand that he had defeated another Scottish army at Dunbar.

From then on Charles was a fugitive. The famous episode when he and Colonel Carlis hid in an oak tree while Roundhead soldiers combed the woods below is a romantic fact of history. All over England pubs called 'The Royal Oak' still remind us of this adventure.

The next six weeks were alarmingly exciting, but after much travelling (at one stage he hid among the stones at Stonehenge) and after many disguises (at one stage he became a man-servant called 'William Jackson') Charles eventually crossed the Channel safely for an exile that was to last for another nine years.

After the death of Oliver Cromwell and the abdication of Richard Cromwell, there was an almost tangible yearning in England to bring back the king and to make a new start. Charles rode into London on his thirtieth birthday to a rapturous welcome. An eyewitness to Charles's return wrote of the 'inexpressible joy: the wayes strew'd with flowers; the bells ringing, the streetes hung with tapestry, fountains running with wine . . . trumpets, music and myriads of people flocking'. At night there were fireworks and illuminations. Anyone suspected of disloyalty had his windows smashed. Charles had had a hard apprenticeship and a long wait. What sort of king did he become?

Well, for one thing, he was head and shoulders more cultured and cosmopolitan than his predecessors. His exile in France had given him sophisticated tastes. Theatres were reopened, having been shut during the time of the Commonwealth. Classical standards were established in all the arts and, almost immediately on his return, Charles set his personal seal of approval to the prestigious scientific body, the Royal Society.

Secondly, his queen, Catherine of Braganza, may not have provided England with an heir, but her dowry was one of the most important ever brought here by a foreign princess: a large sum of money; the foreign cities of Bombay and Tangier; and trading rights to China and the Indies.

And thirdly, Charles's own attitude, mocking, good-humoured, relaxed and self-indulgent, seemed to rub off on to the nation under his rule. The ferocious bigotry of the Puritans was brought to an end. Good manners, rather than sectarian debate, were now seen to be important. Of Presbyterianism he remarked that it was 'not a religion for gentlemen'.

Much has been written about Charles's mistresses. He had many. And he had many bastards: he was kind to all sixteen of them, nine sons and seven daughters, giving many of them honours and titles. To this day the aristocracy of England is peopled with descendants of Charles II. But his extraordinary sexual appetite was not a hole-in-corner shame-faced matter. The nation took his foibles to its heart, and even today the mention of Nell Gwyn – just one of his many mistresses – suggests a notion of jollity and good fun. And Charles **did** bring a sense of fun to the monarchy. He was immensely popular, and he had an intuitive understanding of ordinary people. He said to his brother James, who was a totally different kind of human being, and who once showed concern over Charles's lax security arrangements: 'Don't worry, Jamie. They'll never kill me to make you king!'

However, James was inevitably his heir, for despite the sixteen bastards no legitimate heir was forthcoming. So brother James, aged fifty-one, succeeded to the throne when Charles very unexpectedly died in 1685.

# JAMES II
## 1633–1701   REIGNED 1685–1688
### Son of Charles I and Henrietta Maria

**Charles II's younger brother James was inept and tactless. He is unique in being the only King of England to be driven from the kingdom and to die in exile. He had many faults, but the worst, in most people's eyes, was that of being a Catholic.**

James reigned for almost four years, and in that time his sheer incompetence led to a unique revolution – the 'Glorious Revolution' of 1688 – after which the very nature of monarchy in England underwent a profound and lasting change. Indirectly, then, we must be grateful to him for this.

As a young man, James had shared the same political upheavals as his brother Charles, but being just those few years younger he did not have quite the same sort of involvement. Nevertheless, as he grew up he became Lord High Admiral, strengthened the Royal Navy under his brother, and led two sea battles against the Dutch. He was seen to be a genuinely brave and resourceful commander. Temperamentally, however, James was totally different from his brother. Whereas Charles had been light-hearted and full of good humour, James was rather sour, withdrawn, and inflexible. He had hardly succeeded his brother as king when trouble flared up.

Charles's eldest and favourite bastard, the Duke of Monmouth, son of his first mistress Lucy Walter, made a bid to seize the throne by force. His only claim to the throne was that he was a Protestant, but he tried to bolster up his chances by claiming that his parents had actually been married in secret. He landed at Lyme Regis, declared his Uncle James to be a usurper, claimed the throne, and gathered an army of about 4,000. In Taunton he was actually proclaimed king, taking the title James II, loftily disregarding the properly crowned James II. In an odd way, therefore, for a few weeks England had two King James IIs. The 'Monmouth Rebellion' met its end at the Battle of Sedgemoor, in Somerset, on 6 July 1685, the last

## THE JACOBITES

'Jacobus' is the Latin word for 'James', so when King James II was forced to leave England at the time of the 'Glorious Revolution' in 1688, those who still supported him, even in exile, came to be known as 'Jacobites'. Mostly these supporters belonged to the Catholic faith. The 'kings' who were recognised by Jacobite supporters were James III ('The Old Pretender'), Charles III ('Bonnie Prince Charlie') and Henry IX (Cardinal Stuart).

Jacobite sympathisers would drink a toast 'to the King over the water' and if they wished to conceal their allegiance, their secret sign was to hold their drinking-glasses over finger-bowls, thus toasting 'over water'. Needless to say, when this secret sign was discovered, finger-bowls were banished from English royal tables. It wasn't until this century that the monarch, Edward VII by this time, felt it safe enough to re-introduce finger-bowls for his guests.

In the eighteenth century, when it was a treasonable offence to owe allegiance to the Jacobite cause, sympathisers had many secret devices. One of the most extraordinary is to be found in the West Highland Museum, Fort William, Scotland: it is a tray painted in apparently aimless scrawls, but when a glass is placed in the centre, the reflection bears a remarkable similarity to Bonnie Prince Charlie himself.

# JAMES III
## 1688–1766  'REIGNED' 1701–1766
### Son of James II and Mary of Modena

James Stuart, the so-called 'Old Pretender', was the son of James II. He was the baby who was supposed to have been smuggled into St James's Palace in a warming-pan, and who had been disguised as a bundle of washing when his mother, Mary of Modena, escaped to France. James grew up in France with his parents, and when his father died in 1701 King Louis XIV proclaimed him to be King James III.

His first attempt in 1708 to claim his kingdom was a fiasco, as the Scots refused to let him land. His second attempt was not much better and, after a brief unsuccessful rebellion in his favour at Sheriffmuir in Scotland, James

## THE JACOBITES

was forced to flee back to the continent. He had in fact been proclaimed King James III in the town of Warkworth in England. France refused to grant him any further asylum so he went to Rome where he married Princess Clementina Sobieski, who bore him two sons, Charles and Henry.

James III died in 1766, after a 'reign' of over sixty-four years – which, if it had been a genuine reign, would have been the longest in English history. James III is buried in St Peter's, Rome.

# CHARLES III

### 1720–1788   'REIGNED' 1766–1788

*Son of James III and Clementina Sobieski*

Charles Stuart, otherwise known as the 'Young Pretender' or 'Bonnie Prince Charlie', was born in Rome. Hoping to be more successful than his father in winning support and claiming the throne, he landed in Scotland in 1745, aged twenty-five.

There was a victory over George II's troops at Prestonpans, and Charles held court at Holyroodhouse in Edinburgh. He marched south as far as Derby, but then decided to retreat back to Scotland, where his troops were routed by one of George II's sons, William, Duke of Cumberland, otherwise known as 'Butcher'. This defeat at Culloden in 1746 saw the end of Jacobite hopes, and after several personal adventures Charles fled back to Rome, where he died in 1788. He is buried in St Peter's, Rome.

# HENRY IX

### 1725–1807   'REIGNED' 1788–1807

*Son of James III and Clementina Sobieski*

On the death of Bonnie Prince Charlie the Jacobite line was continued, at least in theory, by his brother, who came to be thought of by Jacobites as 'Henry IX' though he made no such claim himself. He did not marry, as he had become a cardinal in 1747. Therefore on his death the direct Stuart line died out. Cardinal Stuart is buried in St Peter's, Rome.

battle to take place between Englishmen on English soil. The terrible punishments meted out by Judge Jeffreys on supporters of the rebellion did nothing to help King James's popularity, which decreased further as he systematically filled every possible official post with Catholics. Catholic judges, Catholic army commanders, Catholic academics: it was clear that James was bulldozing his way into the reconversion of England.

As always, the king needed an heir, and James had two, Mary and Anne, daughters of his first marriage to Anne Hyde, both of them staunchly Protestant. Naturally, James wanted a son and luckily for him his second wife, Mary of Modena, had become pregnant. The birth was sudden and rather premature. A boy! True, there were many witnesses, but some of them were Catholics! Rumours quickly spread that the queen hadn't really been pregnant at all, and that the child had been secretly smuggled into St James's Palace in a warming-pan. Of course, it suited James's Protestant daughters not to deny the rumours, but warming-pan or not, the baby boy was clearly destined to be the next Catholic King of England. Immediately, there was an outcry of popular opinion that this simply must not happen.

Events moved swiftly. James's Protestant opposers invited Mary's husband, Prince William of Orange, to come to England, with force if need be, to take the kingdom and become its king. Within days William arrived at Brixham, Devon, with his army. James's supporters drained away from him. He travelled to Salisbury on his way to meet William, but suffered such nose-bleeds there for three days that he just couldn't concentrate on mustering his forces. John Churchill, the future Duke of Marlborough, who would have been his commander-in-chief, was so disgusted with James's dithering that he too deserted him.

There was no choice. James returned to London and prepared to flee the country. His wife left first, disguised as an Italian washerwoman, carrying the baby prince as if he were a bundle of laundry. Then James tried to escape, but at his first attempt he was captured at Faversham and had to bribe his way out of a tricky situation. His next attempt was successful and he reached Boulogne on Christmas Day 1688. He was never to set foot in England again. On his way, he had dumped the Great Seal of England into the Thames.

James II tried to regain his kingdom by the back door. He invaded Ireland in 1689 with a small army of Frenchmen, but in the next year he was defeated by William III at the Battle of the Boyne. James then returned to France, where he lived at St Germain-en-Laye, just outside Paris. The French King Louis XIV gave him a pension to help him survive. He died in 1701 aged sixty-seven.

# WILLIAM III AND MARY II

WILLIAM: 1650–1702   REIGNED 1689–1702

*Son of William II, Prince of Orange, and Mary*

MARY: 1662–1694   REIGNED 1689–1694

*Daughter of James II and Anne Hyde*

**William and Mary were unique in reigning jointly. William reigned alone after Mary died.**

William and Mary were cousins, sharing Charles I and Henrietta Maria as their common grandparents. William was the son of Mary, sister of Charles II and James II, who had married the Stadtholder of the Dutch Republic: Mary was the daughter of James by his first wife, Anne Hyde, who had died when James was still Duke of York and Mary was just nine.

And Mary wasn't very much older – only fifteen – when they told her she was to marry her cousin William, who was eleven years older. She is said to have wept for days and even continued weeping during the marriage service, which took place in St James's Palace in 1677, on the twenty-seventh birthday of her husband-cousin. Her uncle, King Charles II, always ready to cheer people up, was standing near her at the wedding service and when the moment came for William to say the words 'With all my worldly goods I thee endow', several coins were spread out, ceremonially, on the open Bible. Charles whispered to her: 'Gather it up and put it in your pocket while you've got the chance.' But poor Princess Mary didn't think it in the least bit funny. She wept all the more. But despite this somewhat unhappy beginning, their marriage was a genuine success. Mary came to adore her rather silent, slightly hunchbacked cousin, who stood several inches shorter than herself.

Strictly speaking, it was Mary who was in line to the throne, but William refused to be subjugated to the role of a mere consort. As for Mary, she was completely dominated by William, and was quite insistent that he should share the throne. Thus the curious situation arose by which the monarchy was shared between them. In practice, of course, it was William who made all the decisions, but Mary remained in control whenever William was abroad.

Mary could hardly be said to have been a political influence. She remained very much under the shadow of William. But they both patronised the arts, including the fashionable new art of gardening. And Purcell wrote for Mary, developing another new fashionable art – opera. Sad to say, Mary did not live long to enjoy her reign. Smallpox killed her, aged only thirty-two, and childless. Purcell composed magnificent music for her funeral, which took place in Westminster Abbey.

As for William, he was never popular. A contemporary said of him:

> He put on some appearance of application: but he hated business of all sorts. Yet he hated talking, and all house games, more. This put him on a perpetual course of hunting, to which he seemed to give himself up, beyond any man I ever knew: but I looked on that always as flying from company and business.

William's silent off-handed manner was intensely disliked. Even his table manners were considered to be boorish and vulgar. Nevertheless, he was an able man, a brave and capable military commander and, despite his silence, a master of languages. He was, as one would expect, very much of a continental, unfortunately involving England in unnecessary wars with his enemy, Louis XIV of France.

Perhaps the most permanent memorial of his reign today is Kensington Palace, for it was William who bought 'Nottingham House' there, having it rebuilt by Christopher Wren, and transforming it into a new royal palace. William suffered greatly from asthma, and hoped that living in what was then the country village of Kensington would help to improve his health. It was during William's reign, too, that the old Whitehall, a beautiful and higgledy-piggledy complex of royal buildings, was completely destroyed by fire. The new Whitehall we know today bears no resemblance at all to the lovely area that was lost. The Banqueting Hall is the only original part that still remains today.

When William was thrown from his horse, an accident in which he broke his collar-bone, and died of consequential pneumonia there was little cause for mourning. The Jacobites, in fact, began to drink toasts to moles ('the little gentleman with the black velvet waistcoat') as a tribute to the animal that had constructed the mole-hill over which William's horse had stumbled. No monument marks the place where he is buried. He was put in the vaults of Westminster Abbey.

# QUEEN ANNE

## 1665–1714   REIGNED 1702–1714

### Daughter of James II and Anne Hyde

**Although herself rather fat, dull and pathetic, Anne, the younger sister of Mary II, presided over a period of elegance and greatness.**

Poor Anne! We can't help feeling sorry for her. She suffered terribly from gout, becoming increasingly so fat and heavy that she could hardly move, and had to be carried, pushed and wheeled about, even having to be lowered through trapdoors. Then those seventeen miscarriages and stillbirths! Of the eighteen children she conceived by her husband, Prince George of Denmark, she must have placed such pathetic hopes on the only one to survive a few years – the sad little Duke of Gloucester. But even he lived only to the age of eleven.

All her contemporaries speak of Anne's dullness. She had no conversation, except tittle-tattle, and took very little intelligent interest in the brilliant achievements of the writers, artists, architects and thinkers, who were creating an age of elegance around her.

Just to list the great names is to recognise that England was now becoming polished, civilised and sophisticated in ways totally unheard of in previous times: Christopher Wren with his new St Paul's Cathedral; James Gibbs with his St Martin's in the Fields; Defoe and Swift; the philosophers Newton and Berkeley; the painters Kneller and Thornhill; essayists and poets such as Addison, Steele and Pope, not to mention politicians and military geniuses such as Walpole and the Duke of Marlborough. One could go on and on. But 'Brandy Nan', as Queen Anne was nicknamed (referring to her love of a tipple), hardly made any impact at all on the events surrounding her.

Great battles were fought and won in Anne's name by the Duke of Marlborough: Blenheim, Ramillies, Oudenarde, Malplaquet. The Treaty of Utrecht was drawn up in 1713, which gave England great power and influence. And in 1707 England and Scotland were at last formally united, in the Act of Union. Time and again Anne was bundled and trundled to St Paul's Cathedral to attend some great service of thanksgiving. But as for the woman herself, she was hardly ever more than an object of mild ridicule. Alexander Pope, with elegant and sarcastic wit, summed it up:

> Here, thou, great Anna, whom three realms obey,
> Dost sometimes counsel take, and sometimes tea.

Jonathan Swift described her court: 'The Queen sits in a circle of twenty visitors with her fan in her mouth, saying three words about once a minute to those about her, and then upon hearing that dinner was ready going out at once.' Indeed, her appetite was enormous. The French Ambassador was amazed that she could stow away so much solid food, and wondered whether she would burst.

For years Anne was inseparable from Sarah Churchill, Duchess of Marlborough. Desperately wanting to put their friendship on an equal footing so that they could do away with courtly formalities, Anne proposed that they should call themselves 'Mrs Freeman' and 'Mrs Morley'. And so they became, until there was an almighty quarrel. Then Anne stripped Sarah of all her offices, and took on another favourite, Abigail Masham, née Hill. Rumours of lesbianism were rife.

It is easy to poke fun at poor Queen Anne, but at least we owe her thanks for the development of Kensington Palace and gardens and the Orangery designed by Wren. We also are indebted to her for founding the races at Ascot: she was a keen horsewoman until she grew too ill and too fat to ride.

After her fashion, too, she was a staunch supporter of the Anglican Church. She dutifully 'touched' sick people to cure them of their ailments. It is well known that the infant Samuel Johnson was one of those whom she touched for scrofula, a disease now long since eradicated.

And finally, we mustn't forget that throughout her life she was noted for her generosity. 'Queen Anne's Bounty' – a fund to help poorer clergymen – was just one example. She constantly supported charities of all kinds, out of her own money. 'As to her privy purse,' wrote one of her courtiers, 'it was the poor's box, a perpetual fund of charity.'

She died unhappy, worried about the succession, and with something of a guilty conscience for having helped to usurp the throne. Her last words hinted at her uneasy mind: 'My brother, my poor brother,' she murmured, referring, of course, to James II, now dead, but whose son, the Old Pretender, was now only too anxious to press his claim to the English throne.

Anne died aged forty-nine, and was buried in Westminster Abbey in a coffin that had to be virtually square in order to accommodate her vast bulk.

# GEORGE I

### 1660–1727   REIGNED 1714–1727

*Son of Ernest Augustus and Princess Sophia*

**George I hated England; he hated poetry; he hated painting; he hated his wife; he hated his son and daughter-in-law. On the whole no one much cared for him either.**

At the time of his succession to the English throne, George I was Elector of Hanover. His right to the English throne came via his mother, Sophia, a granddaughter of James I. When he arrived in England, he presented a distinctly odd appearance, with his vermilion complexion, receding chin, colourless eyes, loud German voice, and light ginger-coloured wig. He came with secretaries and attendants, some negro servants, and two of the ugliest mistresses ever seen at an English court: a fat one, Sophia von Kilmansegg, who was promptly nicknamed 'The Elephant', and a tall thin one, Ermengarda Melusina von Schulenburg, who became known as 'The Maypole'.

George I could not speak English, and so had to struggle with French or Latin to communicate with anyone not knowing German. It is not surprising that during his twelve-year reign he actually spent more time back in Hanover than in England. He was unpopular not just because of his boorish manners and preposterous mistresses, but also because of the fact that he kept his wife, Princess Sophia Dorothea, in perpetual imprisonment in Ahlden Castle in Germany, on suspicion of adultery. Nevertheless, despite his unpopularity, people still preferred the thought of a German Protestant to that of a Catholic Jacobite.

Two good things resulted from the reign of George I: the growing strength of the 'Prime Minister' – Robert Walpole – thus effecting a swing towards the power of Parliament; and the fact that Handel settled in England, thus giving an immense impetus to British music.

George I died on a visit back to Germany. No one ever thought about giving him an English burial. He was simply forgotten.

# GEORGE II

### 1683–1760   REIGNED 1727–1760

*Son of George I and Sophia Dorothea of Zelle*

**Unpopular, unEnglish and rude, nevertheless, George II was brave and crudely self-assertive.**

## 'POOR FRED'

England should have had a King Frederick. King George II's eldest son, Frederick Louis, was expected to succeed to the throne. Born in 1707, he enjoyed popularity; however, like many heirs to the throne, he died prematurely.

He was a keen player of the newly invented game of cricket, and in the summer of 1748 he was hit hard on the chest by a cricket ball while playing at his summer residence, Cliveden House, in Buckinghamshire. An abscess resulted and was the cause of his early death in 1751.

George II hated him, writing: 'I have lost my eldest son, but was glad of it.'

George II was the last English monarch to have been born abroad. He first saw the light of day at the Herrenhausen Palace in Hanover. When he was a boy he little thought he would be King of England, and in fact it was not until he was thirty that his father was, somewhat improbably, invited to England to become its sovereign.

George must have had an awful childhood. His mother was forced into imprisonment for alleged adultery when he was only eleven, and it is doubtful whether he ever saw her again. It is said that he did once try to swim the moat surrounding the castle where his mother was kept, but failed to do so. When his father was King of England, he would not allow George to do the slightest of tasks, and gave him not even the smallest of responsibilities. Naturally, his resentment must have smouldered, and he and his wife Caroline of Ansbach, while they were Prince and Princess of Wales, kept what was virtually a rival royal court, in open contempt and defiance of his father.

His was a long reign, over thirty-three years, and during that time, thanks to his able ministers and military commanders, the strength and influence of Great Britain grew apace.

George threw himself into battle. At the relatively advanced age of sixty-one he led an army of British, German, Austrian and Dutch troops to a conclusive victory over the French at the Battle of Dettingen. 'Don't tell me of danger,' he yelled. 'Now boys! Fire and behave brave, and the French will run.' And run they did. For a while George actually achieved popularity. This was the last occasion when an English reigning monarch fought in battle.

In 1759, the year before George II died, England's military expansion led to conquests in Canada, India and the Caribbean, and we achieved complete mastery of the seas. In many respects it was a successful reign, but this was largely because of the efforts of other men. Power was draining from the monarchy; the real wielders of influence were Walpole and Pitt.

Aged seventy-six, our second Hanoverian monarch died of a heart attack in Kensington Palace while sitting on a loo.

George II was the last king to be buried in Westminster Abbey, but no one troubled to give him any sort of memorial except a small and insignificant paving slab. His son Frederick had died a few years previously after an accident during a game of cricket, so the throne now passed to his 22-year-old grandson, yet another George.

# GEORGE III

## 1738–1820   REIGNED 1760–1820

### Son of Frederick and Augusta of Saxe-Coburg-Gotha

**The grandson of George II was sensitive and conscientious. He tried to do his best for England, and during his long reign he came to be genuinely loved by his loyal subjects. Unfortunately, George III went mad, and had to be replaced by his son in a ten-year Regency period.**

When George III came to the throne as a fresh-faced youngster in 1760 he was the first sovereign since Queen Anne to speak English as a native language. His mother is reported as having told him 'George, be a King!' so despite his early shyness and inexperience, he applied himself diligently and resolutely to restoring the power and influence of the monarchy.

Although he had desperately wanted to marry his friend Sarah Lennox, George allowed himself to be persuaded to seek a foreign princess, Charlotte Sophia of Mecklenburg-Strelitz, to be his queen. They were married just a fortnight before their coronation, and thereafter they lived a lifestyle of conspicuous dullness, faithfulness and domesticity.

They lived in a very small 'palace' – not much more than a large country house – at Kew, and George, who did not care for court life in London, used to ride up to London daily – the first commuter. Meanwhile, Charlotte dutifully produced baby after baby, virtually annually, until they had a family of fifteen: nine sons and six daughters. 'My quiver is full,' he remarked, after the last had been born.

George reigned for almost sixty momentous years. The empire was strengthened; America was lost; Australia was found; France erupted, and guillotined its king. Meanwhile, life throughout Europe was being transformed by the Industrial Revolution. Throughout this time, George III was a keen patron of the arts and sciences. He entertained the boy Mozart and his father when they came to London. His books formed the foundation of the British Museum Library. He also busied himself in agricultural schemes and model farms, so much so that he gained the nickname 'Farmer George'.

It was a personal tragedy that he finally became so mentally sick that he had to be restrained in a strait-jacket and kept as a pathetic prisoner in a padded chamber in Windsor Castle. He had been seen to go up to trees in Windsor Park and talk to them, thinking they were foreign ambassadors. In his final years his long white beard and rambling words 'conversing with angels' gave him the appearance of a crazed King Lear. He lived over ten years in seclusion, and outlived poor Charlotte. But people remembered him with affection.

# GEORGE IV

## 1762–1830  REIGNED 1820–1830

### Son of George III and Charlotte Sophia
### of Mecklenburg-Strelitz

**Fat and self-indulgent, George IV has always been regarded as a grotesque laughing-stock. He reigned for nine years as Regent before becoming king, so the word 'Regency' applies to the period 1811 to 1820, when he was standing in for his mad father.**

From his early teens George IV was sexually voracious, and enjoyed a huge number of mistresses, discarding each one abruptly as he discovered the next. One of his earliest was an actress called Mary Robinson. He fell in love with her as he watched her playing the part of Perdita in *The Winter's Tale* at Drury Lane. Immediately, he pestered her with letters and showered her with presents, signing himself 'Florizel', the name of her lover in the play. The nickname 'Florizel' stuck for a while, but he was usually called 'Prinny' (short for Prince Regent).

## THE ROYAL PAVILION, BRIGHTON

Brighton Pavilion is essential viewing for anyone wanting to understand the world of 'Prinny' – the Prince Regent and future King George IV. Several of Prinny's uncles, including 'Butcher' Cumberland, had enjoyed the new cult of sea-bathing in Brighton, and when Prinny visited it in 1783 he liked the area so much that he came here regularly for almost the rest of his life, installing his secret wife, Mrs Maria Fitzherbert, here.

He took an old farmhouse and turned it first into a classical villa, and then, during his Regency period, his architect John Nash transformed it into the astonishing building we know today as Brighton Pavilion, with its onion-shaped dome, tent-shaped roofs, minarets, and elaborate riot of decoration.

George IV's brother, William IV, also spent time here and added extra lodges to the Pavilion for his wife, but Queen Victoria disliked the place, closed it, and the town of Brighton bought it in 1850.

After nine years of painstaking restoration, the Royal Pavilion was reopened in 1990, glowing anew with vibrant colour. It is probably in better condition than it has ever been.

Brighton is on the Sussex coast, only an hour from London. Prinny himself once commuted to London, but as trains weren't invented at the time (1784) he did it on horseback – a return journey of ten hours.

The only woman for whom Prinny did have a lasting love was a Catholic widow, Mrs Fitzherbert. He actually married her, secretly, but had to have the marriage annulled in order to marry an official wife, foisted on him by Parliament, Caroline of Brunswick, whom he detested at first sight. However, he did his duty by Caroline, who produced a daughter, Charlotte. She sadly died during the birth, thus leaving the throne without a natural heir.

George IV's sex life and drinking orgies were the scandal of his time, and he appeared to have no remorse or inhibition. His treatment of his wife was publicly callous, and at his coronation he gave orders for her to be refused entry to Westminster Abbey. She went round the building hammering at the doors, but had to go away, humiliated.

Despite his appalling behaviour and extravagance, his other claim to fame was as a patron of the arts. He was a genuine connoisseur of painting, architecture, literature, and all the arts. Visitors to England should try to see

Brighton Pavilion, a monument to his eccentric mania for over-the-top building extravagance. It is unique in its odd mixture of Indian and Chinese styles.

George's main gifts to posterity, however, were his improvements to London. We owe a debt of gratitude to George and his architect, John Nash, not only for the weirdly beautiful Brighton Pavilion, but also for the elegant Regent's Park and the magnificent Regent Street, originally built as a new road linking Regent's Park to Prinny's London home, Carlton House.

But by far the most important legacy left to us by Prinny is Buckingham Palace. Originally it had been a relatively modest dwelling, Buckingham House, but George insisted that his own home, Carlton House, sited at the other end of The Mall, was far too small for him. Against all arguments and objections he pushed forward his scheme for enlarging Buckingham House into a new palace, supporting Nash's grandiose plans. Only a man of reckless, ruthless extravagance and egocentricity could have succeeded, and in hindsight we must be grateful to him. London simply wouldn't have been the same without him.

Carlton House was pulled down, but the stone pillars at the entrance can now be seen supporting the portico of the National Gallery. In front of the National Gallery, in Trafalgar Square, is a rather improbable-looking bronze statue by Chantrey of George on horseback, originally intended for the top of Marble Arch when it was in front of Buckingham Palace. George ordered it in 1829 but died before it could be finished. When it was completed it was 'temporarily' placed in its present position.

There is a beautiful white statue of his only child, Princess Charlotte, in St George's Chapel, Windsor. George himself is also buried there, but he has no official memorial. His real memorials are Brighton Pavilion, the vastly improved layout of London, and Buckingham Palace.

As Charlotte had died, the throne passed to George IV's younger brother, William.

# WILLIAM IV

### 1765–1837   REIGNED 1830–1837

*Son of George III and Charlotte Sophia*
*of Mecklenburg-Strelitz*

**William IV was a former sailor. Abrupt and outspoken, irascible, though basically good-natured, unpredictable and eccentric, he was called the original 'Silly Billy'.**

William spent most of his life either as a sailor or else as a rather private individual, living with a successful actress, Mrs Dorothy Jordan, and fathering their ten illegitimate children. He had no reason whatever to suppose that he would become king. However, events were to prove otherwise. His brother, George IV, had produced only one heir, Charlotte, who died at birth in 1817, and then in 1827 his elder brother, Frederick (the 'Grand Old Duke of York'), also died. Hence it was that William came rather unexpectedly and rather late in life – aged sixty-five – to the throne.

His reign was brief, just under seven years. But it was an explosive and momentous time. Much against William's will, the great Reform Bill was pushed through Parliament in 1832. It is impossible to overstate the importance of this. For the first time voting rights were given to the middle classes. It was a colossal constitutional change. In later years further Acts of Parliament were to be passed giving the vote to other classes, and eventually to women as well, but the Reform Bill, in William's reign, marked the first of these great changes. Power was at last passing to the people. Democracy was born.

Clearly, a major result of this change was that the monarch lost political power. William desperately tried to stem the tide of democracy, and at one time abruptly dismissed Parliament in order to try to change the party in power. However, he had to admit political defeat. Since his day, the sovereign has had to adjust increasingly to a neutral role, being 'above politics'.

In himself, William was a colourful character. He had genuinely enjoyed his life at sea, and had joined his first ship as a midshipman, aged just thirteen. He had no privileges, and ate, drank, swore, gambled, whored, just like many a rough-and-tumble teenager in the navy. He actually visited New York while the British flag was still flying over it – the first and only English monarch, albeit a future monarch, to see America as a colony. His life at sea included taking part in a naval battle, and he became a close friend of Nelson, actually giving the bride away at Nelson's marriage to Frances Nisbet in the West Indies.

All his life he hated airs and graces. As he joined the navy he asked to be known simply as 'William Guelph' – his family name. And when he came to the throne he tried hard not to have a coronation at all, eventually making do with a very low-key affair, with hardly any pomp or ceremony. No fuss, no courtly behaviour, no regal dignity. He didn't care whether his crown was put on at any angle, and if he didn't care for anyone he simply swore at him. On one occasion, when the President of the Royal Academy was showing King William round his art gallery, the unfortunate man chanced to point out a portrait of the distinguished naval officer Admiral Napier. William hated Napier, and stood in front of the picture fuming with rage. 'Captain Napier may be damn'd sir!' he roared. 'And you may be damn'd too, sir, and if the Queen was not here, sir, I would kick you downstairs!' And again, when King Leopold of the Belgians sat at table with him, sipping only water, William exploded: 'God damn it, why don't you drink wine? I never let anybody drink water at my table.'

Never an art-critic, he expressed his opinion that 'all pictures of sacred subjects are improper and ought to be destroyed.' And he pooh-poohed his brother's magnificent art collection. 'Ay – it seems pretty – I dare say it is. My brother was very fond of this Knicknackery. Damned expensive taste, though!'

Stories like this are numerous, and they endeared him to his subjects. He appeared to be a bumbling, erratic old eccentric, rambling and roaring out his opinions and never standing on ceremony. Oddly enough, such eccentricities probably kept him on the throne, when throughout Europe many other monarchs were being guillotined or swept into exile. Bluff King William, with his big mouth and pear-shaped head, probably unwittingly saved our monarchy.

When he knew he probably had to produce a legitimate heir, William scoured Europe for possible wives, and finally was accepted by Adelaide of Saxe-Meiningen. It was a happy enough marriage, but alas, no children survived.

One of his pet hates was the Duchess of Kent, widow of his brother Edward and mother of the future Queen Victoria. He bluntly told her to her face that he hoped to God his life might be spared until Princess Victoria became of age, so that there wouldn't be any question of the Duchess herself becoming Regent. With luck, he did manage to survive Victoria's eighteenth birthday, by less than a month. He knew he was dying, but he dearly wished to see another anniversary of the Battle of Waterloo (18 June). He begged his doctor: 'Try if you cannot tinker me up to last over that date.'

William IV died just two days after the anniversary. And as a complete contrast, his eighteen-year-old niece Victoria took the throne, promising 'to be good'.

# QUEEN VICTORIA

## 1819–1901   REIGNED 1837–1901

*Daughter of Edward, Duke of Kent,*
*and Victoria of Saxe-Coburg*

**Granddaughter of George III and niece of George IV and William IV,
Victoria was to become the longest reigning English monarch: 63 years,
216 days. She restored dignity and mystique to the throne and gave her
name and character to a great age in Britain's development.**

What a pity it is that our final memories of Queen Victoria are those of a
dumpy, grumpy, glum-looking, fat little woman who appeared to disapprove
of everything, and seemed determined never to be amused. The fact is that
in many respects she was quite the opposite. Certainly in her young days she
was slim, beautiful, lively, full of laughter and quite as ready as the rest of us
to mock at pompous and silly prudery. But because she lived and reigned for
so long most of her subjects just never remembered her in her prime.

Luckily, there's a vast amount of material about Victoria. Not only was
she such a compelling and fascinating personality that everyone who met
her simply had to record the experience, but also she herself was one of the
most prolific diary-writers of all time. And she actually wrote a book about
herself and her family. The result is that we know more about her life – her
thoughts, her feelings, her day-to-day lifestyle – than that of any other of
our monarchs.

The story of her life, long though it was, can be fairly quickly given. She
came to the throne aged only eighteen. She married her cousin, Prince
Albert of Saxe-Coburg-Gotha, when they were both twenty, and despite her
intense dislike of childbearing, they had nine children. Then, after an idyllic
marriage of twenty-one years, Albert suddenly died of typhus. To say that
Victoria was upset would be the understatement of the century: she was
utterly and totally devastated. For the remainder of her reign – another
forty years – she wore the heaviest of mourning, was hardly ever seen in
public, and lived as a recluse on the Isle of Wight. She did travel to
Windsor and Balmoral, but Buckingham Palace remained dead and empty
and her ministers had to travel to Osborne to see her.

Meanwhile, the British Empire grew in power and strength; new parts of
the world were explored; the industrial revolution transformed society;
railways, telephones, and a multitude of inventions transformed our
lifestyle; the modern world grew up around her.

When she died in 1901, her descendants were so numerous, occupying almost every throne in Europe and Russia, as a result of so many diplomatic marriages, that Victoria had become known as the 'Grandmother of Europe'.

Despite her reclusiveness – or perhaps even aided by it – she acquired an extraordinary mystique, particularly in her later years. She seemed to embody everything that was noble and precious about England and its Empire. Her two jubilees, in 1887 and 1897, marking the fiftieth and sixtieth anniversaries of her coming to the throne, boosted her popularity to unprecedented heights. No previous English monarch ever came to be loved and revered so much as Queen Victoria. Her death stunned the nation. Coming as it did in January 1901, it seemed symbolic of the ending of an age. The twentieth century had arrived.

The basic facts of her life, then, are simply stated. But it is virtually impossible to convey in a short space the vivid intensity of her personality.

Victoria was, of course, astonishingly self-willed. Even as a girl, she had declared that it was her intention 'to be good', and she was blessed (or cursed) with unshakeable opinions on any and every issue, great or small. She had no inhibitions whatsoever about expressing those opinions, or about giving instant reprimands to anyone who offended or opposed her. She was always totally convinced of the rightness of her own views.

Indeed, in almost everything she was a person of extremes. Her love of Albert was ecstatic; her grief at his death as unremitting. She adored her Prime Minister Disraeli; she hated, and humiliated, Gladstone. Earlier on she had adored Melbourne and had hated Peel. In fact, she was frequently quite flagrantly unconstitutional in taking sides on political issues. Could anyone imagine a modern sovereign giving a public rebuke to a prime minister? Victoria did. Gladstone could never forgive her.

Yet she had a tenacious loyalty – sometimes showing a quirkiness which made her ridiculous. Her fondness for her Scottish servant John Brown was quite extraordinary; and she allowed him to make personal and rude comments about her (he habitually called her 'wumman'). And again, she had an Indian servant, Abdul Karim the Munshi (secretary), who despite being quite uneducated was given astonishing privileges in being shown state papers. Her courtiers hated him for putting on airs, and suspected him of betraying confidentialities. When a courtier dared to make a comment, Victoria, then aged seventy-eight, swept everything off her desk in a towering rage, refusing to listen to 'race prejudice'.

Her relations with her family were close, but fraught with tension, again because she always insisted on her own way. Unforgivably, she never allowed her son, the Prince of Wales and future King Edward VII, to take the smallest part in running state affairs. He was fifty-nine when he succeeded to the throne, yet had been given no responsibility or training whatsoever.

Wilful, passionate, self-righteous, uninhibited. Every inch a queen. So, what did she bring to the monarchy? What permanent legacy did Victoria leave?

Well, although she did not consciously construct or innovate – apart, perhaps, from the Albert Hall and the Albert Memorial – nevertheless her name is found permanently embedded around the world: the Australian state of Victoria; the Victoria Falls in Zambia; Mount Victoria in Papua New Guinea; Victoria Island in the Canadian Arctic; capital cities, towns, parks, hospitals, railway stations, even sponge cakes. To compile a full list would be a daunting task. The point is, she dominated an age simply by existing.

More importantly, our whole conception of monarchy underwent a profound change during her long reign. She was not always popular, and indeed survived seven assassination attempts. Nevertheless because of her tenacious devotion to duty and her position as widow-matriarch at the centre of a vast empire and network of royal relations abroad, she became unique, both as a person and as a figure-head.

The concept of the 'royal family'; the idea of royal punctilious attention to detail and duty; the elevation of the monarchy to a beloved ideal: these were the intangible legacies Victoria left behind. She transformed people's notions of what it meant to be 'royal'.

There are statues galore of Victoria, but the visitor will look in vain to find her tomb. Typically, as in life, she chose privacy. And after one of the most magnificent funeral processions of all time, she was buried, next to her beloved Albert, in her tiny private chapel at Frogmore, in Windsor Park.

# EDWARD VII

## 1841–1910   REIGNED 1901–1910

### Son of Queen Victoria and
### Prince Albert of Saxe-Coburg-Gotha

**Bluff, genial and pleasure-loving, Edward waited a long time for a short reign. But it would be quite wrong to belittle him as his mother did.**

If ever there was an example of a personality struggling to escape from a silly and crampingly tactless education, we have it in the story of the future King Edward VII. His father, Albert the Prince Consort – Albert the Good, as Victoria liked him to be called – was an avowed perfectionist, and he was determined that his son should be reared in such a way as to produce the perfect man. Accordingly, the young Edward was subjected to an appalling regime: six hours a day of study, six days a week; no light reading; harsh physical exercise during the rest of the time.

Needless to say, the young boy rebelled, making faces, spitting, throwing stones at his tutor and pulling his beard. He became sullen and morose. And Victoria his mother made it quite plain that she didn't like him, bluntly calling him stupid. To the end of his days, Edward was no book-lover, though he was clearly highly intelligent, a fine linguist, an excellent public speaker, and one who possessed an extraordinarily retentive memory. His childhood, however, was a disaster.

As a young man he quickly learned the pleasures of sex, to the distraction of his parents. Indeed, Prince Albert had only just gone up to Cambridge to give his son a sound ticking-off for having had an affair with an actress when he caught typhoid fever and died. Of course, Victoria blamed Edward for Albert's death, supposing that it was worry over his son's sex-life that had caused Albert to become weakened and catch the fatal chill. 'Oh, that boy,' she wrote in her diary. 'Much as I pity him, I never can, or shall, look at him without a shudder.' For the next forty years Edward as Prince of Wales was kept waiting in the wings, never once being given a proper task to do. Victoria held him at bay.

On the face of it, the main part of Edward's life was simply round after round of pleasure: hunting, gambling, horse-racing, feasting. Frequently there were whiffs of scandal. Certainly, he enjoyed many women, ate extravagantly, and was once caught up in a law-suit about cheating at cards.

All the same, his love of travel was beneficial. As a 'free-lance diplomatist' he helped enormously to further good relations between England and many other countries. After all, most of the kings and queens, dukes and princes were his own cousins and relations, either directly or by marriage. As Victoria his mother kept herself shut up in the privacy of her mourning, Edward was able, abroad, to do something enjoyable and worthwhile, which he wasn't able to do in England. The result of this was that when he did eventually come to the throne, he was a natural go-between among the crowned heads of Europe. It was very largely due to him that the 'Entente Cordiale' between France and England was begun. Alas, despite strenuous efforts on his part, he never quite managed to get on the right wave-length with his cousin the Kaiser, who always mistrusted him and thought he was trying in some way to deceive him.

Edward was a born diplomat, gracious, tactful, punctilious and polite. It has been said that he learned diplomacy by having to deal with difficult parents. All the same, it has to be said that his womanising – he had at least thirteen mistresses – must have given his queen, Alexandra of Denmark, many hours of humiliation and grief. Once, as he was visiting the Moulin Rouge in Paris, one of the dancers brought the house down as she greeted him as an old friend, 'Ullo, Wales', she called out. Edward chuckled and ordered champagne all round.

He was, despite and because of his foibles, immensely popular. As he aged he became enormous, and well deserved his nickname 'Tum-tum'. Legends about his huge appetite were received with relish. Today, the 'Entente Cordiale' is still remembered with nostalgia, and 'Edwardian England' has memories of opulence and dignity. It was a period soon to vanish for ever, but for the upper classes who shared his world of leisure, wealth and dignity, it was a magnificent time to be alive.

The reign of Edward VII was brief: not quite ten years. And when he died in 1910 the storm-clouds of a possible war with Germany were already gathering, much to his concern. The nation sincerely mourned him as he was laid to rest in St George's Chapel, Windsor. Alexandra, his beautiful and somewhat neglected queen, was loved and respected as she lived on for another fifteen years.

# GEORGE V

## 1865–1936   REIGNED 1910–1936

### Son of Edward VII and Alexandra of Denmark

**George V is remembered as the founder of the 'House of Windsor', as it was he who adopted this name for the family during the First World War. The 'sailor-king' was hearty, loud-voiced, small-headed, but dignified, as well as being fanatical over punctuality and duty.**

With George V we come to a period still within living memory. To our present queen, Elizabeth II, he was 'Grandpa England'. They adored each other, and Archbishop Lang remembered seeing King George on his hands and knees while the toddler Princess Elizabeth pulled him along by his beard. To him, she was 'sweet little Lilibet'.

As a young man George didn't expect to be king, because his elder brother 'Eddy' was the heir to the throne. George, second-in-line, was given a tough up-bringing in the navy, and showed genuine aptitude for service life. All his life he continued to have a 'gruff, blue-water approach to all human problems', as his son, the Duke of Windsor, wrote.

However, Eddy died of pneumonia in 1892. It was something of a relief, because he had been embarrassingly mentally backward. In fact, if Eddy had survived and become king, the British monarchy would have been in serious trouble. Queen Victoria, still on the throne when Eddy died, and still determining everyone's lives for them, decided that Eddy's fiancée, Princess Mary of Teck, would now marry George instead. Naturally everyone obeyed, and the marriage of George and Mary (later to be known as Queen Mary) was a rock-solid success.

It was George's misfortune to live through the horrendous years of the First World War. It was a double tragedy for him, because of course many of his closest relations were German. Nevertheless, duty always came first, and he constantly visited the fighting areas to boost morale. He suffered a broken pelvis when thrown from his horse, but continued to meet people and decorate soldiers even from his sick-bed. And when anti-German fever was at its worst, and even the royal family, with all its German connections, was suspected of anti-British activity, he made a dramatic gesture, changing the dynasty's name to that of Windsor, cutting off all remaining ties with Germany, and requiring other members of his family to change their German names for British ones (Battenbergs had to become Mountbattens, for example).

After the war things could never be the same. Modern transport, modern entertainments, modern means of communication, votes for women, socialism: a new world emerged. Stolidly, King George put up with it as best he could. He hated change, but recognised that he couldn't entirely stop it. He stopped Queen Mary wearing shorter skirts and showing her legs, however. And with his own rather old-fashioned beard and Queen Mary's long skirts and curious hats, the royal couple seemed as if they were fossils from the past, which wasn't necessarily a bad thing, because it unconsciously reminded people of days of past glories.

And as for himself, he wore the same collar stud all his life; always went to bed at 11.10 p.m.; expected his sons to wear morning coats when they visited him; refused all foreign food; and roared with fury if ever he found servants had shifted the position of any piece of furniture. (They had to take photos, to make sure just where each piece had to be.) And, just to make doubly sure that he would always, yes, always be on time, he had every single clock at Sandringham put forward exactly half an hour. 'Sandringham time' was an eccentricity everyone had to put up with.

Despite this virtual paranoia about regularity, George did his best to adapt to the changing political world, and did his level best to act as a kind of referee in the post-war turmoil, accepting the first Labour Government under Ramsay Macdonald with good grace, despite his inner misgivings.

The people of England came to love him for his transparent honesty and simplicity, and when he gave the first Christmas broadcast on radio in 1932, his popularity soared. His deep, comfortable voice sounded just as he looked: reliable, old-fashioned, reassuring. When the Silver Jubilee year of his reign came to be celebrated in 1935, he had serious doubts about making any sort of fuss or ceremony at all. He was completely taken back by the enthusiasm of the crowds who greeted him as he rode in the coach back from the thanksgiving service at St Paul's. He turned to Queen Mary, saying with genuine astonishment, 'I believe they really like me!'

He may have been a little naïve, with his stamp collections and pet parrot, but he was certainly no fool. He must have seen the danger signals in the carefree unconventional behaviour of his son and heir, the future King Edward VIII and later Duke of Windsor. 'After I am gone,' he confided to the Archbishop of Canterbury, 'the boy will ruin himself in twelve months.' It was a shrewd prophecy.

# EDWARD VIII
## 1894–1972   REIGNED 20 JAN.–10 DEC. 1936
### Son of George V and Mary of Teck

**The uncrowned king who reigned for 325 days before he abdicated, Edward had been wildly popular as the Prince of Wales before giving up everything for a quiet life with an American divorcee. He is more easily remembered as the Duke of Windsor.**

'King Edward VIII' is a kind of hypothetical memory nowadays. Younger people usually have to be reminded who he was. The 'Abdication Crisis' of 1936 seized the headlines momentarily, but the advent of the Second World War quickly brought much more important issues for people to think about. Nowadays, 'Edward VIII' is not much more than a footnote in history.

It is a well-known fact that British royal fathers and their royal sons have almost always been spectacularly at loggerheads with one another, and this was certainly the case with Edward and his father George V. They were complete opposites. Contrasted with his staid and conventional father,

Edward as Prince of Wales was dashingly modern, a product of the twenties and thirties. He dressed casually, smoked cigarettes, went about hatless (unusual in those days), travelled to ritzy glitzy places, flirted, spoke in a slangy way, often trying to sound American, and generally blew a breeze of the twentieth century into the monarchy. Of course there was nothing wrong with this, although his father and mother were scandalised by it all. On the credit side, David, as he was known to his family and friends, did a good job in adding a new dimension to people's concept of the royals, and he undertook many successful trips abroad, very much as his grandfather Edward VII had done while Victoria had remained at home.

The trouble began when Edward met Wallis Simpson, an American lady who had already divorced one husband, and who was just about to divorce her second, thus clearing the way for her third – David, *alias* Edward, future King of England. Edward seemed utterly mesmerised by her. He constantly showered thousands of pounds worth of jewellery on her. He gave up his friends for her, forbidding the palace switchboard operators to connect them to his phone. He wrote her love-letters galore. And as for Wallis, she lapped up every scrap of his adulation, and simply kicked him under the table if she didn't approve of what he was doing. Astonishingly, the British public were kept completely in the dark about the whole affair, until it had gathered such momentum that the news simply had to break, which it did just in the last months of old King George's reign.

It would be interesting to know what would happen if such a scenario occurred today. In those years, the whole affair seemed unthinkable. For the future king to marry an American was hardly the done thing, but to marry a doubly divorced American was completely unacceptable. Added to which, the unspoken thought was that as she was forty there was little likelihood that she would bear any children. The Prime Minister, Stanley Baldwin, produced an ultimatum: Edward would have to choose either the throne or Wallis Simpson. And, of course, he chose Wallis. At the time, the abdication seemed cataclysmic, but today we can be glad that his much more sensible brother was forced to take on the responsibilities of the crown.

During his brief kingship Edward's ministers and courtiers were horrified by his sloppy and casual approach to royal duties: documents went unread; appointments were abandoned; there was tactless interference in foreign affairs. Visiting Germany with Wallis he notoriously gave the Nazi salute when he met Hitler. Naturally, the Führer was much impressed by him.

Edward abdicated in December 1936, and was married to Wallis the following June, quietly in France. Meanwhile, his brother, desperately unhappy at the situation, gritted his teeth, was crowned as King George VI, and became one of the most successful kings England has ever known.

But what does an ex-king *do*? Well, to begin with, he had to be given a title. 'Duke of Windsor' was his brother's idea: 'I shall create you a Duke,' he said. 'It shall be the first act of my reign.' So for the remaining thirty-five years of his life, Edward VIII became His Royal Highness the Duke of Windsor. His wife Wallis became simply the Duchess of Windsor. The refusal of the new royal family to grant her the coveted title 'Her Royal Highness' was absolute. This enraged Edward and wounded him deeply. He himself always referred to his wife as 'Her Royal Highness', and expected people to curtsey to her. But everyone knew it was a pathetic falsehood. Although she lived to be ninety, Wallis never became royal.

During the Second World War the Duke was given a petty job of no real significance: Governor of the Bahamas. 'Naturally, we loathe the job, but it was the only way out of a difficult situation,' the Duchess is reported to have said. Then, after the war, the couple lived on the outskirts of Paris. They travelled a little, played games, took 'holidays', met friends. It was an empty and useless life, and they knew it.

On a state visit to France in 1972 Queen Elizabeth visited Edward, her Uncle David, in his Paris home. He was dying of cancer, and had only days to live. No one knows what they said to each other, but it must have been a poignant farewell. His corpse was brought back to England and buried quietly in the royal burial ground at Frogmore, Windsor. Fourteen years later Wallis was laid to rest beside him.

# GEORGE VI

## 1895–1952   REIGNED 1936–1952

### *Son of George V and Mary of Teck*

**The younger brother of Edward VIII was kind, shy, conscientious, sensible. He was an exemplary king, husband and father.**

When King Edward VIII abdicated, the line of succession was quite clear: the throne had to pass to his younger brother Prince Albert, the Duke of York, known to his family as Bertie. And Bertie was horrified at the prospect. Never once had he expected to become king. When he realised that his brother was actually going to pass the job on to him he said to his cousin, Lord Louis Mountbatten: 'Dickie, this is absolutely terrible. I never wanted this to happen; I'm quite unprepared for it. David has been trained for this all his life. I've never even seen a State paper. I'm only a Naval Officer, it's the only thing I know about.'

It was true. Bertie had been completely overshadowed by his elder brother, and was quite content to be just a relatively minor royal. He had an appalling stammer, which made it difficult for him to take on public engagements which involved speaking. Nevertheless, he had involved himself in all sorts of charitable activities, particularly among young people. And he was an excellent tennis-player and cricketer.

He had experienced the excitement of active service in the navy during the First World War, taking part in the Battle of Jutland. Then, after the war, he fell genuinely in love with Lady Elizabeth Bowes-Lyon, marrying her in 1923: and marriage for love is a luxury which very few monarchs in our history have enjoyed. Of course, being no contender at that time for the throne, he didn't have to suffer the artificiality of an 'arranged marriage'. The normality of Bertie's married happiness is, regrettably, almost unique in our kingly records.

Bertie had been born at Sandringham in 1895, still in the reign of Queen Victoria, on the very anniversary-date of the death of Albert the Prince Consort. It was inevitable that his string of names (Albert Frederick Arthur George) should start with Albert. However, on becoming king, he chose to be known as George VI. It was an inspired choice, and gave a signal of stability and continuity, following the quiet dignity of his father, George V. The monarchy urgently needed a healing hand after being dealt a near death-blow by the abdication crisis.

Following almost immediately after George VI's coronation came the Second World War. The courage of King George and Queen Elizabeth will never be forgotten as they stayed in London throughout those dangerous years, enduring the Blitz and the damage, as Buckingham Palace itself was bombed. Day after day the king and queen were to be seen moving among the people, inspecting the latest night's destruction and helping to boost morale as they chatted to the Londoners amid the débris. At the beginning of the war plans had been drawn up by Neville Chamberlain's Government to move Court, Government and Parliament to a safe place in the country. But when Winston Churchill took over the premiership he and George VI tore them up. And his wife Queen Elizabeth summed up the impossibility of deserting London in the memorable phrase: 'The children won't leave without me; I won't leave without the King; and the

King will never leave.' No one should ever underestimate the effect of such firmness. George VI and his Queen gave the country an example of unflinching loyalty to duty.

After the war the king shared the austerity years with his people. He gave his assent to change after change as the post-war Labour Government set up the National Health Service, developed the welfare state, nationalised the major industries, and gave independence to India, thus stripping him of his title of 'Emperor'. The British Empire itself ceased to exist, being replaced by a newer association of free states, the 'Commonwealth of Nations'. As a constitutional monarch, of course, he had to agree to all these changes, but it did mean that bit by bit, almost imperceptibly at first, and then increasingly swiftly, the very role and function of the monarchy itself was changing.

For fifteen years George performed the role of constitutional monarch with impeccable devotion. In all the books concerning the history of those years it is virtually impossible to find any criticism of the way he behaved, either in public or in private. He gained enormous respect for the way in which he carried out his duties, overcame his speech-impediment, and handled every difficult situation with modesty and skill.

No one recognised the link between smoking and lung cancer in the years when George was on the throne. He, like most men of his generation, smoked heavily, so it is hardly surprising that he became one of the victims, dying at the relatively early age of fifty-seven. A new chapel, specially constructed on the north side of St George's Chapel, Windsor, to receive his body, was dedicated in 1969.

Honesty and tenacity are not dramatic virtues, but arguably King George VI was one of the best kings Britain has ever had. No great memorial or deed remains, but his lasting influence was that he successfully piloted the monarchy into a new phase of existence.

# ELIZABETH II

## 1926– REIGNED 1952–

*Daughter of George VI and Elizabeth, née Bowes-Lyon*

**Punctilious, persevering, regal but unpompous, our present monarch is a traditionalist who is also an innovator. She possesses a steely self-discipline. Personally, she seems somewhat withdrawn and distant.**

Having reigned for over fifty years, Elizabeth II is the only sovereign most of her subjects can remember.

It seems almost absurdly superfluous to add yet more comment to the millions of words which have been written about her. She has been photographed, filmed, videoed, caricatured, adulated, gossiped about, possibly more than any other person who has ever lived. And yet, paradoxically, despite the crowds, the pomp and ceremony, the intrusive press, she remains an extraordinarily private individual. She probably needs to be, simply to preserve her sanity.

Having now looked at the succession of kings and queens following one another for a thousand years, it is worthwhile to put Elizabeth II in context. To compare her with any of her predecessors will reveal that she has reigned with outstanding skill and determined dedication.

The facts about her life are relatively simple. The first child of Albert, Duke of York, she was born in a private house, 17 Bruton Street, London, now destroyed, with very little prospect of ever becoming a reigning monarch. Of course, from the beginning she had always moved in the topmost royal circles. Her grandmother, Queen Mary, took much care with her upbringing, taking her to museums, concerts, exhibitions, and generally showing her what it was like to undertake royal duties. But it was the abdication of her uncle, when she was a perceptive ten-year-old, that made it abundantly clear that she was next in line to the throne after her father.

Princess Elizabeth was thirteen when the Second World War broke out, and she lived throughout the London Blitz in Windsor Castle, sharing the threat of bombs and wartime rationing (her parents insisted on frugality) with her sister, Princess Margaret. Then, towards the end of the war, she begged to be allowed to do National Service 'as other girls of my age do' and so became Second Subaltern Elizabeth Windsor, completing a course in vehicle maintenance. It must have been a welcome taste of freedom and 'normality'. During the victory celebrations she and her sister slipped out into the London crowds and watched from below as her parents and Winston Churchill appeared on the balcony of Buckingham Palace.

Meanwhile, again as other girls of her age do, she fell in love. This is not a sloppy bit of journalism. Quite simply, she had had eyes on her distant cousin, Prince Philip of Greece, ever since they had first met, when he was eighteen and she was thirteen. King George tried hard to postpone the wedding, like other fathers of his age do. Not that he had anything against Philip, but he just wanted the couple to be quite sure about their intentions, particularly as Elizabeth had apparently fallen for the first boy she had met. But finally he gave in and the wedding in 1947 provided a welcome splash of colour in drab, post-war Britain. Those who remember the event will also remember how beautiful she was. Again, this is not trite royal gossip. It was an extremely popular wedding, and the birth of a son, Prince Charles, almost exactly a year later, was just what the nation wanted. It sealed the continuity of the monarchy so that the future seemed assured. The nightmare of the abdication was now well and truly in the past.

For a very brief spell Elizabeth and Philip were able to enjoy a reasonably normal and private life together. Philip was keen to pursue his career in the navy, and as a serving officer's wife Elizabeth lived for a while in Malta. However, her father's illness began to draw her more into the centre of things, and the royal life of perpetual public engagements began. She and Philip were in Kenya when King George VI died. Quickly she returned, setting foot in England again as Queen Elizabeth II, aged twenty-five, exactly the same age as Elizabeth I had been when she had come to the throne four centuries before. The rest is well known: chronicled interminably, photographed incessantly, gossiped about unmercifully. How on earth can it all be summed up?

Well, to begin with, no age has seen more changes than the decades of Elizabeth's life. Rapid communications and easy transport have made it possible for her to travel more and be seen by more of her subjects than any of her predecessors. Statistics are impossible, because they are always having to be updated. Nevertheless, it's true to say that no monarch in history has travelled more than Queen Elizabeth II. It is a feature of her reign which she shares with her namesake Elizabeth I, whose 'progresses' up and down the country made her so popular.

With this, the glare of publicity has become intolerably intense. Interestingly, it was Elizabeth herself who insisted, against united opposition from all her advisers, on having her coronation televised. The pundits felt that televising the service would be somewhat improper. But Elizabeth saw more clearly than they did that the new medium of television had to be used on such an important occasion. At the time of the coronation, TV was still very new. Thousands of people bought their first TV set in order to watch this coronation, seeing history being made.

From South Africa in 1947, Elizabeth had made a noteworthy broadcast on the occasion of her twenty-first birthday. It took the form of an act of self-dedication to the work which she knew she would have to undertake. 'I declare before you all,' she said, 'that my whole life, whether it be long or short, shall be devoted to your service and the service of our great Imperial Commonwealth to which we all belong.' At the time it seemed little more than a form of words, something of a banal platitude of a promise.

However, several decades later we can see just how deeply she intended to keep that declaration. No sovereign has ever undertaken the monarch's role and duties with such devotion. There are many critics of royalty, but very few have ever been able to fault the tenacious integrity of Queen Elizabeth II in carrying out her lonely and difficult job.

One aspect of royal duties is the sovereign's weekly meeting with the prime minister of the day. The queen has been conspicuously conscientious in briefing herself on all current issues, and woe betide any prime minister who has not done his or her homework. Winston Churchill and Harold Wilson are only two of her prime ministers who have felt embarrassment at the sharpness of her questioning. 'I shall certainly advise my successor to do his homework before his audience,' said Harold Wilson, '. . . or he will feel like an unprepared schoolboy.'

It is salutary that even the highest politician in the land has to feel accountable to someone even 'higher'. Not only does it keep a politician constantly on his toes, but also the fact that it is done privately, and with no shred of party acrimony, adds to the value of these weekly meetings. A further feature, of course, is that a king or queen, over the years, has unrivalled experience, humbling even the most astute politician. No one can pull a fast one over a sovereign who has seen many a statesman come and go.

For many reasons it is regrettable that today there is a growing feeling of dissatisfaction with the monarchy, if not with the monarch. To a large extent this is a result of a bitter propaganda campaign by just a few newspaper editors who use every opportunity to rubbish the queen, the royal family, and the whole institution of monarchy. Cheap gibes, crude headlines and false reporting are relentlessly sensationalising and trivialising the position of the sovereign. Despite Elizabeth's magnificent and unique contribution to royal history, then, there seems to be a curiously ambiguous attitude to royalty today. The crowds still gather and cheer, but the newspapers and television programmes are filled with doubts and sneers.

The future of our constitution is a serious matter, especially as the world increasingly becomes a global village and Britain becomes ever more closely tied to the European community. However, the monarchy has undergone vast changes since the days of that momentous battle when Saxon King Harold was slain at Hastings. Its importance has changed and its role has become more subtle. Who knows what may yet evolve?

Charles III and William V now face the task of leading the monarchy into an unknowable future.

# QUEENS AND CONSORTS

This table lists the queens of England and male consorts from King Egbert's reign in the ninth century. Where known, dates of birth and death are given, as well as the consort's age at marriage. For many of the queens in the period before William the Conqueror, however, dates are difficult to pinpoint, and should be considered as approximate only. (d. = died; b. = born; m. = married)

| Monarch | Queen/Consort | Consort's dates | Consort's age at marriage |
|---|---|---|---|
| Egbert | Redburga (Eadburgh) | | |
| Ethelwulf | Osburga | d. 846 | |
| | Judith of France | b. *c*. 843 | *c*. 13 |
| Ethelbald | Judith of France | b. *c*. 843 | *c*. 15 |
| Ethelbert | unmarried | | |
| Ethelred I | unknown | | |
| Alfred the Great | Elswitha | m. 868/9, d. 905 | |
| Edward the Elder | Egwina | d. 901/2 | |
| | Elfleda | d. 920 | |
| | Edgifu | d. 968 | |
| Athelstan | unmarried | | |
| Edmund I (the Elder) | Elgifu | d. *c*. 944 | |
| | Ethelfled of Damerham | d. after 975 | |
| Edred | unmarried | | |
| Edwy the Fair | Elgifu | m. by 956, d. *c*. 959 | |
| Edgar the Peaceful | Ethelfled | d. *c*. 962 | |
| | Wulfryth (mistress?) | *c*. 945–1000 | |
| | Elfrida | *c*. 945–1002 | |
| Edward the Martyr | unmarried | | |
| Ethelred II (the Unready) | Elfled of Northumbria | *c*. 963–1002 | *c*. 17 |
| | Emma of Normandy | *c*. 985–1052 | |
| Edmund II (Ironside) | Eadgyth | m. 1015 | |
| Canute | Elfgifu of Northampton | | |
| | Emma of Normandy | *c*. 985–1052 | |
| Edward the Confessor | Edith | *c*. 1020–1075 | |

| Monarch | Queen/Consort | Consort's dates | Consort's age at marriage |
|---|---|---|---|
| Harold II | Aldgyth | | |
| | Edith of the Swan Neck | | |
| William I (the Conqueror) | Matilda of Flanders | c. 1032–1083 | 18 |
| William II (Rufus) | unmarried | | |
| Henry I | Matilda of Scotland | 1080–1118 | 20 |
| | Adela of Louvain | c. 1103–1151 | c. 18 |
| Stephen | Matilda of Boulogne | c. 1103–1152 | c. 22 |
| Henry II | Eleanor of Aquitaine | c. 1122–1204 | c. 30 |
| Richard I (the Lionheart) | Berengaria of Navarre | c. 1165–c. 1230 | c. 26 |
| John | Isabella of Angoulême | c. 1187–1246 | c. 13 |
| Henry III | Eleanor of Provence | c. 1223–1291 | c. 14 |
| Edward I | Eleanor of Castile | c. 1244–1290 | c. 10 |
| | Marguerite of France | c. 1282–1317 | c. 16 |
| Edward II | Isabella of France | c. 1292–1358 | c. 16 |
| Edward III | Philippa of Hainault | c. 1314–1369 | c. 14 |
| Richard II | Anne of Bohemia | 1366–1394 | 15 |
| | Isabella of Valois | 1389–1409 | 7 |
| Henry IV | Mary de Bohun | c. 1369–1394 | c. 13 |
| | Joan of Navarre | c. 1370–1437 | c. 33 |
| Henry V | Catherine of Valois | 1401–1437 | 18 |
| Henry VI | Margaret of Anjou | 1429–1482 | 15 |
| Edward IV | Elizabeth Woodville | c. 1437–1492 | c. 27 |
| Richard III | Anne of Warwick | 1456–1485 | 16 |
| Henry VII | Elizabeth of York | 1466–1503 | 19 |
| Henry VIII | Catherine of Aragon | 1485–1536 | 23 |
| | Anne Boleyn | c. 1500–1536 | 22 |
| | Jane Seymour | c. 1507–1537 | c. 29 |
| | Anne of Cleves | 1515–1557 | 24 |
| | Catherine Howard | c. 1522–1542 | c. 18 |
| | Catherine Parr | c. 1512–1548 | c. 31 |
| Edward VI | unmarried | | |
| Jane Grey | Lord Guilford Dudley | 1536–1554 | 16 |
| Mary I | Philip of Spain | 1527–1598 | 27 |
| Elizabeth I | unmarried | | |
| James I | Anne of Denmark | 1574–1619 | 14 |
| Charles I | Henrietta Maria | 1609–1669 | 14 |
| Charles II | Catherine of Braganza | 1638–1705 | 23 |
| James II | Anne Hyde | 1637–1671 | 21 |
| | Mary of Modena | 1658–1718 | 15 |
| Mary II (reigning jointly with) | William of Orange | 1650–1702 | 27 |

| Monarch | Queen/Consort | Consort's dates | Consort's age at marriage |
| --- | --- | --- | --- |
| Anne | George of Denmark | 1653–1708 | 29 |
| George I | Princess Sophia of Zelle | 1666–1726 | 16 |
| George II | Caroline of Ansbach | 1683–1737 | 22 |
| George III | Charlotte of Mecklenburg-Strelitz | 1744–1818 | 17 |
| George IV | Caroline of Brunswick | 1768–1821 | 26 |
| William IV | Adelaide of Saxe-Meiningen | 1792–1849 | 26 |
| Victoria | Albert of Saxe-Coburg-Gotha | 1819–1861 | 20 |
| Edward VII | Alexandra of Denmark | 1844–1925 | 18 |
| George V | Mary of Teck | 1867–1953 | 26 |
| Edward VIII | Mrs Wallis Simpson | 1896–1986 | 40 |
| George VI | Elizabeth Bowes-Lyon | 1900–2002 | 22 |
| Elizabeth II | Prince Philip of Greece | 1921– | 26 |

The Saxon world was a tough, man's world in which literacy was rare and books almost non-existent. For these reasons, very little is known about the early Saxon queens. The *Anglo-Saxon Chronicle* barely mentions them. A curious and somewhat exasperating further difficulty about remembering and studying them is that their names have such a variety of spellings and forms.

# REDBURGA

## DATES UNKNOWN

### Queen of Egbert

Redburga (or Eadburgh), as the first Queen of England, deserves to be better known, but her character and interests will probably never be unearthed. She and Egbert had three children, Ethelwulf (who became the next king), Editha and Athelstan; and the descendants of Redburga and Egbert ruled England for the next 150 years. Egbert's remains are in Winchester Cathedral, but Redburga is not mentioned with him, though it is likely that she too was buried in the old Saxon cathedral.

# OSBURGA

## DIED 846

### First Queen of Ethelwulf

Queen Osburga holds the record among all English queens for providing the country with no fewer than four of its kings. She was the mother of

Ethelbald, Ethelbert, Ethelred I and, the most famous of all, Alfred the Great.

Clearly she was a successful wife and mother (she had other children besides), but it is less clear what happened to her. She may have died, or she may have been simply 'put away' so that her husband Ethelwulf could marry Judith of France.

# JUDITH OF FRANCE
## BORN *c*. 843
### *Second Queen of Ethelwulf*

Judith was aged just thirteen when King Ethelwulf, returning from a pilgrimage to Rome, visited her father's court in France. Her father was King Charles the Bald of the Franks and, as Ethelwulf must have felt it would be politically useful to make a marriage alliance, Judith was pressed into becoming Queen of England, his second wife.

The marriage lasted only two years, as Ethelwulf died shortly after returning to England. They had no children, and Judith was widowed at fifteen. Life, however, had much more in store for her, for she now became . . .

### *. . . Queen of Ethelbald*

As soon as King Ethelwulf died, his son King Ethelbald promptly married the obviously nubile Judith. To marry one's stepmother is unusual to say the least, and it was the scandal of the time. Judith is distinguished, therefore, for being queen to two English kings, father and son.

Her marriage to Ethelbald was also a short one, for he died young, aged about twenty-six. Judith was now widowed for the second time, aged about seventeen.

By this time her father felt it was time for her to come back home: he demanded her return and promptly placed her in a nunnery. However, Judith was not destined for a cloistered life. She eloped and married Baldwin I, Count of Flanders. One result of this union was a son, the future Baldwin II, who grew up to marry Aelfthryth, a daughter of King Alfred the Great. Generations later a descendant of theirs, Matilda, became the wife of William the Conqueror. Thus the royal line of the Normans can claim descent from the old Saxon kings.

# ELSWITHA
## DIED 902
### Queen of Alfred the Great

'Ealshswitha of the Gaini' was a descendant of the Mercian kings and she married Alfred when he was only eighteen, four years before he became king. We do not know how old Elswitha was, but she outlived Alfred by three years, thus experiencing the whole of his turbulent and exciting reign.

The problem of the Danish invasions must have preoccupied them both, but as Alfred became more and more successful the pair of them enjoyed a relatively settled life in Winchester, which Alfred made his capital. She brought up two sons and three daughters; her elder son, Edward, succeeded to the throne. The descendants of Elswitha and Alfred were to rule England right up to the time of the Norman Conquest.

# EGWINA, ELFLEDA, EDGIFU
## DATES UNCERTAIN
### Queens respectively of Edward the Elder

Very little is known of the wives of Edward the Elder; perhaps the first was merely a mistress. At all events, they were conspicuously fertile and between them produced at least eighteen children. Egwina gave Edward three children, including the future King Athelstan; Elfleda gave him ten children; and Edgifu gave him five more, including two more future kings – Edmund I and Edred.

Fertility, of course, is the *sine qua non* of queens, so in these terms alone Edward's reign was a conspicuous triumph, and Edward himself was keenly aware of the diplomatic advantages of marrying off his children into other royal families. His daughters married kings of France, Burgundy, Provence, and another married the Holy Roman Emperor, Otto the Great.

# ELGIFU
## DIED c. 944
### First Queen of Edmund I (the Elder)

Note that variant spellings of Elgifu include Aelgifu, Elgiva, Algyva and Aelgytha. Quite apart from being married to a king and giving birth to two future kings (Edwy and Edgar), Elgifu's claim to fame rests on the fact that she was venerated as a saint.

William of Malmesbury, the twelfth-century monk and historian, wrote that Elgifu founded the famous nunnery at Shaftesbury and recorded the fact that she died there. He praised her for her generosity, wisdom, and gift of prophecy; he even went on to compose verses in honour of her miracles. She has also (wrongly) been called Abbess of Wilton. The Feast Day of St Elgiva is 18 May.

Elgifu's life was short: her husband Edmund was aged only twenty-three when she died, so it was only natural that he should marry again.

## ETHELFLED OF DAMERHAM
### DATES UNKNOWN, d. AFTER 975
### *Second Queen of Edmund I*

Almost nothing is known of Edmund's second wife, Ethelfled. She and Edmund were to enjoy only two months of marriage before he was stabbed to death by Leofa, an outlawed thief. They had no children.

## ELGIFU
### DATES UNKNOWN, d. *c.* 969
### *Queen of Edwy the Fair*

Edwy's reign was a disaster. He was about fifteen when he came to the throne and about nineteen when he died. Sometime during his reign, and certainly by 956, he married Elgifu – yet another queen of that name – but no details survive, except for the fact that she was his stepmother's daughter. No children are recorded.

## ETHELFLED
### d. *c.* 962
### *First Queen of Edgar the Peaceful*

Ethelfled died in childbirth after just three years of marriage, so she never knew that the boy she bore would become king, saint and martyr, and would eventually find rest in a Russian Orthodox Chapel in Brookwood cemetery: she was, in fact, the mother of King Edward the Martyr.

Ethelfled was the daughter of one of the king's deputies, Ealdorman Ordmaer. We do not know when she died, but she left a grieving nineteen-year-old husband, who turned next to a nun for solace.

# WULFRYTH

## *c. 945–1000*

### *Second Wife/Mistress of Edgar the Peaceful*

It is a little unclear whether Edgar actually married Wulfryth (sometime around 961) or merely abducted her from a nunnery at Wilton and gave her a nice little daughter, Edith. Edgar had previously tried to seduce another nun, Wulfhilda, but she had put up such resistance that Edgar turned his attention to Wulfryth instead.

Certainly, Wulfryth had a daughter by Edgar, but shortly after the birth she returned to Wilton Abbey where she eventually became its abbess. Tongues must have wagged, but in fact both Wulfryth and her daughter ultimately came to be thought of as saints. The veneration of St Edith of Wilton developed into a local cult.

St Wulfryth did not last long in Edgar's affections and, as she had returned to her nunnery, he decided to marry a third wife.

# ELFRIDA

## *c. 945–1002*

### *Third Queen of Edgar the Peaceful*

Elfrida was a daughter of another of Edgar's deputies, Ealdorman Ordgar of Devon, and she was the widow of Ealdorman Athelwold of East Anglia. Edgar's third marriage, in 964, therefore, was something of a political move; nevertheless, it lasted, and the couple had two children, one of whom, Ethelred, was to become King of England, known for ever after as Ethelred the Unready. Interestingly, Elfrida was crowned with her husband King Edgar by Archbishop Dunstan in Bath Abbey on 11 May 973. This is the first recorded instance of a coronation of a Queen of England.

Edgar's reign was conspicuously successful in many ways, and it is a tragedy that he died so young, aged only about thirty-two. His death left Elfrida as a young widow with a son aged only seven. Meanwhile, Edgar's older son Edward, by his first wife Ethelfled, succeeded to the throne aged about twelve.

This state of royal affairs must have galled Elfrida, being so near and yet so far from regal power. If only her own son Ethelred could somehow become king! After all, there were plenty of people willing to support his claim. Whether or not Elfrida plotted her step-son's assassination we shall never know; however, the opportunity to remove the obstacle to her ambitions presented itself a few years later in 978, when Edward, now a young teenager, visited his stepmother at Corfe Castle. As he rode into Corfe, Elfrida's co-conspirators were ready and waiting. The young king, still on horseback, was offered a drink and was brutally stabbed as he accepted it. He fell from his saddle, but his foot became caught in the stirrup and he was dragged along the ground as his horse galloped off. It is not clear whether Elfrida was actually present at the murder, but certainly she must have connived at it.

Thus Elfrida became the archetypal wicked stepmother. Her son was now king, but everyone knew that she had blood on her hands. That she acknowledged her guilt is perhaps shown by the fact that in 980 she founded a famous Benedictine nunnery at Amesbury, near Stonehenge, in expiation of her crime. She even placed her abbey under the patronage of St Mary and St Melor, St Melor being a young Cornish prince who had been murdered as a result of jealous ambition, in circumstances closely resembling Elfrida's own wicked deed. Elfrida herself became a nun and died at Wherwell Abbey in Hampshire, which she also founded.

# ELFLED OF NORTHUMBRIA

## c. 963–1002

### First Queen of Ethelred II (the Unready)

Little is known of Elfled of Northumbria: she was probably too busy bringing up her thirteen children by Ethelred the Unready. One of her sons, Edmund 'Ironside', succeeded Ethelred and became king. Elfled must have died before 1002, for in that year Ethelred married his second wife, Emma of Normandy.

# EMMA OF NORMANDY

## c. 985–1052

### Second Queen of Ethelred II (the Unready)

Emma was one of the great characters of her time and has the unique distinction of marrying two Kings of England (Ethelred and Canute) and

Seven Saxon kings were crowned on or beside this ancient Coronation Stone, at Kingston upon Thames, Surrey: Edward the Elder; Athelstan; Edmund I; Edred; Edwy; Edward (Saint and Martyr); and Ethelred II (the Unready). (*Photo*: David Hilliam)

Edward I captured the Stone of Scone in 1296 and ordered this Coronation Chair to be made to incorporate it. Since then, it has been used in the coronation ceremony of every English monarch. Tradition links the Stone with the cushion on which Jacob rested at Bethel; but it was certainly used for many Scottish coronations before coming to England. It has now been returned to Scotland, and is on view in Edinburgh Castle. (*Photo*: Hulton Getty)

Six mortuary chests in Winchester Cathedral contain the oldest kingly bones in England. The contents were tipped out during the Commonwealth by Parliamentarian soldiers, and the skulls and bones were jumbled up as they were put back. Somewhere here are the bones of King Egbert, the first King of all England. (*Photo*: John Crook)

Possibly these are the bones of several other early Saxon kings as well as those of King Egbert. Mixed up here may be the bones of Egbert, Ethelwulf and Edmund I. The bones of King Canute, Queen Emma and William II (Rufus) are also contained somewhere in these mortuary chests. (*Photo*: John Crook)

A terrifying omen occurred in 1066 soon after King Harold had been crowned. We know now that it was Halley's Comet, shown here on the Bayeux Tapestry. It was widely believed to be a sign of God's displeasure that Harold had broken his solemn oath to recognise the right of William, Duke of Normandy, to the English throne. Months later, the Norman Conquest was to destroy the Saxon world. (*Photo*: Michael Holford)

The death of Harold was a turning-point in English history. The Saxon civilisation was ruthlessly replaced by that of the Normans. The most unforgettable date in British history is 1066, the fateful year of the battle of Hastings. This extract from the Bayeux Tapestry shows the death of Harold. (*Photo*: Michael Holford)

Traditionally, the 'Rufus Stone' marks the spot where King William II was killed by an arrow. The alleged assassin, Sir Walter Tyrell, fled the country. A local charcoal burner found the king's body and took it on his cart to Winchester Cathedral. The original stone was set up in the eighteenth century, but this has recently been encased in a new cast-iron cover, shown here, which clearly tells the story of the king's death. (*Photo*: Mary Hilliam)

Edward I ordered a memorial cross to be erected at each spot where the body of his queen, Eleanor of Castile, rested on its journey from Harby in Nottinghamshire to Westminster. There were twelve crosses in all. Only three of these still survive: at Geddington, Northamptonshire; Hardingstone, just outside Northampton (shown here); and Waltham. The one outside Charing Cross station is a nineteenth-century replacement. (*Photo*: Mary Hilliam)

ION SINE SOLE
IRIS.

The Rainbow Portrait of Elizabeth I is on view at Hatfield House, Hertfordshire. It was in the grounds of this house that Elizabeth learned that she had become queen, on the death of her half-sister Mary. The dress she wears in the portrait is covered with eyes and ears, to show how watchful she was; the serpent on her sleeve is the emblem of wisdom; and the rainbow in her hand is the symbol of peace. The motto, *Non Sine Sole Iris*, means 'No rainbow without the sun' – the sun, of course, being the queen herself. The portrait is attributed to Isaac Oliver (1565?–1617). (By courtesy of the Marquess of Salisbury)

The execution of Charles I at Whitehall. The Banqueting House, shown here, is the only surviving part of Whitehall, and is open to visitors. A scaffold was built in the street outside. Some of the spectators managed to dip their handkerchiefs in the king's blood before they were hustled away by the Parliamentarian soldiers. (Ashmolean Museum, Oxford)

The posthumous history of Cromwell's skull is told on p. 201. There is every reason to believe that the skull, with a spike still sticking out of the top, is genuine. Its final owner felt that it needed a better resting-place than the ebony box in which it was kept when he inherited it, so the skull was given to Sidney Sussex College, Cambridge, where it is now decently interred. (*Photo*: Edwin Smith)

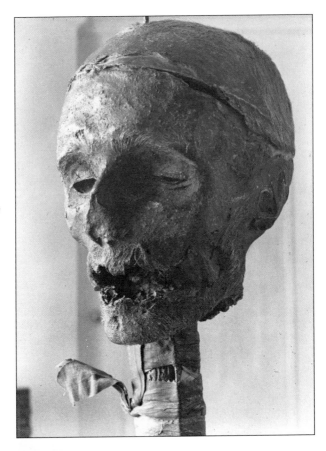

Probably the most famous illegitimate son of any English king, James Scott, Duke of Monmouth and Buccleuch, was the offspring of Charles II and his first mistress, Lucy Walter. He was beheaded after he had led the unsuccessful rebellion against his uncle, James II. After the execution it was realised that there was no portrait of Scott, so his head was quickly sewn back on to his body to enable an artist to take his impression. All subsequent portraits, including this one by Sir James Kneller, owe a debt to that first painting. (By courtesy of the National Portrait Gallery, London)

**Left**: 'The rare and awful visits of Albert Edward, Prince of Wales, to Windsor Castle'. This cartoon by Max Beerbohm captures the strained relationship between Queen Victoria and the future Edward VII. She attributed the death of her husband, Albert the Prince Consort, to her son's wayward behaviour. 'I never can or shall look at him without a shudder,' she wrote. (*Photo*: V & A Picture Library). **Right**: Alice Keppel was Edward VII's last mistress. Queen Alexandra was tolerant enough to bring her to Edward's deathbed in the king's final hours. Alice Keppel was an ancestress of Mrs Camilla Parker-Bowles. (*Photo*: Hulton Getty)

Edward had Langtry Manor, Bournemouth, built in 1880 for his current favourite mistress, Lillie Langtry, 'The Jersey Lily'. It is now a hotel, with much memorabilia of the royal connection. The future king had a special peep-hole made so that he could inspect guests before he came down to dinner. His four-poster bed is a special feature of the hotel. (*Photo*: David Hilliam)

being the mother of two other Kings of England (Hardecanute and Edward the Confessor). She was a truly remarkable person, and it's a great pity that she is so little remembered nowadays. In her lifetime she was greatly admired, and when she died she was buried with great honour among the Saxon kings in Winchester Cathedral.

In her young days she was remarkably beautiful and was known as the 'Fair Maid', but as she grew older she gained a reputation for wisdom, and became known as the 'Old Lady'. She was the Queen Mother of her times.

She was the daughter of a Norman duke, and so it was largely through her and her son Edward the Confessor that Norman influence became strong in England, paving the way for the invasion of 1066.

Emma's marriage to Ethelred the Unready came at a turbulent and eventful time in English history, marked by the brutal invasion of the country by the fierce Danes. Both she and Ethelred had to escape to the continent, back to her family. When Ethelred died in 1016 his successor and Danish opponent Canute determined that he too would marry her. It says much for her attractions. The rest of Emma's story is told below, under the title Second Queen of Canute.

# EADGYTH

## DATES UNKNOWN

### *Queen of Edmund Ironside*

Eadgyth was queen only briefly, during Edmund Ironside's short rule. She was Swedish-born and the widow of Earl Sigeferth, who had been conveniently murdered. Edmund Ironside had had a secret love affair with her, and at the time of his brief occupancy of the throne the couple had two sons, Edmund and Edward, who may have been twins.

The Danish Canute was determined to rid himself of any potential rivals, so after Edmund Ironside had been disposed of, he imprisoned Eadgyth and banished her two children to Sweden with a 'letter of death'. Luckily for them, the King of Sweden spared them and their subsequent lives make fascinating reading. Edward became known as 'Edward the Exile' and has been called 'The Lost King of England'. He did ultimately return to England, was murdered in 1057, and was buried in St Paul's Minster.

Eadgyth herself was buried in Shaftesbury Abbey, a place of pilgrimage for it was also the place where Edward the Martyr had his shrine.

# EMMA OF NORMANDY
## *c. 985–1052*
### *Second Queen of Canute*

Emma of Normandy was King Canute's second queen. The first was Elfgifu of Northampton, whose relationship with him is thought to have begun soon after his arrival in 1015. Although it is unclear whether they were actually married, she did bear him a son, Harold ('Harefoot'), who succeeded his father as King of England from 1035 to 1040. And, whether mistress or wife, when Canute married Emma he did not cast Elfgifu aside, but quite openly maintained two consorts.

It seems astonishing that Emma should marry her former husband's enemy, but the marriage was very successful, and she and Canute became greatly respected. She was widowed again twenty years later and lived on in Winchester.

The most astonishing episode in her long and eventful life was a trial which took place in the old Saxon cathedral in Winchester. Although she was an elderly lady by then, Emma had been accused of having an affair with Alwine, Bishop of Winchester, and so her son Edward the Confessor insisted that she should undergo a terrifying form of trial by ordeal.

Within the nave of the old cathedral nine ploughshares were heated to become red-hot and Emma was required to walk upon them with bare feet. To everyone's relief, she did this without sustaining any injury, and so was declared innocent. She was so delighted that she gave nine manor-houses to the monks of the cathedral (one for each ploughshare). Bishop Alwine gave nine more manors: no doubt he was just as relieved as she was. The site of one of these manor-houses, the Manor of God-Begot, is in Winchester's High Street: today it is a restaurant. The name means 'House granted to God'.

Queen Emma's remains are in one of the mortuary chests on view in Winchester Cathedral, together with the bones of her second husband, King Canute. Also lying in the same chest are the remains of her great friend, Bishop Alwine. Death did not divide them. More details about Emma are given above, under the title Second Queen to Ethelred II (the Unready).

# EDITH
## *c. 1020–1075*
### *Queen of Edward the Confessor*

Edward the Confessor, brought up in a Norman monastery, had taken a vow of chastity, so married life can't have been very much fun for Edith, daughter of the powerful Earl Godwin and sister of Edward's successor, King Harold, who was slain at Hastings.

The first biographer of Edward speaks rapturously of Edith as sharing in his good works of charity, and in fact spurring him on to even greater acts of generosity to the poor. The very name 'Edith' means 'gift of happiness', but alas, she bore no children, and this lack of sons contributed to the uncertainty over the royal succession.

Apparently, Edith preferred to sit at the king's feet rather than occupy the throne at his side, and would only six next to him in church or at table. Obviously she knew her place. On the death of her husband, Edith went back to live in Winchester, an honoured widow, and in November 1066, just a month after the Battle of Hastings, it was Edith who performed the final act of submission to the Conqueror. Winchester was then the capital of England, so it was necessary for William to seal his conquest by capturing and occupying it. He moved cautiously, rather expecting further battles as he marched through the Hampshire countryside. But the Saxon army had been demolished, and Winchester gave in without a struggle. It was left to Edith, queen of the Confessor, to hand over the city keys to William. It was a moment of high significance.

It's good to know that the Conqueror was kind to Edith. She lived on in Winchester in her house to the north of the High Street, and on her death in 1075 her body was taken to Westminster with great honour.

# Aldgyth and Edith of the Swan Neck
## Dates Unknown
### Queen and Mistress respectively of Harold II

It may look strange to put both women together, but the fact is that for most of Harold's life Edith was for all practical purposes his wife. He met her when he was in his early twenties, and it is believed she came from Norfolk. We don't know whether or not they were married, but certainly they lived together and had four strong sons, Godwin, Edmund, Magnus and Ulf, and two buxom girls, Gunhild and Gytha.

When he became king, then, Harold was aged about forty-six and had a fully fledged family. But as he struggled to unite his kingdom he had great trouble with Morcar and Edwin, Lords of Northumbria and Mercia. They were openly in revolt. In trying to pacify them it was Harold's own suggestion that he married their sister, Aldgyth, in York Minster. It was clearly a political marriage, and neither Harold nor Aldgyth pretended to have any love for each other. But the fact that they did marry seems to suggest that Harold had not actually gone through a marriage ceremony with the real love of his life, Edith of the Swan Neck.

We do not know much about Aldgyth, and in any case she was queen for only a few months, being soon widowed when Harold was slain at Hastings. But we do know that when news of William's invasion reached London she was quickly packed off for safety, and fled to Chester. A few months later she had a baby boy and called him Harold. But while Aldgyth went off to Chester, Edith of the Swan Neck (what a romantic name!) helped Harold to prepare and then she and Harold's mother, Gytha, travelled down to Hastings to watch the battle.

During that battle they waited and watched under a massive oak tree, later called the Watch Oak. And they must have been sickened by what they saw. On that day the old lady Gytha lost three sons and a nephew, and the corpses on the battlefield were so mangled and jumbled together that she simply couldn't recognise them. It was left to Edith of the Swan Neck to unfasten the chain mail on one of the victims. Only then could she identify the tattoo marks on that body, and tell the world that this was indeed the man who had loved her.

# MATILDA OF FLANDERS
## c. 1031–1083
### Queen of William I (the Conqueror)

Matilda of Flanders was very petite, in fact she was probably just over 4 feet tall. She was only about sixteen when William proposed, and he was about twenty. At first she refused, but he galloped to her father's home in Lille and set about her. He knocked her down, grabbed her plaits, pulled her round the room and gave her a good sound kicking. After that he rode off leaving her to reconsider his marriage proposal. She agreed.

They were cousins, and in those days it was a sin to marry your cousin. However, William was determined, and the marriage went ahead in defiance of the Pope, who had explicitly refused his permission. They were both excommunicated, and the Pope pardoned them only after each had promised to build an abbey. The two abbeys are still in existence today, in Caen, Normandy. It was a happy and faithful marriage, and Matilda bore William four sons and six daughters, some in France when she was still Duchess of Normandy, and some in England when she was the Conqueror's queen.

When William conceived the idea of invading England she threw herself enthusiastically into the project, and at her personal expense she presented him with a beautiful specially built flag-ship – the *Mora*. On the prow there was a gilded figure-head of their little boy, the ten-year-old Rufus, with a trumpet in one hand and a bow and arrow in the other, firmly pointing towards England. She was heart and soul behind her husband, and later, when he was firmly in control in England, William rewarded her by having her crowned as queen in Winchester Cathedral.

Sad to say, as the family grew up there were feuds and Matilda often sided with her sons. Eventually, she went back to Normandy and spent most of her last years there. However, William was a faithful husband, and when she died he was so grieved that he vowed he would give up his favourite sport, hunting. And he kept his vow.

It's impossible to know for certain whether or not Matilda had a hand in making the Bayeux Tapestry, but her name has been associated with it down the centuries.

Matilda still lies in the Abbaye aux Dames, the abbey she built in Caen as penance for marrying her forceful and energetic cousin.

# MATILDA OF SCOTLAND
## 1080–1118
### *First Queen of Henry I*

Matilda's mother was descended from Alfred the Great and her father is well known to students of English literature, for he was none other than the Malcolm who followed Macbeth as King of Scotland. He makes the final speech in Shakespeare's play.

During her teenage years Matilda was known as Edith, and was a none-too-willing nun in Romsey Abbey, Hampshire, where her aunt was abbess. Her aunt tried to force her to take the veil, but Edith tore it off and stamped on it behind her aunt's back. But if ever she had unwelcome suitors, she quickly put it back on again, to shoo them away.

She must have thought differently about Henry though, and when she married him, three months after his coronation, she became an excellent consort and provided him with four children: two girls and two boys.

She was full of charity and good works. One of her main interests was encouraging road-building. It was still early days in the Norman re-organisation of England.

One permanent memorial she left behind was the bridge at Stratford-le-Bow in London. It was the first arched bridge in England and was called a bow bridge. The bridge gave its name to the area. Perhaps luckily for her, Matilda died before her husband and before *The White Ship* disaster in which her two sons, William and Richard, drowned. But it was her daughter, also called Matilda, who became 'Lady of the English' during Stephen's reign.

## ADELA OF LOUVAIN
### *c.* 1103–1151
### *Second Queen of Henry I*

After his heir had drowned, King Henry was desperate for another son, so he remarried, this time to a daughter of a French count, Godfrey of Louvain. Adela (sometimes called Adelicia or Adelaide) was only eighteen; Henry was fifty-three.

No son came; Henry died; and for a year Adela lived as a nun at Wilton, near Salisbury. Then, as she was still young, she came out of mourning, married William de Albini, Earl of Arundel, and seven of their children were to survive. Among the descendants of this marriage came two girls destined to become tragic queens: Anne Boleyn and Catherine Howard. Adela spent her final years in a convent in Flanders.

## MATILDA OF BOULOGNE
### *c.* 1103–1152
### *Queen of Stephen*

There were so many Matildas at this time! This one, a Countess of Boulogne, was rather a shadowy figure. She gave Stephen her full support during the civil war, and helped to organise a rescue bid when he was lying captive in Bristol Castle. She produced three sons and two daughters and died two years before Stephen. She was buried in Faversham Abbey, which she had helped to found.

## ELEANOR OF AQUITAINE
### *c.* 1122–1204
### *Queen of Henry II*

Everything about Eleanor was quite spectacular. Her long life was filled with every kind of excitement. A brief account cannot do her justice. There are many biographies of her: she simply compels attention.

To begin with, she was brought up in the south of France, where poetry and the arts were so much more sophisticated than in the barbaric north. Aquitaine was a land of troubadours and courtly love, where marriage was merely incidental. Her tastes, her morals, her lifestyle: everything about her was different, and she brought a new dimension to the English court. Two things stand out: she was sensationally beautiful and outstandingly rich.

Before ever she came to England Eleanor had been Queen of France and when her husband King Louis went to the Holy Land on the Second Crusade (1147–1149) she insisted on going too and actually led a contingent of women to form a special 'ladies' crusade. Louis was quite out of his depth both in war and marriage, and his crusade was a complete disaster.

As for Eleanor, high-spirited and uninhibited, the high-spot of the crusading adventure came when she fell passionately in love with her uncle Raymond, who happened to be Prince of Antioch – one of the Crusader States. Raymond was ten years older than Eleanor, and it was clear to everyone that there was a powerful physical attraction between them.

Eleanor shattered Louis by refusing to go on to Jerusalem with him. She refused to leave Antioch. Almost incredibly, she demanded a divorce! Such behaviour was outrageous, and Louis' reaction was swift. He ordered his army to prepare, secretly, to leave the city of Antioch. Without warning, Eleanor was woken up at midnight and forced to accompany Louis to Jerusalem, without even saying goodbye to Raymond. She was in disgrace.

As Louis and Eleanor passed through Rome on their way back to Paris, the Pope tried to bring about a reconciliation. He even prepared a double bed for them both, and ordered them to make love. But it was no good. Eleanor found that Louis would rather have been a monk.

However, Eleanor's life changed dramatically when she met Henry Plantagenet, heir to the throne of England. The passion was mutual, despite the fact that she was twelve years older. Quickly she pressed insistently for a divorce from Louis, who put up no resistance, and just two months later she married Henry Plantagenet in Poitiers Cathedral.

Two years later Henry II and Eleanor were crowned, magnificently, in Westminster Abbey. Her silks and velvet, jewels and brocades, all from exotic lands, astonished everyone.

Henry's reign was an exhausting and turbulent one, in which Eleanor shared fully, as well as giving Henry five sons and three daughters. She had to put up with Henry's restlessness, his temper, and his mistress-hunting. Eventually, the marriage fell apart, especially as their sons grew up. She sided with them against their father, so Henry virtually imprisoned her in various castles, mostly in Salisbury or Winchester for the last sixteen years of his life. She was sixty-seven when Henry died and she could be released. Yet, astonishingly, her life was now just about to enter its most active period.

Her favourite son, Richard the Lionheart, was now king, but needed every bit of help she could provide. He was hardly ever in England, so she simply took over the kingdom and ruled in his name, passing popular laws, pardoning prisoners, making sure that things ran smoothly.

Knowing that England needed an heir, she organised a marriage for him with Princess Berengaria of Navarre. Somebody had to take the initiative, so she personally made the journey to Navarre, south of the Pyrenees, conducted all the negotiations and then set off with the bride-to-be to find Richard, who was somewhere in the Mediterranean on the way to his Crusade. She got as far as Sicily with Berengaria and then had to get back to England to sort out trouble which was brewing with her too-ambitious son, John.

Then news came that Richard was being held captive on the continent for a huge ransom. Eleanor raised an enormous sum to set him free: it cost everyone in England a quarter of a year's pay. However, with her powerful personality she not only managed to get people to pay up, but when Richard was finally released she travelled about the country with him, the pair of them enjoying huge popularity, despite the crippling cost.

She survived her son Richard, saw her other son John crowned as his successor, then went back to Aquitaine and arranged another splendid marriage, this time with her granddaughter Blanche of Castile to the grandson of her former husband, King Louis. She was energetic to the end. Her tomb in Fontevrault, next to her husband Henry II, has a magnificent effigy, a tribute to a great queen.

# BERENGARIA OF NAVARRE
## c. 1165–c. 1230
### Queen of Richard I (the Lionheart)

As Queen, Berengaria never saw England. She was born in Navarre, married in Cyprus, lived in France, and was buried in an abbey she had built at L'Epau, near Le Mans.

Her life was a strange and rather sad affair. Her reputation for beauty was widespread so when she agreed to marry Richard it might have seemed a perfect match. He was handsome, brave, and the most popular warrior-king in Christendom. Eleanor, Richard's mother, travelled with her to Sicily, handed her over to Richard's sister, and went back to England. Then the bride-to-be was taken to Cyprus where she and Richard were married. She was crowned Queen of England and Cyprus.

But Richard was gay. He had no time for her. He went on to his Crusade, and left her to follow after. And when he lost the campaign he pushed her off to England by boat, saying that he would travel by land and meet up with her later. Berengaria must have been devastated. She never reached England. She probably never wanted to.

There was a sort of reconciliation, and Richard promised to change his lifestyle. But it was too late. Berengaria was actually with him when he died. She must have known that her life as queen had been a sham.

She was only about thirty-four when Richard died, but she never remarried. Instead, she retired to a nunnery and spent the rest of her life helping the poor, and especially caring for abandoned children.

Writers have wrongly spread the idea that Berengaria never set foot on English soil. However, on the contrary, in her widowhood she often visited the court of King John, who allowed her to go anywhere she wanted throughout the country. In fact, in 1220 Berengaria joined the huge crowd that gathered in Canterbury Cathedral to witness the translation of Thomas Becket's bones to his new shrine.

In 1229 she built a beautiful abbey in L'Epau, and it was here that she lived out her final days as a nun, giving herself a new name – Juliana. Her effigy – which was formerly in Le Mans Cathedral – was taken back to L'Epau Abbey in 1970, where it can be seen today in the chapter house. All in all, it was a curious life for an English Queen.

## ISABELLA OF ANGOULÊME

### c. 1187–1246

### Queen of John

Isabella was an attractive young teenager of about thirteen when John married her in Bordeaux. John had fallen quite madly in love with her and quickly abandoned his previous wife, whom he had married for money. In the first rapture of passion for Isabella he spent whole days in bed with her, totally neglecting his other duties.

They had five children and John had about twelve bastards as well. But he was not only lecherous and cruel but also spitefully jealous. Once, when he thought Isabella was having an affair, he had the man hanged and then suspended the corpse over her bed. The marriage lasted sixteen years and ended when John was poisoned. It must have been a great relief to Isabella.

Their little nine-year-old son, Henry, was heir to the throne. It was a dangerous time, so rather than wait for someone else to claim the kingdom Isabella acted promptly. She was in Gloucester at the time, quite a long way from London, so she quickly proclaimed little Henry king and immediately had him crowned in Gloucester Cathedral. There was no actual crown to hand, so she simply used one of her golden collars. Isabella was still only thirty, so she was delighted to go back to Angoulême and marry the lover she had been forced to jilt when John demanded her as his wife. It was a happy reunion, and she bore her new husband six sons and five daughters. Isabella's fecundity was remarkable.

Then came disaster. She was accused, probably wrongly, of conspiring to poison the King of France. She fled to Fontevrault Abbey, a place of sanctuary, and lived in hiding in a secret chamber there for the last two years of her life, dying aged about sixty. Years later, when her son King Henry III visited Fontevrault, he was upset to find that she had been buried in the open cemetery there, and ordered her remains to be moved inside the abbey to lie alongside the other royals. He must have remembered that hasty coronation she had given him as a boy. She has a noble effigy there.

# ELEANOR OF PROVENCE
## c. 1222–1291
### Queen of Henry III

Fourteen-year-old Eleanor arrived in England on a cold January day in 1236 to marry King Henry III in Canterbury Cathedral, and immediately after the wedding service the royal couple set off for London, where Eleanor was to be crowned in Westminster Abbey. Henry himself was aged twenty-nine, and had been king for twenty years. He had made at least five unsuccessful attempts to find a bride, so he must have been pleased to have found himself a wife at last.

A contemporary account tells us of the elaborate preparations for Eleanor's coronation: 'the city was adorned as never before with silk hangings and with banners, crowns, palls, tapers and lamps, and with certain marvellous ingenuities and devices; the streets were delivered from dirt, mud, sticks, and everything offensive'. Eleanor's arrival and coronation were marked with extravagant excess. Unfortunately, everything else she ever did was equally marked with wasteful ostentation. Thus she became one of the most unpopular queens who ever shared a monarch's throne. People attributed much of their increased taxation to her extravagance, and it was widely believed that her influence over King Henry was a result of witchcraft.

On one occasion, during a particularly violent demonstration, she was going under London Bridge in her barge, and the citizens above pelted her with rotten eggs, garbage and stones, shouting 'Down with the witch! Let's drown her!' She was rescued, and had to shelter in Old St Paul's until it was safe for her to come out. It was felt that she was far too foreign, gave jobs to her large retinue of followers from Provence, and generally refused to fit in with English ways.

Eleanor produced six sons and three daughters and survived her husband Henry by almost twenty years. She lived out the rest of her time in a nunnery in the little Wiltshire town of Amesbury, close to Stonehenge. It was the legendary resting-place of Queen Guinevere, and had many connections with other royal ladies.

Perhaps Eleanor had learned her lesson about extravagance, as the old chronicler tells us that: 'My Lady Eleanor, Mother Queen of England, now for Christ's sake despised the withering flower of this world, wherein she formerly delighted, and on the Feast of the Assumption was made a nun at Amesbury.' She died there, aged sixty-nine, and her heart was buried at the Greyfriars' Church in London.

# ELEANOR OF CASTILE

## c. 1244–1290

### First Queen of Edward I

Nowadays people remember this Eleanor as the queen for whom the beautiful 'Eleanor Crosses' were made, the most famous of which gives the name to 'Charing Cross' in London.

When Edward and Eleanor first met, she was a lively little ten-year-old Spanish girl, and he was a tall, long-legged teenager of fifteen – even his nickname was 'Longshanks'. Edward and his mother (another Eleanor – Eleanor of Provence) had been told by a fortune-teller that if they were to enjoy good fortune, they had to arrive at Burgos, in Castile, where Eleanor's father was king, precisely on 5 August 1254. Accordingly, they arrived spot on time, and the two youngsters were married.

It seems incredible to think of a little girl being taken in marriage to a strange far-off country and leaving her parents and friends behind. Eleanor must have felt frightened and lonely. However, when she got to England everyone was kind to her, and King Henry III, her new father-in-law, made sure that her room in Guildford Castle had glass put into its windows, and a special fire-place with a chimney was made for her.

Obviously, Eleanor had to be educated and grow up before she could be a proper wife for Edward, so he went off for a few years, indulging in his favourite pastimes, tournaments and war. Then began a marriage which was genuinely shared. They went off together on a crusade, during which Eleanor saved Edward's life and nursed him back to health. They had many adventures together, and she bore him a daughter while they were in Acre, one of sixteen children. Then, on the way back to England they learned that Henry III had died, so in effect they were now king and queen.

Edward's reign was filled with warfare for he was determined, if possible, to create a united kingdom. He fought fiercely and successfully in Wales, and made his young son (their fourteenth baby) Edward the first 'Prince of Wales' as a gesture of reconciliation. Eleanor had given birth to him in Caernarvon Castle.

Next he turned to Scotland, with rather less success, and wrote to ask Eleanor to come up north to join him. Alas, they never met again. She was taken ill on the way and died in the little Nottinghamshire village of Harby.

Edward was desolate. He rushed back south, but could do nothing except make arrangements for her funeral. She had to be taken back to Westminster in stages, and he ordered a beautiful memorial cross to be erected in each of the stopping-places. In all, there were twelve: at Lincoln, Grantham, Stamford, Geddington, Northampton, Stony Stratford, Woburn, Dunstable, St Albans, Waltham, Cheapside, and – best known of all, the final village just before Westminster itself – Charing. Of course, the village became known by the name of the memorial, Charing Cross. Today it is the name of a busy railway station. And in the forecourt, surrounded by parked cars and taxis, there is a tall monument – a memorial to Eleanor. It is a Victorian replacement of the one which originally stood at the top of Whitehall, on the site now occupied by a statue of Charles I on horseback.

Edward's love for his wife was marked by yet another romantic gesture. He ordered two wax candles to burn for ever by her tomb in Westminster Abbey. They burned for two and a half centuries, and were extinguished only at the time of the Reformation.

# MARGUERITE OF FRANCE

### c. 1282–1317

*Second Queen of Edward I*

Edward, much as he had loved Eleanor, needed a companion, so he took a second bride, Marguerite, a sixteen-year-old Princess of France. Edward himself was sixty by now; nevertheless, they had three children.

Marguerite was twenty-six when Edward died, and she lived for only another ten years, during which time she busied herself helping the poor and encouraging the arts. She spent much of her time and wealth helping to rebuild the church of the Greyfriars in London, where her mother-in-law's heart had been buried (Eleanor of Provence), and she herself was buried there in 1317. However, it was an ill-fated church; it was burnt down in the Great Fire of London, and its replacement, designed by Sir Christopher Wren, was destroyed in the Blitz.

# ISABELLA OF FRANCE

### c. 1292–1358

*Queen of Edward II*

The story of Isabella's life is filled with unspeakable cruelties. Indeed, her nickname was 'The She-Wolf of France'. Nevertheless, she suffered cruelty as much as she inflicted it.

Isabella's father was King Philip the Bold of France, and when she married Edward II her hopes must have been high. But when she realised that her new husband was openly and crazily in love with his gay partner, Piers Gaveston, she wrote home to her father in misery.

She put a brave face on things, and did in fact bear Edward two sons and two daughters. But after Gaveston was captured and beheaded by the barons who hated him, Edward took up two new partners, the Despensers, father and son. Isabella had probably had just about enough, and took to herself a lover, Roger Mortimer.

Aiming to revenge herself on Edward, Isabella recruited an army in France and after a struggle Edward was defeated. Hugh Despenser was hanged on a gibbet 50 feet high. First his genitals were cut off and then he had to watch his own bowels being burnt in front of him. Then he was beheaded and the four quarters of his body were sent as warnings to various parts of the country. Then Edward himself was murdered in Berkeley Castle.

Of course, Isabella's son Edward now became king. He was only fourteen, but obviously he'd had enough of all this royal sleaze. The first thing he did was to arrest her lover Mortimer and have him hanged. Then he put Isabella herself under house arrest in a fortress at Castle Rising, Norfolk. She stayed there for thirty-one years and went mad.

She too was buried in the church of the Greyfriars, as her two immediate predecessor queens had been. But Isabella had the posthumous satisfaction of lying beside her dead lover, Roger Mortimer, for he also had been laid to rest in Greyfriars, after his remains had been hanged in chains at Tyburn.

# PHILIPPA OF HAINAULT
## c. 1314–1369
### Queen of Edward III

Hainault, where Philippa came from, is in Flanders. The Hainault in London has no connection with this at all. Like many Dutch or Flemish women, Philippa was a hearty, buxom girl with lovely flaxen hair. No one ever spoke ill of her, and her influence was wholly good.

A story about her gives some indication of her character. When she entered England as a bride in 1328 there was a great tournament held in her honour. A badly made scaffold on which she and her ladies were sitting suddenly gave way and she fell alarmingly to the ground. Luckily, no one was hurt, but Edward III, her bridegroom, was absolutely furious and ordered the scaffolding contractor and his carpenter to be hanged.

Philippa fell to her knees and flatly refused to get up until he had changed his mind and pardoned them. And so, writes the historian Jean Froissart, who knew her well, 'the people learnt to love her as no Queen was ever loved before or since'. At the time of this incident Philippa was only fourteen. It must have taken courage and determination to risk upsetting her new husband like that.

As she grew into a mature woman, Philippa brought wealth to England by encouraging the wool trade with her native Flanders, and acted as a well-trusted regent when Edward was abroad.

Edward and Philippa had thirteen children, including the Black Prince, who was Prince of Wales and heir to the throne, John of Gaunt, who was Duke of Lancaster, and Edmund, who was Duke of York. Fortunately, she didn't live to learn of the death of her eldest son, the Black Prince, and could never have foreseen the power struggle between the descendants of her other sons, the Lancastrians and Yorkists, during the Wars of the Roses in the years ahead.

Philippa was only fifty-five when she died in Edward's arms. Visitors to Westminster Abbey will find her tomb near Edward the Confessor's shrine, with her splendid effigy in white marble.

# ANNE OF BOHEMIA
## 1366–1394
### First Queen of Richard II

The death of the Black Prince in 1376 was a terrible blow for the monarchy. He would have made a strong and splendid king. When he died, his son Richard was only ten years old, and was much too young to take up the full responsibilities of kingship after the death of his grandfather, Edward III in 1377. Thus began more than a century of squabbles for power.

Richard and Anne were both only fifteen when they married, and the young couple seem to have been very fond of each other, sharing artistic tastes. She had a mania for extravagant clothes and introduced the horned head-dress into England. This absurd-looking affair stood 2 feet high: two cardboard horns decorated with gold and silver lace and blazing with jewels. As for Richard, he introduced shoes with long pointed toes, at least 18 inches long. This was the age of Chaucer. Pictures of the time show the astonishing and fantastic fashions which were being worn, largely as a result of Anne and Richard. Anne also introduced the side-saddle for women. Again, it was a silly fashion, and footmen had to run alongside to help ladies keep their balance.

Anne was only twenty-eight when she died of the plague, childless, in her palace at Sheen, in present-day Richmond. She was given the most extraordinary funeral yet seen in the country. A vast sum was spent on wax candles and torches, specially imported from Flanders, and the roadways of Fleet Street, The Strand, and Charing Cross were flaming with light as the long procession passed along towards Westminster Abbey. All the peers and their wives were commanded to attend and to wear long-trained black cloaks and hoods. As for Sheen Palace, where Anne died, Richard simply couldn't bear to go there any more, and ordered it to be demolished.

# ISABELLA OF VALOIS
## 1389–1409
### Second Queen to Richard II

Isabella must have been a bewildered little girl when she was told she must marry the King of England. After all, she was not quite eight years old. But marry she must, so she had to leave her father, Charles the Foolish of France, and go and live in Windsor Castle as Queen of England. She probably had a vague understanding that her marriage was a part of a peace-making deal between England and France. Richard, her husband in name, visited her from time to time, and made a fuss of his little queen. But it must have been lonely, frustrating, and perhaps rather embarrassing for Isabella.

Then, all of a sudden, her position changed. Richard was no longer king, then he disappeared: she didn't know whether he was alive or dead. A new and strange king appeared out of nowhere, calling himself Henry IV. Isabella found herself being moved out of Windsor, having to settle into a place called Sunninghill.

Enemies of the new King Henry plotted to overthrow him and persuaded her to accompany an army of rebels, but it was no good. At Cirencester the plot fell apart, the ring-leaders were beheaded and Isabella was packed off back to London under lock and key.

It was then that the usurping King Henry had a brilliant idea: he would marry his son and heir, Prince Hal, to Isabella. It would be a perfect match! After all they were both the same age – just eleven years old. But by then Isabella had had enough of being told what to do. She put her foot down and utterly refused to have anything to do with Prince Hal. The very fact that a new marriage was being planned for her must mean that Richard was dead, so she went into mourning. And as far as she could, she ignored the new regime.

What on earth does a king do with a foreign child-widow who is also a dispossessed queen? Eventually, Henry simply let her go back to France, where she belonged. She married again, this time to a proper husband, Charles, Duke of Orleans, and died in childbirth aged twenty. Little did she know that in a few years' time the famous battle of Agincourt would take place, after which Prince Hal, now King Henry V, would marry her younger sister, Catherine, and would imprison her husband Charles in the Tower of London for a quarter of a century.

# MARY DE BOHUN
## c. 1369–1394
### First Wife of Henry IV

History books do not often mention Mary. After all, she died five years before Henry became king, so she never knew that royalty was in store for both him and her little son Henry, the future victor at Agincourt.

Her ancestor had come over from Normandy with the Conqueror and had been made Earl of Hereford for his help. So, overthrowing kings was in her blood too.

Mary bore Henry seven children in all, and was only twenty-five when she died, giving birth to their daughter Philippa in Leicester. She was buried with great ceremony in the church of St Mary de Castro in that city.

# JOAN OF NAVARRE
## c. 1370–1437
### Second Wife and Queen of Henry IV

Henry IV did not need to marry Joan. He had his heirs. Nevertheless, he felt it would be a good political move, so when Joan's husband, the Duke of Brittany, died, he invited her over to become his consort. Besides, it looks good in the public eye to have a queen to accompany you.

Joan, daughter of Charles the Bad, originally came from Navarre, so she is often referred to as Joan of Navarre; but sometimes, with reference to her previous husband, she is also known as Joan of Brittany.

Henry and Joan were married in Winchester Cathedral by Bishop William of Wykeham, who had founded Winchester College a few years before. Then, three weeks later, Joan was crowned in Westminster Abbey. On the whole, everything went well in this marriage, though there were no children. They enjoyed ten years together before Henry died rather suddenly at a relatively early age. She was to survive him by twenty-four years.

Apparently, she got on well with her step-son, who became Henry V, and for a while she was treated with love and respect. Then came the worst years in her life. The victorious Henry, basking in the glory of his military successes, suddenly had her arrested, stripped of everything she possessed, and forced into imprisonment. She was accused of being a witch!

For three years her life must have been a misery; she knew as well as anyone that the penalty for witchcraft was to be burnt alive. Evidence against her was flimsy, but she languished in prison until the last weeks of Henry V's life, and then his conscience must have pricked him, for he had her released at last.

The rest of Joan's life was spent in comfort. She lived to see her serious-minded grandson Henry VI reach his sixteenth year and then she died, mercifully unaware of all the troubles he would suffer during his unhappy reign. She is buried with her husband Henry IV in Canterbury Cathedral.

# CATHERINE OF VALOIS
## 1401–1437
### Queen of Henry V

For many, Catherine of Valois is known about only because of the memorable courtship scene in Shakespeare's play, *Henry V*.

After Agincourt, a part of the spoils of victory was the hand of the French princess in marriage. Henry and Catherine were married in Troyes just as soon as the final peace-treaty was signed. She was the daughter of Charles VI of France (Charles the Foolish) and was the much younger sister of Isabella, who had married Richard II some years before.

As her coronation in Westminster Abbey took place during Lent, the feasting after the ceremony had to be a fishy affair. Contemporary accounts give a fascinating description of the various dishes at the banquet: 'eeles in burneur [*beurre noir*, or burnt butter], pike with herbage, lamprie powdered, martine fried and leech lumbard flourished'. The second course was 'Gellie [jelly] coloured with columbine flowers, white potage or creame of almonds, breame of the sea, coonger, fresh salmon, halibut, gurnet, rochet boiled, smelts fried, creius [prawns] and lobster'.

Catherine seems to have been treated well and as a keen lover of music she had a dulcimer, lute and *harpette* (small harp) sent over from Paris, for which she paid £25.

Henry and Catherine were married for only just over two years before he died of dysentery, but in that time they had been happy to see the birth of a son and heir. Naturally, therefore, the little baby was recognised as Henry VI. Superstitiously, Henry V had forbidden Catherine to have her baby at Windsor: he thought it would bring bad luck. But that was just where the baby was born.

At the death of her husband, Catherine was still only twenty-one. However, she bravely took on the responsibility of bringing up the royal heir, and travelled many miles showing him off to the crowds and drumming up loyalty. But to be a widow at that age is not a happy situation. Within a few months Catherine took a lover, and in very great secrecy she married him. His name: Owen Tudor. At that time the name Tudor held no significance at all to anybody. Owen was just a common soldier who had been promoted to be one of Henry V's personal bodyguards. In fact, Catherine was marrying a servant.

Three children were born to Owen and Catherine before the secret was out. At first, all hell broke loose. Catherine was banished to a nunnery and Owen was clapped in Newgate gaol. Later, however, Henry VI pardoned them both, acknowledged their children and made one of them Earl of

Richmond. And it was his son, Henry, the 2nd Earl of Richmond, who became the first of the Tudor kings, Henry VII.

Catherine, banished to Bermondsey Abbey, became ill after the birth of her fifth child by Owen Tudor, and died there in 1437, aged thirty-five. It had been a strange life. She was buried in Westminster Abbey with a beautiful alabaster memorial, but this was destroyed on the orders of her grandson Henry VII, during extensions to the Abbey. Perhaps he did not want people to look at it and speculate too much on his rather dubious ancestry. At the same time, her coffin lid was accidentally raised, exposing her parched corpse. For generations it became a tourist attraction to see and touch Catherine's gruesome remains, and the famous diarist, Samuel Pepys, actually kissed her on his birthday in 1669. In his diary he wrote:

> On Shrove Tuesday, 1669, I to the Abbey went, and by favour did see the body of Queen Katherine of Valois, and had the upper part of the body in my hands, and I did kiss her mouth, reflecting upon it that I did kiss a Queen: and this my birthday and I thirty-six years old and I did kiss a Queen.

Catherine's remains were not properly laid to rest until Queen Victoria's reign.

# MARGARET OF ANJOU
## *c.* 1429–1482
### *Queen of Henry VI*

Like so many of our queens, Margaret was little more than a girl when she left her foreign home to take part in the turbulent affairs of England. She was only fifteen. Her father was René, Duke of Anjou, brother of the Queen of France, so Margaret's marriage to our King Henry VI was a part of yet another political package-deal as England and France struggled to make peace in the aftermath of Joan of Arc.

Henry and Margaret were married quietly in Tichfield Abbey, near Southampton, and then were given a royal welcome when they arrived in London. At first, everything looked promising. Henry was busy planning his new projects at Eton and Cambridge, and in the year following the marriage Henry was specially honoured by the Pope: he was given the papal Golden Rose in recognition of his services to religion and education.

However, little by little Margaret must have realised just how weak-willed and foolish her scholarly husband was. He pardoned his enemies, gave huge amounts to the poor, let people off their debts. And then he completely lost his wits for eighteen months. Margaret gave birth to their one and only son, Edward, during the time Henry was unconscious, so when the king recovered she had to introduce him to his own baby and tell him what name she had chosen for him.

The Wars of the Roses then began in earnest and Margaret realised that she had to take some sort of control, for Henry, even sane, was certainly no soldier. The following years were hectic: battles, defeats, victories, deaths and imprisonments. After two attempts at being king, Henry finally lost out to Edward IV and was quietly murdered in the Tower of London. As for Margaret, who had fought so bravely and organised resistance to the rebels, she had the misery of seeing her son killed in the final battle at Tewkesbury and she herself was held captive in the Tower. She had a reputation for cruelty and vindictiveness but, after all, she had only tried to do her duty.

Eventually, her aged father René paid out a vast ransom for her and she returned to France. A French writer who saw her at the time tells us that 'the once peerless Margaret had become a horror to look upon. Grief had turned the whole volume of her blood to water; her once superb eyes were swollen and red with weeping, and her skin covered with blotches like leprosy'. She died aged fifty-one and was buried in the tomb of her father and mother in Angers Cathedral.

# ELIZABETH WOODVILLE
## c. 1437–1492
### Queen of Edward IV

Elizabeth's life had more than its fair share of excitement and terror, but eventually fate was kind to her. She was the first Englishwoman and the first commoner to marry an English king since before the Norman Conquest. In fact, the situation was so extraordinary that Edward married her in extreme secrecy and it was only months afterwards that he had to confess what he had done.

According to tradition, the story began when Elizabeth, then the young and beautiful widow of Sir John Grey, decided to ask the king personally to intervene in restoring some land to her sons. She waited by a tree, later known as the Queen's Oak in the forest of Whittlebury, Northamptonshire, and when the king came by on his way to hunt deer, she stepped out and dared to accost him.

By all accounts she was ravishingly attractive with long blonde hair right down to her feet. Edward was captivated. They were married at the Manor House in the tiny village of Grafton in Northamptonshire (now called Grafton

Regis). When the secret came out they had to out a brave face on it, and Elizabeth quickly took to her new position. She produced ten healthy children.

Unfortunately, Edward's brother Richard disliked her intensely, thinking her an upstart, so as soon as Edward IV was dead he lost no time in putting the young uncrowned King Edward V in the Tower of London, declaring Elizabeth's marriage to Edward IV illegal and her children bastards. Elizabeth was frantic. She literally had nowhere to go, so she fled with all her children (except Edward, who was in the Tower) to seek sanctuary in a part of Westminster Abbey.

Anyone who has had to look after a crowd of young children in a cramped space will appreciate the difficult situation Elizabeth was in. She had no furniture, only primitive toilet and washing facilities, and relied on the embarrassed monks to feed her. And she was accompanied by Elizabeth, aged 17, Richard, aged 11, Anne, aged 8, Cicely, aged 6, Katherine, aged 4, and Bridget, aged 3. They sat on rushes. But worse was to follow. Elizabeth was now peremptorily ordered to send her other son, the eleven-year-old Prince Richard, to leave her and go to join his elder brother in the Tower of London.

These brothers are of course famed in history as the 'Princes in the Tower', murdered by their infamous uncle so that they wouldn't get in his way as he grabbed the throne to become Richard III.

The scene as Elizabeth said goodbye to her son Richard is described by Sir Thomas More, writing within living memory of the event:

> And therewithal she cried, 'Farewell, my sweete sonne. Let me kiss you ere you go – for God knows if we shall ever kiss again,' and so fell to kissing him and to weeping sore; and the child, poor innocent, wept as fast as herself.

They took him away and she never saw him again. Thomas More continues:

> She swooned and fell to the ground . . . and sobbed and filled the whole place with her pitiful sorrow. She beat her breast, and tore her fair hair, calling on her sweet babes by name. Then, kneeling down, she cried on God to avenge her.

These were Elizabeth's worst years. She had to move out and go to another part of Westminster, and for two years she was known as 'Dame Grey, lately calling herself Queen of England.' What humiliation!

Richard III's defeat at Bosworth came as a godsend to her. Her dignity was restored and one of the children who had been with her in that dreadful scene in Westminster Abbey, Elizabeth of York, became Henry VII's bride, thus reconciling the feuding families of York and Lancaster.

Elizabeth Woodville lived on to see three sturdy grandchildren born, including Arthur and the future Henry VIII. These little boys were aged six and three when she died; they probably reminded her at times of her own unlucky sons, Edward and Richard, lost in the Tower for ever.

## ANNE OF WARWICK
### 1456–1485
### *Queen of Richard III*

Like Elizabeth Woodville, Anne Neville was English. She was the daughter of the Earl of Warwick ('Warwick the Kingmaker'). In 1470, when she was fourteen, as part of her father's political scheming, she had been married to Henry VI's son, Edward, then aged seventeen, thus briefly becoming Princess of Wales. However, five months later she was widowed when Edward was killed (or murdered?) at the Battle of Tewkesbury.

She was still a useful political pawn, so, just a year later, aged fifteen, she was snapped up by Richard – then Duke of Gloucester – who was soon to manoeuvre himself into being king on the death of his brother, Edward IV.

Richard and Anne were crowned in Westminster Abbey in July 1483, walking barefoot from Westminster Hall to the abbey, where they both stripped naked to the waist in order to be anointed with holy oil. It must have been an embarrassing moment for Anne, but then she was used to doing her duty.

Richard was determined to seal the process of acquiring royalty, and gave Anne and himself a second coronation, in York, just to make it doubly sure. But the reign was shortlived. And Anne's part in it was even shorter. Both her son and she herself died just before the Battle of Bosworth, and thus the long line of Plantagenets came to an end.

## ELIZABETH OF YORK
### 1466–1503
### *Queen of Henry VII*

Elizabeth was nineteen and Henry twenty-nine when they married. Despite the fact that it was a calculated move on Henry's part to put an end to the

Wars of the Roses, the marriage was a happy one, fruitful and loving. No one ever accused either of them of being unfaithful.

After a wretched and terrifying childhood (Elizabeth was one of Edward IV's children, terrorised by the usurper Richard III), Elizabeth's years as wife and queen were relatively tranquil. Four children survived: Arthur, Margaret, Henry, Mary. And Elizabeth and Henry planned great futures for them all.

Arthur, Prince of Wales and heir to the throne, had to be found a wife of undoubted regal birth and political value. Catherine, Princess of Aragon, seemed the perfect choice, so it was with great pride and hope for the future that Elizabeth and Henry welcomed the fifteen-year-old Spanish princess for her marriage to their son. He was just the same age as his bride.

The wedding, in Old St Paul's, was one of the most magnificent ever seen. Catherine herself gave a lively demonstration of Spanish dancing, with 'snapping bones after the manner of her country' – castanets had arrived. But alas, the marriage was to last just five months. Arthur died, probably of the plague, and Elizabeth was so grieved that it totally undermined her health. She lived for less than a year, and died shortly after giving birth to an eighth child. Henry gave her a superb funeral, and her tomb in Westminster Abbey is one of the finest in the land. But her universal memorial is in virtually every household, although few people are aware of it. It is her portrait which we see as the Queen on every pack of cards.

# CATHERINE OF ARAGON
## 1485–1536
### First Queen of Henry VIII

The happy Spanish princess who astonished the English court at her wedding, with her fantastically shaped dresses, her castanets and her stately dancing, was destined, as queen, to die lonely, banished, and wounded with insult.

She had originally been brought to England to become the wife of Prince Arthur, the elder son of Henry VII. At the time of this wedding both she and Arthur were just fifteen. When Arthur died, just four months later, she wrote home to her father to say that she didn't want to marry again in England. However, Henry VII was determined not to lose her: she was far too valuable a political pawn. He decided that she would make just the right wife for Arthur's younger brother, Henry. At the time of Arthur's death the future Henry VIII was only ten years old, so this meant keeping Catherine waiting around in England for him to grow up a bit. Ironically in view of later events, the Pope was persuaded to grant a special dispensation to allow her to marry her husband's younger brother. Twenty-one years later, no amount of persuasion could make the Pope give another special dispensation to allow Henry to divorce her.

Henry VII died in April 1509. By then, his heir, now Henry VIII, was coming up to his eighteenth birthday and Catherine was twenty-three. Obviously, it was just the right moment to get married. The wedding took place quietly at Greenwich. Then, just a fortnight later, there was magnificent pageantry and rejoicing as the young newly-weds were both crowned in Westminster Abbey on a lovely day in June.

In the early years their marriage was a joy. Both were young, artistic, and kept a brilliant court. London became a cultural centre as never before. Henry was constantly surprising her with ingenious masques and unusual entertainments. Even the birth of a girl was a cause for merriment and rejoicing. 'There will be other children,' he said. But the miscarriages and deaths went on and on. Henry persuaded himself that the marriage was cursed, and his neglect worsened into abuse.

Catherine's dignity and courage, steadfastness and adamantine refusal to bend to Henry's will in the matter of divorce will always earn her as much admiration as pity. Her daughter Mary inherited much of this steely strength. Catherine died aged fifty of cancer, and was buried well away from London, in Peterborough Cathedral. At the news of her death, the Spanish Ambassador wrote back to Spain saying that 'Henry went mad with delight, dressed himself from head to foot in yellow damask, and stuck a white feather in his yellow velvet cap'.

# ANNE BOLEYN

### c. 1500–1536

### *Second Queen of Henry VIII*

It was widely believed that Anne was a witch. She had so much influence over the king that only sorcery would explain it. Even Henry himself believed this. There were even physical oddities about her, which seemed to suggest that there was something unnatural about her: she had a large mole on her neck, and six fingers on her left hand. . . .

By playing hard to get, Anne inflamed Henry to a furious lust. Her sister Mary had already been one of his mistresses, but Anne was firm: it was to be marriage and queenship for her, or else nothing. She had been one of Catherine of Aragon's ladies-in-waiting, so she knew her way about court pretty well. The marriage was in secret and Elizabeth was born eight months later.

Of course Anne simply had to get pregnant again, but this time she suffered a miscarriage and the king was getting impatient. Her enemies – and there were plenty of them – got together and hatched a plot. Everyone knew how hot-tempered and jealous Henry could be, so a few accusations of adultery would do the trick. Preposterously, Anne was accused of having sex with five other men, including her own brother. She knew she was trapped, and the rest of her short life had the inevitability of a Greek tragedy.

Her brother and three more of the accused men were all beheaded on Tower Hill. The fifth, a court musician, was taken away to be tortured. He was told that he would be spared if only he would declare the queen to be guilty. Poor man, in his agony he said just what they wanted, and was promptly hanged and quartered for his pains.

The spot on Tower Green where Anne was beheaded is gazed upon by thousands of visitors today. An exceptionally skilful executioner was brought over from France especially to do the job, and he managed to sever her head with a single blow. Nobody had remembered to order a coffin, so she was pushed into an old arrow-chest, rather too small for her, and her remains were taken into the chapel vault.

A legend grew up that Anne's body was secretly taken for reburial in Sale Church in Norfolk, near Blickling Hall, where her ancestors are laid to rest. However, when Queen Victoria had the Tower vault thoroughly tidied up during her reign, all the Tudor victims were found to be still in their original places, though rather mixed up with dust and bits of broken coffins. Victoria had all the various bones sorted out and put in nice neat urns.

# JANE SEYMOUR

## c. 1507–1537

### Third Queen of Henry VIII

Henry again went wild with glee at the death of Anne Boleyn. Tradition tells how he waited under a tree in Richmond Park for a gun-signal to tell him that the execution of Anne had taken place, and then he galloped off as fast as he could to Wolfe Hall in Wiltshire, home of the Seymours, to celebrate his betrothal to his third wife, Jane. The Spanish Ambassador described Jane as 'no great beauty, of middle stature: so fair one might almost call her pale.'

Henry and Jane were married at York Place, in the Queen's Closet. She had been a lady-in-waiting to Anne Boleyn, just as Anne had served Catherine of Aragon, so she was used to the ways of court.

Jane was aged about thirty when she gave birth to Edward. It was a difficult birth, but it was her moment of triumph. She had given the king what he had always wanted: a son and heir. The celebrations went on and on. Edward was born on a Friday and christened on the Monday. As soon as the christening was over in the Chapel Royal, Hampton Court, all the company of guests trooped into Queen Jane's bedroom, where she was propped up in bed. The excitement and fatigue must have been simply too much for her. Within days she was dead of puerperal fever.

Of all Henry's wives, it is Jane who is buried next to him in St George's Chapel, Windsor.

# ANNE OF CLEVES
## 1515–1557
### Fourth Queen of Henry VIII

Henry had been married once as a duty and twice for love. Now it was time for duty again, and his chief adviser, Thomas Cromwell, decided that it would be useful to forge a link with Protestant Europe. Holbein produced a portrait of the proposed bride, the king granted his approval, arrangements were made for a coronation, and so without further ado Anne set sail for England.

To say that Henry was disappointed on her arrival would be a gross understatement. He was livid. He roared his displeasure at Cromwell, saying he would not be husband to that 'Dutch cow'. Another memorable insult he hurled at him was that she was nothing but a 'great Flanders mare'. Cromwell trembled for his life, and was duly executed a few months later.

Nevertheless, despite all the fuss, Henry and Anne did come to an astonishingly amicable arrangement. They both realised that they had made a mistake, so Anne settled for becoming Henry's official 'sister'. They divorced, but remained on good terms with each other. Anne was given a comfortable income and was honoured at court. She wrote home: 'The King's highness whom I cannot have as a husband is nevertheless a most kind, loving and friendly father and brother.'

Anne lived on into the reign of Queen ('Bloody') Mary and was buried in state in Westminster Abbey.

# CATHERINE HOWARD

*c. 1522–1542*

*Fifth Queen of Henry VIII*

Catherine was eighteen when she married Henry: he was forty-nine. Someone remarked at the time that 'he caresses her more than he did the others'. Once more, Henry had married for love; or perhaps it was lust. At any rate the physical attraction was intense, while it lasted.

By all accounts Catherine's upbringing was astonishingly lax. She had virtually no education. Her father, Lord Edward Howard, a distinguished soldier, had lost his wife and had to farm out his numerous offspring. His old stepmother Agnes, Duchess of Norfolk, volunteered to take Catherine off his hands. 'Old Agnes', as she was called, lived in a large house in Lambeth, but although she had some ten or twelve young ladies as personal companions, the circumstances were somewhat poverty-stricken and slack.

Catherine and the twelve other young ladies all slept together in one large room containing two enormous beds. Catherine would steal out of the room when the old lady was asleep and lock her in, and then the youngsters ran riot, bringing young men in, dancing, revelling, having midnight feasts. There was Henry Mannox, a music-teacher, Francis Dereham, who could play the mandoline, and Thomas Culpepper, a cousin, who used to show them how to dance.

One night the old Duchess was woken up by the noise and suddenly appeared out of nowhere. She beat Catherine, cuffed the maids, and ordered the gentlemen off the premises. Francis Dereham, perhaps the chief offender, fled to Ireland, leaving behind a box containing some revealing letters.

All this sounds extremely trivial, and perhaps it was, but the whole scene was made part of the terrible indictment which led to Catherine's trial and execution. No one will ever know just how guilty Catherine was, but she was silly enough to have brought all three of those young gentleman friends with her into Henry's court. Francis Dereham even became her secretary.

Henry seems to have gone quite mad with rage and jealousy when he heard about Catherine's involvement with these men. Catherine was not even allowed to speak in her own defence. The end came with terrifying suddenness. Even before Catherine reached the Tower the severed heads of Culpepper and Dereham had been stuck on spikes over the central arch of London Bridge. As for Catherine, she spent the last night of her life practising exactly how to lay her head on the block. It was the same block of wood which had been used six years before, by Anne Boleyn.

It had been an eighteen-month marriage. Catherine was just twenty when her pathetic remains were laid in the vault of the Chapel Royal, St Peter ad Vincula, just yards from where she was beheaded.

# CATHERINE PARR
## 1512–1548
### *Sixth Queen of Henry VIII*

Catherine had already been twice married before she became Henry's sixth wife. Both her previous husbands had died young and Catherine herself, or Lady Latimer as she should properly be called, was still only thirty-one, young enough to provide a few more longed-for heirs. She seems to have been a kind, gentle, sensible person. Everyone spoke well of her. She was well educated and had firm opinions. She made it clear that she was not particularly anxious to marry Henry and told him frankly it would be better to be his mistress than his wife. She knew it was dangerous.

As everyone knows, Catherine did manage to survive, but it was a very narrow escape. She too was almost sent to the Tower, partly for being too argumentative over religious matters, and partly because she was not producing the babies Henry still hoped for. By this time he had become impossibly short-tempered, living in constant agony with his ulcerous leg. In fact, it was largely Catherine's skill as a nurse that saved her life.

It must have been a tremendous relief for Catherine when Henry finally died. Ageing dictators are fearsomely unpredictable. Still uncrowned, she resumed the life she had wanted to live. Before Henry had demanded her, Catherine had been just about to marry Thomas Seymour, brother of Jane Seymour. It was a love match, and she deserved to be happy. So, within a month of Henry's death, Catherine and Thomas Seymour were married, though so secretly that we do not know the exact date.

At first all went well, and Catherine became a kind of stepmother to the royal children, Princess Elizabeth and Lady Jane Grey, who was descended from Elizabeth Woodville. But then an incident took place which upset her profoundly for the rest of her life. Princess Elizabeth, the future queen, was growing up fast, and was a lively, sparkling teenager, aged fourteen. Thomas Seymour was no saint, and loved to romp with her, and one day Catherine came across them both in an exceedingly embarrassing embrace.

The princess was sent in disgrace to Hatfield House and Catherine, heavily pregnant for the first time in her life, withdrew to Sudeley Castle in Gloucestershire. She was totally devastated by what she had witnessed, and at times literally lost the will to live. Very soon after giving birth, she died of puerperal fever, as Jane Seymour had done. There were, of course, sinister but unprovable rumours that Thomas Seymour had poisoned her.

# LORD GUILFORD DUDLEY
## 1536–1554
### Consort of Lady Jane Grey

No, he never was king, but he wanted to be, hoped to be, and might well have been king.

The whole point of the Duke of Northumberland's plot to put Lady Jane Grey on the throne was to make his own son, Guilford Dudley, King of England. To that end he arranged for Lady Jane and Guilford to be married. At first, Jane refused point blank: after all, she was already betrothed to Lord Hertford. However, she was literally and physically beaten into submission by her parents.

They were married just six weeks before Edward VI died. Jane was fifteen and Dudley sixteen. It is clear that Jane had no idea about the plans which were being made for her; she didn't even know that Edward was dying. But Dudley knew the position clearly enough.

The moment Edward died, Jane was told that she was to be queen. It took some considerable persuasion to convince her that this was so, and then, while she was reluctantly trying on the crown, the Marquis of Winchester happened to remark: 'Another shall be made to crown your husband withal.' Instantly Jane saw the whole situation for what it was. Young though she was, she realised with perfect clarity that she had been duped. She told Guilford that to make him king would be quite unconstitutional and needed the authority of Parliament. As for herself, she would be prepared to make him a duke, but certainly not king. Guilford burst into tears. 'I will not be a duke, I will be King,' he blubbered, and rushed out of the room to find his mother.

But events overtook both Queen Jane and her would-be King Guilford. When Mary took her rightful place on the throne she did not wish either of them any harm. Nevertheless, they posed a threat, a Protestant threat, and while they lived, perhaps they would become a rallying-point.

Consequently, Jane and Guilford were both imprisoned in the Tower of London. After six months, Guilford Dudley was beheaded. His still bleeding corpse was trundled past Jane's window in a hand-cart. Minutes later, she too was executed, having 'reigned', uncrowned, for nine days.

# PHILIP OF SPAIN
## 1527–1598
### *King Consort of Mary I*

Philip *was* a king. By the time he died he was King of Spain, Portugal, Sicily, Sardinia, Naples, Milan, the Netherlands; Guinea, Angola and Mozambique in Africa; Ceylon (present-day Sri Lanka), Goa, Malacca, Macao and the Philippines (named after himself) in Asia; the Azores, Canaries and Cape Verde Islands, the West Indies, Florida, and all the Central and South American countries in the New World. What's more, when he married 'Bloody' Mary he was actually declared to be King of England.

Queen Mary was infatuated with Philip. True, she had been engaged for years to Philip's father, the Emperor Charles V, but that was years before, when she was a child. For her, it did not matter that there was an eleven-year age gap between them. The wedding in Winchester Cathedral was an occasion of supreme pomp and ceremony. The venue had been chosen carefully. London might well have been dangerous, because the people were wary of Catholic Spain. Moreover, the Archbishop of Canterbury was not available: he was in prison. And in any case Winchester was nearer to Spain.

At the ceremony Philip was dressed exquisitely in white satin worked with silver, a gold collar studded with diamonds, and round his knee was the Garter, for he had been invested in the Order as soon as he had arrived in England. He was still only a prince when he entered the cathedral, but before the ceremony started a herald announced to all those assembled that the Emperor Charles had just created Philip King of Naples. Thus a king would be marrying a queen, and there would be no discrepancy in rank.

Philip spent the next months trying to ingratiate himself with the people. He had brought with him a gift of thirty-four chests of gold, each a yard long, which he paraded ostentatiously through the streets of London. But, apart from Mary, no one was really deceived. Philip literally had no time for England or his wife. Even during his brief stay in England he had begun to flirt with her ladies-in-waiting. One of them, the young and beautiful Lady Dacre, thwacked him soundly with a stick to beat him off. He stayed in England for just fourteen months. He did return later, just for a few weeks, but then he stayed away for good.

Even before he had come to England Philip had been married before, to the Infanta Mary of Portugal, but she had died after three years, giving birth to their son, Don Carlos. Then, when Mary Tudor died, he married Isabella of France. And when she died, he married a fourth wife, Anna, daughter of the Emperor Maximilian II, and had another son by her.

He spent much of his final years completing his enormous palace, the Escorial, just outside Madrid, and sent his heavy fleet of ships, the Armada, to try to invade England. His defeat was total. All in all, he did not enjoy a happy relationship with England.

# ANNE OF DENMARK
## 1574–1619
### Queen of James I

Like so many queens, Anne was a foreign princess who had to leave her home as a teenager, and hardly ever saw her own land or family again. Three times the ship carrying her to Scotland was swept back to sea, and almost sank. Witchcraft was thought to be the cause, and one woman suspected of all the mischief was convicted and burnt. James was so impatient to have Anne that he braved the sea himself, set sail for Norway, where she was stranded, and they were married in the unlikeliest place – the hall of the old bishop's palace in Oslo.

When eventually James and Anne got back to Scotland James was so hard up that he could hardly afford a coronation service. He had to write to the Earl of Mar, begging him to lend him a pair of silk stockings. And he had to borrow spoons from Anne's courtiers for the coronation feast afterwards. It had been a bleak and poor court in Edinburgh, so it must have been a welcome change of lifestyle for them when they were invited south to become the King and Queen of England. The coronation itself, however, was a very quiet affair, because London was suffering from the plague.

It was the London of Ben Jonson and Inigo Jones – innovators in staging glittering new forms of courtly entertainment. Anne thoroughly enjoyed these elaborate masques, dressing up and taking part in them herself. They were curious mixtures of dance, music, pageant and highly artificial poetry, with names like 'Pan's Anniversary', 'The Temple of Love', and 'Albion's Triumph'. Today we would find them boring and rather silly – but at least they did represent a new and cultured kind of court.

Anne had her unhappiness though. As for most women in those days, several of her children died, but the death of Henry, heir to the throne, hit her with particular grief. He was a fine lad, aged eighteen, and died probably of typhoid fever contracted after swimming late one night in the Thames. His death paved the way for his younger brother, who was to become Charles I.

Anne's later years were clouded by her husband's crude ways. He never washed his hands; he loved to get drunk; he loved his homosexual friend 'Steenie' to the point of obsession. Anne's health declined and she died aged forty-five. She insisted on dying in a Danish bed she had imported from her native land: it must have reminded her of happier days. Poor as always, James simply couldn't afford the sort of funeral he felt he ought to give her, so her body lay unburied at Somerset House from March until May. Then she was taken to Westminster Abbey for burial, but he gave her no memorial.

# HENRIETTA MARIA
## 1609–1670
### Queen of Charles I

Henrietta Maria, the daughter of the King of France, was lively, haughty, petulant, self-willed, graceful, beautiful – and fiercely Catholic. She was aged fifteen when she arrived in England, having already been married by proxy to Charles I in Notre Dame in Paris. It is really quite extraordinary how so many kings and queens have married each other as complete strangers.

Henrietta was having breakfast, having just landed in England from Calais, when Charles arrived from London to meet her. She had prepared a few English phrases to greet him, but forgot the words and broke down in tears. Charles, always the perfect gentleman, took her in his arms and comforted her. They inspected each other and stood back to back to see how much taller he was – she reached to his shoulders. Then Charles suggested she might have high heels and inspected her feet – and by this time she had quite recovered herself and burst out into giggles. They rode on to Canterbury for a second marriage, and then off they went to London.

Charles, although king, had not yet been crowned, so preparations were fully in hand for the traditional coronation ceremony in Westminster Abbey. Then it was that Charles realised that the giggly little girl he had married possessed a fiery temper and a stubbornness which even he could not shift. She knew that the coronation would be a Protestant affair, and so, as a Catholic, she absolutely refused to take part in it. She not only refused to be crowned, but also refused even to be present. There were violent rows. She would even smash window panes with her bare fists, saying that she would rather die than have the crown placed upon her head by a heretic.

Charles was appalled, but there was nothing he could do about it. As for the courtiers and people of England, they too were shocked. They remembered all too clearly that it was only a short time ago that people were burning one another for having different religious beliefs. It was a bad beginning, and the relationship between them was cool for a number of years. It was not until Charles's favourite, the Duke of Buckingham, was assassinated that they drew closer together. Children came, Charles, James, and as many as seven others, but some died young.

The trouble with Henrietta was that she was continually giving Charles unwanted advice, and much of it was bad advice, too. She hated Parliament, and simply did not understand it. She encouraged Charles to ignore it and rule as a king should, by himself. She little thought just how disastrous such a course of action could be. . . .

Henrietta did not witness her husband's execution. She had already fled to France, and when Cardinal de Retz visited her to tell her of Charles's death he found her in bed, trying to keep warm. She had no fuel, no food, no money. In vain, she asked Cromwell for an allowance. He sent word back that as she hadn't been crowned, she wasn't properly a queen, and so had no claim on the public purse. Perhaps, after all, it served her right!

She lived to see her son Charles restored to the throne, and she lived again briefly in London. But she was above all a princess of France, and when she died she was buried among her ancestors at St Denis, just outside Paris.

# PROTECTRESS ELIZABETH CROMWELL
## DATES UNKNOWN
### Wife of the Protector, Oliver Cromwell

Oliver Cromwell, at the height of his powers, was king in all but name. True he had refused to wear the crown, but he did sit on a throne, rode in the royal coach, wore purple velvet edged and lined with ermine, and was addressed as 'Highness'.

Elizabeth, his wife, had to accustom herself to a station in life that she could not have imagined in her wildest dreams when she married Oliver in 1620. However, she was a practical housewife, and she knew that her job was to entertain ambassadors, attend state functions, support the new régime. And she too, like all of Cromwell's family, was a 'Highness'. She had the title 'Protectress'.

Tittle-tattle must have abounded. It was something of an embarrassment to be elevated so high, so quickly. She must have been acutely aware of the wagging tongues that invariably referred to her as 'Old Joan'. Accordingly she had a number of secret staircases and trap-doors made at Whitehall and Hampton Court, so that she could glide about these palaces unnoticed and pounce upon her servants 'and keep them vigilant in their places and honest in the discharge thereof'.

She busied herself keeping house. Oliver busied himself keeping the country. There was no frivolity, no masques or balls, no mistresses. Practical and hardworking, Elizabeth kept cows in St James's Park, and organised dairy-maids making butter; she had teams of 'godly maidens' sewing clothes and palace furnishings; and she kept a long list of useful dishes which would come in handy when preparing for specially important visitors.

Her father, Sir James Bouchier, had been a wealthy London merchant, so she was quite used to living comfortably. All in all, life was kind to her.

## MRS DOROTHEA CROMWELL
### DATES UNKNOWN
*Wife of Richard Cromwell*

History books never even mention Dorothea. Why should they? She made no mark on history. However, history made a heavy mark on her. Richard, her husband, struggled to hold the country together after the death of his father. Dorothea was present in Westminster Hall when he was given a magnificent installation as Lord Protector II, and for a while at least she must have been given the title of Protectress.

But Richard's position was impossibly difficult, and after just three months he resigned. Parliament still owed his father a huge sum of money, but poor Richard was forced to flee to the continent to avoid being arrested for debt. All the unpopularity of the Cromwellian revolution fell on his head.

Dorothea waited fifteen years for his return, but died without ever seeing him again. She is buried with their eight children in Hursley parish church, near Winchester.

# CATHERINE OF BRAGANZA
## 1638–1705
### *Queen of Charles II*

Mistresses, mistresses: everyone knows about Charles and his mistresses. But if you ask most people who his wife was, very few will even remember her name. It was Catherine, a 23-year-old princess of Portugal. Of course, it was a political move. It helped to line up Portugal and France against Spain. The Spanish were bad-tempered about the match, as they had hoped one of their own princesses would be chosen. Someone overheard the Spanish Ambassador say that he hoped the marriage would be barren. It was.

Poor Catherine had to put up with all her husband's concubines and bastards. Charles made it plain that he did not intend to forsake any of his friends or pleasures so Catherine simply had to swallow her pride, however difficult it must have been for her.

Not speaking English, surrounded by Portuguese monks, suffering ill health, submitting to humiliations heaped on her by her husband, Catherine is probably one of the least-known English queens. She was pretty, and she adored her husband when they were married. But no one could call her time in England happy.

As Charles lay dying Catherine came to his bedside to say goodbye to him. She was so overcome with emotion that she had to be carried away fainting. She sent word to Charles to beg his forgiveness. 'Alas poor woman!' replied the king. 'She ask my pardon? I beg hers with all my heart: take her back that answer.'

After his death, Catherine lived for a few years in Somerset House, and then decided she would be much happier back in Portugal. She is buried in Santa Maria de Belém, in Lisbon.

# ANNE HYDE
## 1637–1671
### *First Wife of James II*

According to widespread belief, Anne Hyde's mother was a 'tub-woman' – that is, a woman employed to carry out beer from a brewhouse. The story goes that she was a good-looking girl and the brewer took a fancy to her and married her. He died soon after, leaving her a large fortune. The lucky young widow went to one Mr Hyde, an up-and-coming lawyer, to ask how to manage her affairs, and he promptly married her himself. Mr Hyde rose high in his profession; so high, in fact, that he became Lord Chancellor and Earl of Clarendon. And from this marriage came a daughter, Anne.

It was just at the time of the Restoration that the future James II, brother of Charles, managed to make Anne pregnant. These were days when princes did not marry commoners, and although both Anne's father and James's mother, Henrietta Maria, were shocked at the thought of a marriage between them, Charles told his brother that he had to go through with it.

The marriage was successful, though James was frequently unfaithful. Among their eight children were two girls, both of whom were destined to become queens in their own right: Mary II, wife of William III; and Queen Anne.

Anne Hyde never lived to see her husband crowned, so was never really a queen herself. She died in 1671, aged thirty-four, very painfully, of cancer.

# MARY OF MODENA
## 1658–1718
### *Second Wife and Queen of James II*

James was still the Duke of York when he married Mary of Modena, daughter of an Italian duke. His first wife, Anne, had died two years before, and he considered the attractions of several possible candidates to become his second wife. The short-list was whittled down to two: fifteen-year-old Mary of Modena, and her Aunt Leonora, who was fifteen years older. The fact that they both wanted to become nuns seemed irrelevant, so James empowered a representative, Lord Peterborough, to go to Modena and marry one or other of them, by proxy. The bride's name was left blank on the documents he took with him.

Lord Peterborough chose Mary, and she was duly brought back to London, facing a hostile mob who hated the thought of another Catholic princess. Rumour had it that she was the Pope's eldest daughter. It was an odd situation. She was fifteen; her husband was forty; she had two step-daughters to help look after, as well as her father-in-law's mistresses and Portuguese wife, who demanded tactful handling. She was also well aware that her religion automatically made her unpopular.

James II and Mary had a splendid coronation. James decided not to have a grand procession, but to spend all the money instead on Mary's robes and jewels. It cost him £100,000. All sorts of sinister omens are reported to have occurred during the coronation, including the toppling of the crown from off James's head, and the blowing down of the Royal Standard from the White Tower.

The fact is, people were getting jittery about the possibility of a Catholic heir being born. Both Mary and James were Catholic, and James was doing his utmost to spread Catholic practices into England as much as possible. And it was then that the people's worst fears were realised: Mary gave birth to a son. Rumour spread that the queen hadn't really been pregnant at all, and that she had smuggled this baby boy into the palace in a warming-pan, just so that he could grow up and become a Catholic king.

Revolution burst around her. By this time Mary, one of James's daughters by his first wife, had married a fiercely ambitious Protestant prince, William of Orange, who now pressed his claim, landing at Torbay in Devon, having been invited by James's Protestant enemies to take the throne.

Leaving before her husband, Mary fled to the continent with her little baby (later known to historians as the 'Old Pretender'). James joined her in France, and they all lived in exile unhappily ever after.

# PRINCE GEORGE OF DENMARK
## 1653–1708
### *Consort to Queen Anne*

George of Denmark was loyal, faithful to his wife, possessed of a huge appetite, was unutterably dull and stupid, and drank like a fish. 'I have tried him drunk,' said Charles II to Lord Dartford, 'and I have tried him sober – but oddsfish! There is nothing in him.'

The trouble with George was that there was literally nothing for him to do. Granted, he performed his matrimonial duties with meticulous regularity, and made his wife Queen Anne pregnant each year from 1683 to 1700. But apart from making model boats and beating his little boy when the child felt giddy, there is nothing much worth recording about him.

He wasn't much good at conversation either. His usual remark, on hearing any news, good or bad, was 'Est-il possible?' And eventually 'Est-il-possible' became his nickname.

Poor old Est-il-possible suffered from asthma. A malicious courtier suggested that he was forced to breathe hard lest people should think he was dead, and bury him by mistake. He died six years before Anne and was buried in Westminster Abbey.

# SOPHIA DOROTHEA OF ZELLE
## 1666–1726
### *Divorced Wife of George I*

Princess Sophia Dorothea never came to England. She was locked up in prison. Her story is a tragic one. She was only fifteen when she was forced to marry her 22-year-old cousin George, and she hated him from the moment they met. The dislike was mutual; nevertheless, they did have two children, a boy and a girl, and the boy became our George II.

In the circumstances it was inevitable she should take a lover, and she fell desperately in love with a Swedish count, Philip Königsmarck. The secret affair lasted for five or six years. The couple planned to elope to France, and all would have been well for them except for the fact that Philip also loved someone else – a Countess Platen. The countess discovered their plans to elope and in a fit of jealousy she planned to have Philip murdered in a corridor leading to the princess's apartments.

No sooner had the assassin done his job than old Countess Platen rushed out of her hiding-place, from where she had witnessed the murder, and planted her high-heeled shoe on the dying Philip's mouth. She exposed the plot and of course Sophia Dorothea was in total disgrace. Aged twenty-eight she was sent to prison in the castle of Ahlden, and remained there for the next thirty-two years. She was, however, allowed an 8-mile walk every afternoon, always on the same road. She was sixty when she died, just a year before George. She was never Queen of England, but was allowed to call herself Duchess of Ahlden.

# CAROLINE OF ANSBACH
## 1683–1737
### *Queen of George II*

Caroline of Ansbach was thoroughly inspected by her prospective father-in-law, the future George I, before she was considered suitable for marriage. 'As soon as I entered the room he took a wax light and examined me from head to foot,' she wrote. We can assume that she passed the test, for George allowed his son to marry her. The year was 1705 and they were both aged twenty-two. At that time none of them had any idea that the monarchy of Great Britain would be theirs.

It was to be another twenty-two years before they were to be crowned king and queen in Westminster Abbey, and then Caroline proved a strong character, helping George positively in his royal duties: perhaps even too much so, for a popular rhyme was chanted behind his back:

> You may strut, dapper George, but 'twill all be in vain,
> We know 'tis Queen Caroline, not you, that reign.

In fact, Caroline was a good queen, encouraging all the arts, including the newest one in her time – gardening. She was extremely keen on horticulture and landscaping. We are indebted to her not only for work on the gardens at Kew but also the completion of Kensington Gardens. She had waters diverted so that the Serpentine could be made. Her royal gardener was Charles Bridgman, who invented the ha-ha (a kind of sunken fence) and who paved the way for Capability Brown. Queen's Walk, on the eastern side of Green Park, is named after her, as she had it laid out with a little pavilion for her use.

Her later days were marked by open hostility between herself and her son Frederick, Prince of Wales, and his wife. 'I wish the ground would open this minute and sink the monster into the lowest hole in hell,' she remarked. But then, she openly called her future son-in-law a 'bed-bug' and a 'dirty little animal'. She had firm opinions.

Despite his many mistresses, George II loved and respected her. As she lay dying she begged him to marry again after her death, but the old king told her he couldn't possibly think of it – he'd simply have mistresses instead.

## CHARLOTTE SOPHIA OF MECKLENBURG-STRELITZ
### 1744–1818
*Queen of George III*

George III was a shy young man of twenty-two, blushing easily, when he came to the throne. The monarchy had to skip a generation when his father, Frederick, Prince of Wales, died aged forty-four as a result of a cricket ball accident. At first young George was very much under the influence of his ministers and his mother Augusta, the Dowager Princess of Wales. Augusta must have felt somewhat cheated of the chance to become queen, so she was determined to maintain her influence for as long as she could.

A king's first duty is to marry, so Augusta scoured the courts of Europe for a suitable bride. The tiny Duchy of Mecklenburg-Strelitz seemed to have just the right girl: picked from relative obscurity, such a bride would never dare interfere with affairs of state; and being just seventeen years old, there would be plenty of time for babies to arrive.

Young as he was, George had already had two affairs: in fact he had actually gone through some sort of secret marriage service with the first girl he had fallen in love with – a beautiful Quakeress called Hannah Lightfoot. Indeed, there were rumours of a son, who had been bundled out of the country to South Africa. And then there was Sarah Lennox, a ravishingly lovely young lady-in-waiting at court. George was still passionately in love with Sarah, even as his new bride arrived in England for him.

Nevertheless, George's mother had been firm. 'George,' she had said, 'be a King!' and so, if that entailed marrying a foreign princess whom he had never even seen, then marry her he would. He was determined to do his duty. Charlotte Sophia of Mecklenburg-Strelitz duly arrived. Certainly no beauty, she had such a wide mouth that everyone called her the Crocodile! They married within hours of meeting each other. During the wedding service people looking closely at George noticed that when a prayer was said containing the words 'Abraham and Sarah' he blushed bright scarlet on hearing the name 'Sarah'.

However, George was faithful. The little German girl may not have been beautiful but she certainly proved to be fertile. Within less than a year she had produced an heir to the throne – the future George IV. And then, almost annually, there followed an astonishingly large succession of babies: after George came Frederick, then William, then Charlotte, then Edward, and Augusta, and Elizabeth, and Ernest, and Augustus, then Adolphus, and Mary, and Sophia, then Octavius, and Alfred, and finally came Amelia. Charlotte Sophia was still only thirty-eight when she had her last child. 'My quiver is full,' said George.

Charlotte and George were probably the most private and domestic of all our kings and queens. Certainly, they kept a formal court for special occasions, but they enjoyed family life in a quiet, modest residence in Kew. George himself liked strolling out and talking to the local farmers, thus earning himself the nickname 'Farmer George'.

This way of life may have seemed rather less than royal, but both Charlotte and George were genuinely interested in meeting people and were popular. Across the Channel, their exact contemporaries Marie Antoinette and Louis XVI were living a greatly different lifestyle, and met a predictably different reaction from their French subjects.

As the family grew, George took over a new home, again quite modest in size, called Buckingham House. Later on, this house was to be enlarged beyond anyone's imagination by their precocious and extravagant firstborn son, George IV, who turned it into Buckingham Palace.

Throughout their marriage Charlotte was kind, sensible, and tolerant. She had a great deal to put up with: first of all, the interminable childbearing; then her husband's madness (he grew more and more eccentric until he became quite insane for at least the last ten years of his life); and then, finally, the scandals and unpopularity surrounding her son, who became Regent as his father lingered into senility and madness. But perhaps her greatest regret was that she had never been allowed to have any part in the affairs of state. Everything important was kept from her. She had to glean what news she could from the newspapers.

Charlotte died in 1818, two years before George. She had been a dutiful queen for fifty-seven years.

# CAROLINE OF BRUNSWICK
## 1768–1821
### *Queen of George IV*

When Caroline came to England in 1795 to marry her cousin George, he had no desire whatsoever for a wife. He had a vast range of delectable mistresses, and in any case he already had a wife – his secret wife, Mrs Fitzherbert. However, Parliament insisted that he should marry a proper wife, so somewhat reluctantly he agreed, rather out of pique, choosing virtually at random. Although Caroline was his cousin he had never met her, though a small painting was sent, giving him a rather flattering preview. Everyone who knew Caroline was aghast at the choice. She had an appalling reputation for bad manners and loose morals; her head was too large for her body, her teeth were rotten, and she stank.

No one could quite pluck up the courage to tell the Prince of Wales the full truth about Caroline. He simply sent his favourite mistress at the time (Lady Jersey) to bring her back to England and deliver her to him at St James's Palace. He did not bother to meet her himself, but when she was ushered into his presence, one glance at her was enough. 'I am not well,' gasped the Prince. 'Pray get me a glass of brandy!' He gulped it down and staggered out of the room, horrified at the predicament he had landed himself in.

The relationship went from bad to worse. He had to go through with the wedding, but according to Caroline's own account of the wedding night the Prince got himself so sozzled that he fell insensible, and stayed that way until morning. That the marriage was consummated was proved by the birth of a daughter, Charlotte, but George and Caroline lived together only briefly and then Caroline was provided with a large house on Blackheath.

Scandalously, Caroline now began to entertain men friends on a large scale. Tales of her wild parties and prolific adultery circulated everywhere. Caroline had taken up charitable work, adopting a number of local orphans and foundlings. On the surface this looked good and gave her a reputation for being a lady bountiful. However, the real motive behind all this was to hide the fact that she was giving birth to children of her own.

The high point of all the scandal-mongering was reached when it became widely believed that she had given birth to a son. Of course, if this were so, then one day he might claim the throne. An enquiry, discreetly called a 'Delicate Investigation', was set in motion and the first witness, a Lady Douglas, gave testimony that Caroline had privately confided to her that all this was true, and that Caroline had told her that she had disguised her pregnancies by stuffing cushions up her clothes and making out that she was usually fatter than she really was.

Lady Douglas informed the Commission of Enquiry that a boy had been born in 1802, that the child was registered as 'William Austin' and that Caroline was bringing him up, pretending he was the son of a dockyard worker's wife. In Lady Douglas's opinion, the father was Rear-Admiral Sir Sidney Smith, for Caroline had told her what a fine bedfellow he was.

Many notable men were caught up in this Delicate Investigation, much to their discomfiture, but the Prince managed to rescue the reputation of one, George Canning, a future Conservative Prime Minister, by deleting his name from those who were to be interrogated. Canning had been terrified that he would be ruined by what would be revealed.

Eventually the Commission decided that very little could be proved, and Caroline was grudgingly let off, except that one affair, with a Captain Manby, did seem to have taken place. However, it must be recorded that William Austin remained in her care for the rest of her life, and accompanied her wherever she went. All the Delicate Investigation did was to make Caroline extremely popular, for people always take sides, and her husband, the Prince of Wales, was seen to be the persecuting villain. Caroline continued behaving as outrageously as ever.

She was abroad in Italy when her husband the Prince Regent at last succeeded his father. By now Carline's behaviour was becoming almost obscene, and she had caused horrified amusement at a ball by dancing topless. George was outraged and ordered that her name should never again be mentioned: the date of his coronation was approaching and he ordered that she must not be considered to be his queen. Even the churches were not to mention her in their prayers. Naturally, Caroline resented this. She returned to England, hoping to take her place alongside George at the coronation.

One of the most preposterous episodes ever witnessed at Westminster Abbey then took place. George ordered all the doors of the Abbey to be closed against Caroline, and the crowds outside, who had heard all about her wild Italian adventures, jeered and hooted as she went from door to door, banging on them and shouting to be admitted. 'Go back to Italy!' the people yelled.

In abject humiliation she had to go home. Nineteen days later she was dead. They shipped her body back to Brunswick.

# ADELAIDE OF SAXE-MEININGEN
## 1792–1849
### *Queen of William IV*

William IV had never expected to be king, and lived quietly and unmarried with his partner, an actress called Mrs Jordan, and their ten children. However, as it became more and more obvious that he would have to be the next monarch, duty demanded that he should find himself a proper wife. Proposal after proposal went out to prospective brides, and with monotonous regularity refusal after refusal came back. Meanwhile, he had fallen desperately in love with an English heiress, Miss Wykeham. Both his brother, George IV, and Parliament refused permission for William to marry Miss Wykeham, so he had to continue his search for a bride. At last his patience was rewarded by an acceptance; it was to be the 26-year-old Princess Adelaide of the small German Duchy of Saxe-Meiningen.

William was fifty-two; unmarried with ten illegitimate children; hopelessly in love with Miss Wykeham; desperately in debt; and on the brink of marriage to an unknown princess exactly half his age. He was miserable. His state of mind is reflected in a letter he wrote to his eldest illegitimate son:

> The Princess of Saxe-Meiningen is doomed, poor, dear, innocent young creature, to be my wife. I cannot, I will not, I must not ill use her. . . . What time may produce in my heart, I can not tell, but at present I think and exist only for Miss Wykeham. But enough of your father's misery.

Such is the background of the marriage of William and Adelaide.

No princess ever entered England with less fuss or ceremony. She arrived in London one July evening in 1818 accompanied by her mother, and settled into Grillon's Hotel in Albemarle Street. The Prince Regent, the future George IV, came round as soon as he could, after a dinner party at Carlton House, and William himself, summoned from Kew, arrived at about midnight. They all enjoyed a happy supper together – and it was clear that despite everyone's fears, Adelaide would fit in and make an acceptable wife.

William hated ceremony. They were married very quietly in old Queen Charlotte's private room at Kew Palace, where an old toilet-table was draped over and turned into an altar with a couple of candles and a prayer book. After this, there was an outdoor family picnic near the Chinese pagoda in Kew gardens. It was a genuinely happy occasion.

The coronation, though it took place in Westminster Abbey, was also a relatively unpompous occasion. William wanted to do away with the ceremony altogether, calling it a 'useless and ill-timed expense'.

Adelaide was a perfect consort in difficult circumstances. Although she had the highest moral standards herself she was tolerant and kind to all William's illegitimate children, and provided a welcome air of respectability to the court after the scandalous times of George IV. The only sad thing about her brief, six-year reign was that she failed to provide William with an heir: two little daughters died in infancy.

After William died, Adelaide enjoyed the freedom to travel and do some sight-seeing. She gave £10,000 of her own money to build the Anglican Cathedral in Valetta in Malta, which she visited in 1838.

No memorial exists for her in St George's Chapel, Windsor, where she is buried, but her name is still vigorously alive in Australia, where the beautiful city of Adelaide was designed and founded in her honour while she was still queen.

# PRINCE ALBERT OF SAXE-COBURG-GOTHA
## 1819–1861
### *Consort of Queen Victoria*

Victoria and Albert were both twenty when they were married, both of them deeply in love. Victoria wrote: 'He is perfection in every way – in beauty, in everything. . . . Oh, how I adore and love him . . .'. And it's true to say that she felt the same way about him for the rest of her life.

Albert was her cousin, coming from Bavaria, son of the Duke of Saxe-Coburg-Gotha, and had studied in Brussels and Bonn. Studious, intellectual, humourless. Stiff, earnest, hardworking. His personal motto: 'Never relax, never relax, never relax.' And in Victoria's eyes he could do no wrong.

They had nine children, and their progeny were to fill royal palaces everywhere. At the end of her life Victoria was called the 'Grandmother of Europe'.

It is easy to poke fun at dull people who treat everything with deadly seriousness, so although Albert worked himself to the bone on a huge number of projects, the people of England really had very little time for him. He was too clever and cultured. His main achievement, perhaps, was in being the inspirational force behind the Great Exhibition of 1851, by far the largest gathering of arts, sciences, skills and industry which the world had ever seen. It was a triumph of organisation, and gave an enormous boost to British commerce. The profits went to form the various museums which are still major tourist attractions in London today. The Albert Hall was also built out of these profits.

He helped design Balmoral and Osborne House on the Isle of Wight, he painted, composed, drew up plans for workers' dwellings, sat on committees, made speeches; he was relentlessly, remorselessly *good*. Albert the Good. But, rather like the dodo, Albert became chiefly famous for being dead.

Albert's death at forty-two came suddenly. Bertie, their eldest son and future Edward VII, had just discovered the facts of life with an actress (why must it always be an actress?) and Albert was desperately worried. The situation gave him 'the greatest pain I have yet felt in this life'. So, one winter's day, Albert travelled up to Cambridge, where Bertie was briefly studying, to give his son a right royal ticking-off. 'You must not, you dare not be lost,' Albert told him. 'The consequences for the country, for the world, would be too dreadful!'

## OSBORNE HOUSE, ISLE OF WIGHT

Anyone wishing to become fully acquainted with the life of Queen Victoria must visit Osborne House. Every square inch proclaims her presence. Victoria and Albert bought Old Osborne House in 1845 and Albert immediately set to work to redesign and rebuild it according to his own fastidious tastes. It was complete within a few years and here Victoria's family grew up. The royal children were given a furnished 'Swiss Cottage' to play in and to learn housekeeping and cookery. It was perhaps the world's first 'Wendy House'.

At Osborne Victoria spent the idyllic years of her married life, and when in 1861 Albert suddenly died, she spent the forty years of her widowhood here. And it was here that she died, cradled in the Kaiser's arms (her favourite grandchild) and surrounded by her family.

Accordingly, virtually nothing was changed. Shortly after Albert's death she wrote: '. . . *his* wishes – *his* plans – about *everything*, *his* views about *every* thing are to be my *law*! And no human power will make me swerve from *what he* decided and wished.'

Visitors should allow plenty of time to take everything in: the house is crammed with Victoriana and as well as all the formal rooms we can also see her personal lift (worked by hand by a servant in the basement!), her shower and bathroom, the nursery suite, the Swiss Cottage and toy gardening-tools, and even Victoria's own private bathing-machine. And among the pictures is the famous portrait of Victoria on horseback, attended by the notorious old rogue, John Brown.

Her successor, Edward VII, disliked the place and quickly gave it to the nation. For a while it was a Royal Naval College but this was closed. However, parts of it are still in use as a Convalescent Home.

Alas, the weather was cold in Cambridge and Albert caught a chill. Within a fortnight he had died of typhoid fever. Victoria was distraught. No human being in public life has ever mourned a spouse so dramatically, so completely, so permanently. For the rest of her life – almost forty years – she led the life of a recluse, living mostly in Osborne House or Balmoral, the two houses they had built together. In all that time she visited London only very rarely; she never attended a court ball; she never went to a theatre or a concert. She slept with his nightclothes, and she kept a marble model of his 'sweet little ear' on her writing-desk.

It can be claimed that Albert's death influenced the country at least as much as his life. For decades a pall of silence and hushed respectability fell over the English court. No greater contrast could be imagined between the hoots of derision which had been hurled at the licentious George IV and the reverential awe enjoyed by Victoria in her widowhood.

The image of the Royal Family as a role-model of perfection was, perhaps, Albert's final legacy.

The Albert Memorial, just opposite the Albert Hall, is the public edifice to his memory. But almost uniquely for royalty, his grave is a private one, in the Royal Mausoleum at Frogmore, a secluded part of Windsor Park.

# ALEXANDRA OF DENMARK
## 1844–1925
### Queen of Edward VII

Victoria considered Alexandra to be 'one of those sweet creatures who seem to come from the skies to help and bless mortals'. Certainly, Alexandra was a remarkable woman. She had to be, to marry Bertie.

As a boy and teenager, 'Bertie' – the future King Edward VII – proved to be wayward and uncontrollable. He was the despair of his parents, Victoria and Albert, and they realised that they had to find someone with very special qualities to fit the demanding role of wife and future consort.

The trouble was, if they suggested anyone as a bride, Bertie would be sure to disagree. He had already rejected Elizabeth of Wied, who wasn't beautiful enough. Cunningly, it was arranged that Bertie should happen 'quite accidentally' to meet Alexandra while visiting the cathedral of Speyer in Germany. They met, and Bertie was enchanted. So much so that when they next met, rather more formally, he proposed to her immediately.

They were married without fuss, as it was still only months since Albert had died. 'Alex' was nineteen, and Bertie twenty-two. The nation was in raptures, and Alfred Tennyson, the Poet Laureate, wrote an appalling poem of welcome:

> . . . Saxon or Dane or Norman we,
> Teuton or Celt, or whatever we be,
> We are each all Dane in our welcome of thee,
> Alexandra!

For the first forty years of their marriage, they were the Prince and Princess of Wales. It was a long wait to reach the throne, and Queen Victoria resolutely refused to give Bertie any kind of responsibility or work of any kind. The frustration for Bertie was intense, and he sought every kind of extravagant pleasure, simply to keep himself occupied: racing, hunting, eating, gambling, drinking, travelling, and naturally enough, women.

Alexandra was monumentally tolerant. Gracious and kind, she suffered various health difficulties, especially deafness and lameness, but she kept her strikingly beautiful looks to the end of her life. Everyone knew how unfaithful Bertie was, but she kept a silent dignity and accompanied him, when asked, without complaint. She was a byword for regal conscientiousness.

Prince Albert had begun the modern royal tradition of service to the community, which we take for granted nowadays. However, this concept of monarchy is a recent innovation, and Alexandra was the first consort queen to involve herself deeply and sincerely in charitable works since those medieval queens who retired to nunneries.

She started up a special branch of a military nursing service; she supported hospitals and the International Red Cross; she visited quite ordinary people in their sick-beds. And in 1913, to mark the fiftieth anniversary of her arrival in England, she founded 'Alexandra Rose Day' to support work in hospitals.

On coming to the throne her husband abandoned the name Albert and became known as King Edward VII. Both Alexandra and Edward were extremely popular in their different ways: Alexandra because of her virtues, and Edward despite his faults.

To the end of his days Edward was a glutton and a womaniser. When his health finally collapsed he was in Biarritz, accompanied by his long-standing mistress, Mrs Alice Keppel. He was brought home, and when it was evident that he was soon to die, Alexandra, with quite extraordinary selflessness, invited Mrs Keppel to his death-bed to take her last farewell.

Alexandra herself lived on until 1925 and died just before her eighty-first birthday.

# MARY OF TECK
## 1867–1953
### *Queen of George V*

Those who can remember the coronation of Queen Elizabeth II will also remember the majestic, queenly figure of her grandmother, Queen Mary, for she died only a few weeks beforehand, unfortunately not quite living long enough to see that impressive ceremony. She was almost eighty-six when she died, a living link with the past, for when she was born Queen Victoria was still in the first half of her reign, Dickens and George Eliot were busily writing and Gladstone and Disraeli were still in their prime.

Mary was born in Kensington Palace, in the same room where Queen Victoria had also been born, and was a great-granddaughter of George III. Her father was Duke Francis of Teck, but she was brought up in England, and so had the advantage, in royal eyes, of being both royal and English. She seemed right to be consort for the heir to the throne: beautiful, high-spirited, artistic and moral.

The heir, however, was a little-known, rather backward young man, Prince Albert Victor Christian Edward, known as 'Eddy' in the family. He had always been somewhat sickly, and almost as soon as Mary and Eddie had become engaged, Eddy caught pneumonia and died. Frankly, it was no great loss. It may well have been something of a relief. However, life must go on, and the next in line to the throne was Eddy's brother George, quite a different personality. Queen Victoria, still alive, still eager to organise, swiftly suggested that Mary, or 'May' as they called her, should marry George. Thus, on 6 July 1893, Mary and George were married in the Chapel Royal, St James's Palace. Thus began more than forty years of genuine wedded happiness.

Queen Mary was an exemplary consort to George V. Together they presented an image of rock-solid respectability. Duty, courage, faithfulness: all the traditional virtues. During the First World War, which broke out quite soon after they became king and queen, they did their utmost to set an example, observing food rationing, banning alcohol from their table, growing potatoes in their flower beds, and constantly visiting hospitals and factories. George even changed his name, so that they should not seem to be so 'German'. The name of Windsor was adopted.

After the war there were difficult times and George tried hard to preserve an impartiality in dealing with the clash of politicians, sometimes running into constitutional difficulties: but no one ever doubted his integrity. As for Mary, she continued to work for many charities, helped to beautify London's parks, and with her artistic knowledge was a major influence in restoring Buckingham Palace, which had been badly neglected during Victoria's long absence from it. Visitors to the palace today will appreciate the long, beautifully lit picture gallery. It was dark, gloomy and badly overcrowded until Queen Mary transformed it.

King George V died in 1936. Queen Mary had naturally expected her son Edward, the wildly popular Prince of Wales (known to family and friends as David), to succeed him, but this was not to be. True, he became king, because the succession is instantaneous: 'The King is dead – long live the King!' However, after reigning uncrowned for less than a year he abdicated in favour of his younger brother, who became George VI. From that day onward Mary hardly ever saw David again.

Mary's final years were darkened by the abdication of her eldest son, Edward VIII, and the death of her youngest son, the Duke of Kent, in a plane crash. She lived through the Second World War and then bereavement came yet again when her middle son, George VI, died of cancer. Her tall figure, draped in mourning, was an unforgettably melancholy sight.

Her official memorial is in St George's Chapel, Windsor. She and George lie side by side, carved in gleaming white marble – splendidly life-like effigies. Hers was actually carved and put in place while she was still alive – a macabre touch.

However, Mary of Teck's intangible memorial is the great tradition of duty and service which she personally instilled into her granddaughter, who was of course to become Elizabeth II. It had been increasingly obvious that Elizabeth would inherit the throne, so old Queen Mary (she would not accept the title Queen Mother) took it upon herself to make sure that she took the two little princesses, Elizabeth and Margaret, to Hampton Court, the Tower of London, Greenwich, and told them all the stories of history. And she gave her great-grandson, Charles, a silver christening mug that had once belonged to George III, her own great-grandfather.

When she knew she was dying, and when Elizabeth realised that 'her old Granny', as Mary called herself, would not live to see the coronation, a deeply touching and private little ceremony took place. Elizabeth called for the royal crown and other articles she would wear, and solemnly put them on for the old Queen to see.

After so much tribulation, Mary died knowing that the throne would be secure.

# MRS WALLIS SIMPSON
## 1896–1986
### *Wife of the Duke of Windsor*

Edward, the Prince of Wales, son of George V and heir to the throne, met a married American woman in 1931 at a house party. It was a cold, damp, winter weekend, and the Prince, making conversation, asked her if she was missing the comforts of American central heating. To his astonishment, she looked him in the eye and replied: 'I am sorry, Sir, but you have disappointed me. Every American woman who comes here is always asked that same question. I had hoped for something more original from the Prince of Wales.'

From that moment, Edward was hooked. It almost seemed as if he spent the rest of his life trying to undo that first impression of disappointment: he showered gifts upon her, particularly the priceless jewellery which he had inherited; he gave up many of his friends for her; he travelled to rich villas and Mediterranean resorts with her. When, five years later, he was confronted with the choice of becoming either King of Great Britain and Emperor of India or Mrs Simpson's third husband, he chose the latter.

The story of the abdication has been told so often. What it boiled down to was that Edward had become completely mesmerised by Wallis Simpson. She kept him captivated for the rest of his life. Of course, the royal family was aghast. The whole world was dumb-founded. And it fell to Edward's younger brother to pick up the pieces, become king and keep the monarchy going.

King George VI and Queen Elizabeth (later to become the Queen Mother) were duly enthroned, much against their will, and went on to become two of the most highly respected monarchs in our history, but they never forgave Edward VIII for thrusting them so cruelly and unexpectedly into the royal limelight.

Edward took the title Duke of Windsor and apart from a brief period during the Second World War when he served as Governor of the Bahamas, he did nothing of value for the rest of his life, living in exile with Wallis in Paris. Although Edward was styled 'His Royal Highness the Duke of Windsor', the honour of being a 'Royal Highness' was pointedly withheld from Wallis. She was simply the 'Duchess of Windsor'. It rankled deeply with them both. The Duke always tried to make up for it by referring to Wallis as 'Her Royal Highness', but he could never quite deceive himself, nor could he deceive Wallis. 'Royal Highness' she was destined never to be.

Nevertheless, a tribute came from Adolf Hitler, with whom they once had tea. 'She would have made a good Queen,' he said. It was a solitary opinion.

Wallis, Duchess of Windsor, came to Buckingham Palace only once: for the Duke's private funeral. She then returned to Paris, and we are told that for the last eleven years of her life she never slept. When she died in 1986, her corpse was brought to England to be laid to rest beside Edward, Duke of Windsor.

# QUEEN ELIZABETH THE QUEEN MOTHER
## 1900–2002
### *Queen of George VI*

Her grandson, Prince Charles, put it in a nutshell: 'She is one of those extraordinarily rare people whose touch can turn everything to gold.' Indeed, it can be said that Elizabeth the Queen Mother added an entirely new dimension to the very concept of royalty.

Her marriage to the Duke of York in 1923 was seen as something of a break with tradition. Despite her noble Scottish background she was a 'commoner' marrying into royalty. It was a welcome sign of the times, for people remembered that she, like so many of themselves, had lost a much-loved brother in the First World War. Her arrival seemed like a breath of fresh air. She was British, and one of 'us'.

In fact, Elizabeth had been reluctant at first to accept the Duke's proposal of marriage. She voiced her concern with clear-sighted perception, saying that she feared 'I should never again be free to think, speak or act as I really feel I should think, speak and act.' Bertie, as the Duke was known in the family, had to propose three times before she could bring herself to say 'yes'.

As for her ancestry, she was born Lady Elizabeth Angela Marguerite Bowes-Lyon, daughter of Lord and Lady Glamis. She can trace descent from the Scottish King Robert II. However, her mother was English, and she had been born in England. Photographs of the young Elizabeth show just how beautiful she was. Anecdotes recall how she charmed away the stuffiness of the royal family. George V, fanatical over punctuality, adored her, and once protested that he himself had been too early, when in fact it was she who had been late to arrive at table.

In the ordinary course of events Elizabeth would have been just a relatively minor member of the royal family, worth a tiny footnote in the pages of twentieth-century history. But as everybody knows, the abdication of Edward VIII pitchforked the Duke and herself into positions neither of them wanted. It is said that the Duke broke down completely when confronted with the news of his brother's abdication. From then on Elizabeth provided support for her husband in a manner equalled by no other queen.

Right through the war they stayed in London, sharing the dangers of the Blitz. When Buckingham Palace itself was bombed, Elizabeth remarked: 'Now I feel I can look the East End in the face.' It was a typical reaction.

## BUCKINGHAM PALACE

The surprising fact about Buckingham Palace is just how relatively recently it has become the focus of royalty in London. Queen Victoria was the first monarch to live here, but she virtually abandoned it after the death of Prince Albert. Her son, Edward VII, was born and died here; and Prince Charles was born here in 1948.

Originally, it was a comparatively modest town house, belonging to John Sheffield, Duke of Buckingham. King George III first bought 'Buckingham House' in 1762 and extended it to house his growing family and large library. During this period it was known as the 'Queen's House' and Queen Charlotte gave birth to twelve of her fifteen children here.

It is to George IV that we owe the present Buckingham Palace. When he came to the throne in 1820, he was living in Carlton House, at the east end of The Mall. He decided that he needed a much more elaborate palace, and entrusted the enlargement of Buckingham House to his favourite architect, John Nash. Parliament was horrified at the expense, which grew and grew as Nash's plans were implemented. Work began in 1825 and the palace was not quite completed when George IV died in 1830.

William IV disliked the place, and never lived there. When the Houses of Parliament were burnt down in 1834 he even suggested that Buckingham Palace would make a good substitute.

Queen Victoria, however, moved in almost immediately after her accession, and it was under her direction that further enlargement took place. The railings round the front court were not erected until 1906. The Mall was widened and the Victoria Memorial was unveiled by George V in 1911, and it was not until 1912 that work on the front of the palace was eventually completed.

The ceremony of Changing the Guard takes place daily at 11.30, and Buckingham Palace itself is now usually open to the public during the summer months.

Day after day, at the height of the bomb attacks, George and Elizabeth toured the devastation, talking to the ordinary people of London, whose determination they shared. People will never forget that sympathy; that common bond. Victory came, but also the years of austerity, and then widowhood.

Elizabeth's first reaction to the death of her husband was something akin to Victoria's. She withdrew to Scotland, toying with the idea of living in retirement in a ruined castle, the Castle of Mey, which she had just acquired. However, her vitality, her love of family, her sense of duty, and her sheer *joie de vivre* gradually returned. She settled at the heart of things, in Clarence House, a stone's throw from Buckingham Palace. Her exuberance blossomed anew and she became more involved in public service than ever before. She became president, patron, colonel-in-chief, or whatever, of well over three hundred organisations, who looked to her for inspiration and support.

In the last decades of her long life, which spanned the whole of the twentieth century, she became a unique national institution – the 'Queen Mum'. It is probably true to say that no other consort or royal widow has ever received so much public affection. Proof of this came in August 2000, when she became the first royal centenarian. As she celebrated her 100th birthday, London came to a halt while thousands crowded outside her home, Clarence House, and Buckingham Palace, where she appeared on the balcony with the royal family.

More proof of how deeply she was loved came when she lay in state in Westminster Hall after her death in 2002. Hundreds of thousands queued for miles to have the opportunity to file past her coffin. They came in such unexpectedly large numbers that even the palace officials were astonished. In fact Westminster Hall had to be kept open for much longer than had originally been intended, for several days and right through the nights, to enable the mourners to pay their last respects.

Someone once described the Queen Mother as being a 'marsh-mallow with a core of good Scotch granite'. Her charm was always apparent – but it was the granite that we respected and loved.

# PRINCE PHILIP, DUKE OF EDINBURGH
## 1921–
### *Husband of Elizabeth II*

Philip and Elizabeth are in fact distant cousins, having Queen Victoria as a common ancestor. Queen Mary pointed out, with more detailed precision, that they are third cousins through their descent from Queen Victoria, second cousins once removed (from Christian IX of Denmark), and fourth cousins once removed through collateral descendants of George III.

What it meant was that when Philip was a teenager of eighteen, and a naval cadet at Dartmouth, the young Princess Elizabeth, aged just thirteen, was allowed to meet him, owing to their distant kinship. From that moment, she never had eyes for any other boy. That may sound too much like a tinsel fairy-tale to be true, but it is actual fact. Indeed, King George VI was rather worried that his daughter had simply fallen for the first boy she had met, and tried his hardest to delay an engagement, and then to delay a public announcement. But Elizabeth had made up her mind. In 1947 they were engaged.

Philip was born a prince. A prince of Greece. His father, who had died in 1944, had been Prince Andrew of Greece, and his mother was Princess Alice, a great-granddaughter of Queen Victoria. However, Philip had been educated in Britain, at Gordonstoun, a somewhat unusually tough and physically demanding public school. To all intents and purposes he was English, and as he wanted a career in the British Royal Navy, he was keen to become naturalised as a British citizen.

The first problem before Elizabeth could marry him, therefore, was what name he should adopt. If he renounced his Greek citizenship and his title of prince he would at least need a name on a passport. Now that he was about to marry, the need for a suitable name became more urgent, in view of any future children.

Philip was reluctant to assume his cumbersome family surname: Schleswig-Holstein-Sonderburg-Glücksburg. This name may come as something of a surprise but in fact Philip's ancestry is pure Danish; he does not have a single drop of Greek blood in his veins. The College of Heralds, trying to help, looked into his ancestry and found that he was related to a previous Duke of Oldenburg, and suggested that he might use an English version of this and call himself 'Oldcastle'.

However, as everyone knows, he became simply 'Mountbatten', taking on the name of his Uncle Dickie, who had just become Viceroy of India. It seems obvious now, but it took the ingenuity of the Labour Government's Home Secretary at the time, Chuter Ede, to come up with this solution.

Anyone with an eye for historical detail will note therefore, that when Elizabeth Windsor married Philip Mountbatten each of these surnames was only just thirty years old: for the Battenberg family had been required to change their name at the same time as George V had changed his.

Just before the wedding King George made Philip Duke of Edinburgh, and gave him a few more titles besides, but of course he lost his Greek title of prince when he became naturalised. It was not until 1957, ten years after their marriage, that Elizabeth conferred upon him the title of Prince again, this time a British Prince, in recognition of his public services.

Elizabeth and Philip were to enjoy only just over four years of freedom before they had to take over the roles of Queen and Consort. Two children were born, Charles and Anne, and Philip was set for a naval career.

The death of George VI in mid-life cut short any hopes for an independent naval career for Philip. Since then he has been active, incredibly active, in travelling, speaking, sponsoring. He is the president, patron, colonel-in-chief, chancellor, chairman, governor, admiral, ranger, general, commander-in-chief, captain-general, chief, trust member, etc. of close on six hundred organisations. In addition to accompanying the Queen on her innumerable tours, he has undertaken a vast number of independent trips by himself. For many years, it was calculated that he worked a fourteen-hour day, travelled an average of 75,000 miles a year, carried out about 300 engagements and made about 80 speeches annually.

His most lasting innovation has been his Duke of Edinburgh Award Scheme, which has given personal challenges to well over a million youngsters not only in Great Britain but also in the twenty-five Commonwealth countries around the world. 'It has probably done more for people than anything else I have been involved in,' he once said.

Detractors of the monarchy should pause to consider this aspect of voluntary public service now carried out by most of the royals. It is a relatively recent phenomenon of monarchy, arguably having been begun by Victoria's Prince Albert.

The Duke of Edinburgh's contribution to the life of the country has often been quietly performed, without attracting blaring headlines. However, no previous consort, surely, has ever been involved in so many activities or been so energetic over such a long period of time as Prince Philip.

# ROYAL BONES

## THE KINGS OF WESSEX

The early kings before Edward the Confessor are virtually lost in a remote period of our history. However, they were great men of their times, and must have been buried with honour. Listed below are the resting-places, where known, of the Kings of Wessex, from Cerdic (who landed in 508 AD in what is today known as Hampshire) to Egbert, the first King of all England.

| Monarch | Resting-place |
|---|---|
| Cerdic | |
| Cynric | |
| Ceawlin | |
| Ceol | |
| Ceolwulf | |
| Cynegils | Winchester Cathedral |
| Cenwalh | Winchester Cathedral |
| Queen Seaxburgh | |
| Cenfus | |
| Aescwine | |
| Centwine | |
| Cadwalla | died in Italy and was buried in Old St Peter's, Rome |
| Ine | died on a pilgrimage to Rome |
| Ethelheard | |
| Cuthred | |
| Sigeberht | |
| Cynewulf | |
| Beohrtric | Wareham, Dorset |
| Egbert | Winchester Cathedral |

## SAXON KINGS OF ENGLAND

Here are the resting-places of the Saxon Kings of England from Egbert to Harold II, killed by the Normans at the Battle of Hastings in 1066:

| Monarch | Resting-place |
|---|---|
| Egbert | Winchester Cathedral |
| Ethelwulf | Winchester Cathedral |
| Ethelbald | Sherborne Abbey |
| Ethelbert | Sherborne Abbey |
| Ethelred I | Wimborne Minster |
| Alfred the Great | Originally in the old Saxon Minster in Winchester, then at Hyde Abbey, Winchester. Now lost |
| Edward the Elder | Winchester Cathedral |
| Athelstan | Malmesbury Abbey |
| Edmund I (the Elder) | Glastonbury Abbey |
| Edred | Winchester Cathedral |
| Edwy the Fair | died (and possibly buried) at Gloucester |
| Edgar the Peaceful | Glastonbury Abbey |
| Edward the Martyr | Originally at Wareham, Dorset, then reburied in 981 in Shaftesbury Abbey. Recently reburied again in Brookwood Cemetery, Surrey |
| Ethelred II (the Unready) | Old St Paul's, London. Now lost |
| Edmund II (Ironside) | Glastonbury Abbey |
| Canute | Winchester Cathedral |
| Harold I (Harold Harefoot) | St Clement Dane's, London |
| Hardecanute | Saxon cathedral in Winchester |
| Edward the Confessor | Westminster Abbey |
| Harold II | Pevensey seashore; later, Waltham Abbey. Now lost. Perhaps in Holy Trinity Church, Bosham, East Sussex |

## KINGS AND QUEENS SINCE 1066

Listed opposite are the resting-places of the kings and reigning queens of England since 1066:

| Monarch | Resting-place |
| --- | --- |
| William I (the Conqueror) | Abbey of St Stephen, Caen, Normandy |
| William II (Rufus) | Winchester Cathedral |
| Henry I | Originally Reading Abbey. Now lost |
| Stephen | Originally Faversham Abbey. Now lost |
| Empress Matilda | Rouen Cathedral |
| Henry II | Fontevrault Abbey, France |
| Richard I (the Lionheart) | Fontevrault Abbey, France |
| John | Worcester Cathedral |
| Henry III | Westminster Abbey |
| Edward I | Westminster Abbey |
| Edward II | Gloucester Cathedral |
| Edward III | Westminster Abbey |
| Richard II | Westminster Abbey |
| Henry IV | Canterbury Cathedral |
| Henry V | Westminster Abbey |
| Henry VI | St George's Chapel, Windsor |
| Edward IV | St George's Chapel, Windsor |
| Edward V | possibly in an urn in Westminster Abbey |
| Richard III | Grey Friars' Abbey, Leicester. Now lost |
| Henry VII | Westminster Abbey |
| Henry VIII | St George's Chapel, Windsor |
| Edward VI | Westminster Abbey |
| Mary I | Westminster Abbey |
| Elizabeth I | Westminster Abbey |
| James I | Westminster Abbey |
| Charles I | St George's Chapel, Windsor |
| (Oliver Cromwell | Westminster Abbey, then dug up and lost) |
| (Richard Cromwell | Hursley parish church, Hampshire) |
| Charles II | Westminster Abbey |
| James II | St Germain-en-Laye, France |
| William III | Westminster Abbey |
| Mary II | Westminster Abbey |
| Anne | Westminster Abbey |
| George I | Herrenhausen, Hanover, Germany |
| George II | Westminster Abbey |
| George III | St George's Chapel, Windsor |
| George IV | St George's Chapel, Windsor |

| Monarch | Resting-place |
| --- | --- |
| William IV | St George's Chapel, Windsor |
| Victoria | Royal Mausoleum, Frogmore, Windsor |
| Edward VII | St George's Chapel, Windsor |
| George V | St George's Chapel, Windsor |
| Edward VIII | Royal Burial Ground, Frogmore, Windsor |
| George VI | St George's Chapel, Windsor |

# EGBERT
## DIED 4 FEBRUARY (?) 839   AGED *c.* 69
### *Winchester Cathedral, Hampshire*

Some of the oldest royal bones in the country lie in six small wooden chests on view in Winchester Cathedral. They rest high up on top of a kind of screen each side of the area between the choir-stalls and the altar.

A casual visitor can easily miss them, but in these almost inconspicuous boxes lie the remains of some remarkably famous people – certainly great names of the times in which they lived.

No one can be quite certain exactly who lies where, but according to the inscriptions on the sides of these boxes, the contents include the remains of no less a personage than King Egbert, the very first King of England; also King Cynegils of Wessex, who died as long ago as 643, and who founded Winchester's Saxon cathedral.

And among other early kings whose bones are contained in these boxes are King Edmund, a son of King Alfred the Great, King Canute and his wife Queen Emma, and also King William II, usually called William Rufus.

Identification is impossible, however, because Parliamentarian soldiers smashed the boxes open in 1642 and scattered the contents. One of the boxes states that the jumbled kingly remains were 'promiscuously' put back into their containers in 1661.

# EDWARD THE MARTYR
## MURDERED 31 MARCH 978   AGED *c.* 15
### *Brookwood Cemetery, Surrey*

You wouldn't expect to find the bones of a King of England in a cutlery box in the strong-room of the Midland Bank (now HSBC) in Woking. Nevertheless, a few years ago this is where they were stored. It's a complicated story.

King Edward the Martyr was only fifteen when he was pulled off his horse and stabbed by order of his stepmother at the gates of Corfe Castle in Dorset in 978. His bones have an extraordinary history. At first he was buried in nearby Wareham, but after miracles started happening his remains were taken to Shaftesbury and reburied at the abbey there.

He was declared a saint in 1001 and his holy bones were venerated in Shaftesbury Abbey until Henry VIII's time, when the buildings were broken up and sold. However, the nuns took such good care to hide St Edward's remains that his coffin was never discovered. Never, that is, until a small lead casket was unearthed in 1931 under a stone in what had been the abbey's north-east transept. The casket contained a skull and other bones. It seemed obvious that these were the lost remains of King Edward.

Immediately the remains became the object of a complicated legal tussle between two brothers who contested ownership. For years the former King Edward lay jumbled up in a cutlery box in the vault of a branch of the HSBC Bank in Woking.

Eventually, the legal wrangle was settled, and now King Edward, Saint and Martyr, has the distinction, unique among the Kings of England, of belonging to a sect of the Russian Orthodox Church. He lies in a beautiful newly built shrine in Brookwood Cemetery, near Woking in Surrey, and his bones are venerated there on four occasions a year: 31 March 978, the date of his martyrdom; 4 March 981, the date when his body was taken from Wareham to Shaftesbury; 3 July 1984, the date of his enshrinement at Shaftesbury; and 16 September, the date when his bones were finally enshrined at Brookwood.

# ETHELRED II (THE UNREADY)
## DIED 23 APRIL 1016   AGED *c*. 48
### *Old St Paul's, London*

Ethelred's mother had been the wicked Queen Elfrida, who had murdered Edward the Saint and Martyr, her stepson. She had done this simply out of motherly concern, to put her own son Ethelred on the throne. Of course, she did feel some pangs of conscience afterwards, so she fled to Amesbury, near Stonehenge, and founded a nunnery where she lived until her death. Ethelred duly became king.

As a baby Ethelred had caused some concern when he peed in the font while he was being baptised – obviously an omen of disaster. Saint

Dunstan, who was present to see Ethelred's infant indiscretion, immediately predicted horrendous slaughter of the English during Ethelred's lifetime. Sure enough, Ethelred's reign was marked by Danish invasions and horrible battles and massacres. Ethelred was forced to flee to France, but returned briefly, dying in London and being buried in old St Paul's Cathedral.

Presumably, Ethelred's bones are somewhere underneath the St Paul's we know today, but it's worth remembering that Sir Christopher Wren's building is in fact the *fifth* cathedral to be constructed on this site. Ethelred was buried in the *third* cathedral, a Saxon building, which was destroyed by fire in 1087. The building which is often referred to as 'Old St Paul's' was the *fourth* cathedral, built by the Normans, and finally destroyed by the Great Fire of London in 1666.

# EDMUND II (IRONSIDE)
## MURDERED *c.* 30 NOVEMBER 1016    AGED *c.* 23
### *Glastonbury Abbey, Somerset*

Edmund was the son of Ethelred the Unready, and he got his nickname 'Ironside' for his courage in battle against the Danes. He had to compromise with King Canute, however, and the two men shared the kingdom after the Battle of Ashington.

It was a pity that Edmund didn't have an iron bottom as well as iron sides, because his assassination was particularly uncomfortable, according to some accounts. He had gone to a privy late one night (a primitive lavatory which consisted of a wooden board with a circular hole made in it, placed over a rather smelly pit) and was sitting down easing his call of nature. Hidden underneath, in the pit below him, lurked the son of one of his enemies, waiting for the royal bottom to present itself. With a sharp dagger the assassin stabbed the king twice in the bowels and fled.

Edmund was buried in Glastonbury Abbey, leaving Canute in full control.

# CANUTE
## DIED 12 NOVEMBER 1035    AGED *c.* 43
### *Winchester Cathedral, Hampshire*

The bones of King Canute lie in one of the wooden chests in Winchester Cathedral (see Egbert above).

Canute died in Shaftesbury and was buried first in Winchester's old Saxon Minster. Later, his remains were ceremonially transferred to the new Norman cathedral, together with the bones of other Saxon kings and dignitaries.

When Parliamentarian soldiers broke these chests open during the time of the Commonwealth, these remains were scattered all over the cathedral floor. They were put back, in new chests, but all jumbled up. Sad to say, no one can now say exactly whose bones are whose.

The beautifully painted chests we see today were made in the sixteenth century – the original chests lie inside them.

## HAROLD I (HAROLD HAREFOOT)
### DIED 17 MARCH 1040    AGED 24
#### St Clement Dane's, London

The Danish King Harold Harefoot was Canute's son by Elfgifu of Northampton. His was a short reign, just five years. He was only twenty-four when he died, to be succeeded by his half-brother Hardecanute, who loathed him.

One of the first things Hardecanute did when he became king was to dig up Harold's body, chop off its head and chuck it into a bog. Luckily, some fishermen came across it, and Harold's remains were then buried in the London church called St Clement Dane's, just opposite the present-day law-courts, where Fleet Street and Aldwych meet.

St Clement Dane's gets its very name from the fact that a Danish community lived hereabouts and, like Harold Harefoot, were buried here.

## HARDECANUTE
### DIED 8 JUNE 1042    AGED c. 24
#### Winchester Cathedral, Hampshire

The Danish King Hardecanute was Canute's son by his wife Queen Emma. There are many spellings of his name, which can be confusing – Hardicanute, Harthacnut, etc. He reigned for only two years and, like his stepbrother Harold, he was only about twenty-four at the time of his sudden death.

Hardecanute was a notoriously heavy drinker, and choked to death 'with horrible convulsions' while getting drunk at a wedding feast in Lambeth. He could well have been poisoned. He was buried near his father, King Canute, in the old Saxon Minster in Winchester, but there is no mention of him there nowadays.

# EDWARD THE CONFESSOR
## DIED 5 JANUARY 1066    AGED 62
### *Westminster Abbey, London*

Edward spent much of his time building his abbey in Westminster, so it was inevitable that he should be the first to be buried there, only a few days after it was completed. Of course, the original building was much smaller than it is today. It was Henry III, two centuries later, who greatly enlarged it and who further encouraged the cult of the Confessor.

Nowadays, the Confessor's shrine is tucked away behind the main altar, and it is easy to forget that it was once the most magnificent centre-piece in the whole abbey, decorated with gold, precious stones and beautiful marble. The Confessor was declared a saint in 1163, and for centuries thousands of pilgrims visited his shrine, kneeling in the recessed arches on each side, and reaching up inside to get as close as possible to the saint. Many stayed overnight near the shrine, hoping for miracles to occur.

This great medieval shrine was created by King Henry III, who was passionately devoted to the memory of Edward, and who even named his own son after him, later to become Edward I. In a great ceremony in 1269 Henry III himself, together with his brother, sons and nephews, carried the holy bones of Edward from their original resting-place in the abbey to the glittering new shrine.

At the time of the Reformation the shrine was dismantled and Edward was again reburied, rather inconspicuously, elsewhere in the abbey, but during the reign of the Catholic Queen Mary I the tomb was reassembled in a bungled sort of way and the saint's body was brought back into an honoured position again. The coffin is still there, not beneath the ground, as you might suppose, but raised high up.

# THE LEGEND OF EDWARD THE CONFESSOR'S RING

For a medieval saint it seems to have been something of an occupational hazard to be dug up after burial, and to have one's coffin rifled for relics and valuables. The more venerable the saint was in life, the more vulnerable he was in death. Edward the Confessor is a prime example.

A famous story told about Edward is that once, as he was walking near Westminster Abbey, he gave away a valuable ring containing a large sapphire to an old beggar who asked him for alms. Years later, some English pilgrims met the same 'old beggar' in the Holy Land, who explained that he was none other than John the Evangelist. He gave them the ring, and asked them to go back to England and return it to King Edward, and to warn him that in six months' time he would die.

This story is depicted in many churches – one of the the best examples is in the St John Window at York Minster. The ring became Edward's personal symbol.

When Edward was buried in 1066, all sorts of precious articles were buried with him, and he was laid to rest wearing this holy ring – naturally a great temptation for future generations.

His coffin was first opened in 1102, just thirty-six years after his death, and his body was found to be perfectly preserved (no surprise, for this seemed to happen to most saints' bodies). The Bishop of Rochester tried to pull a hair from Edward's beard (which was 'white as frost'), but no amount of tugging would pull it out. The good bishop was 'gently reproved' by the Abbot for boldness. Later, in 1163, when Edward's corpse was moved to a new shrine, the ring was taken off his finger and taken into the treasury of Westminster Abbey. It is unclear exactly what happened to it, but tradition has it that 'St Edward's Sapphire' survived to be placed at the very top of the Imperial State Crown which is now worn on important state occasions by the present Queen. If this is genuinely King Edward's sapphire, then it is older than the Tower of London, where it is kept.

Sadly, St Edward's tomb has suffered many accidents and indignities over the centuries. It was shifted about unmercifully during the troubled times of the Tudors, then, in 1685 at the coronation of James II, some scaffolding fell on it and broke it open. A Westminster choirboy put his hand inside and, feeling among the saint's bones, pulled out a large crucifix which he gave to James II who 'was pleased to accept the gift.'

James tried to take this priceless holy relic with him as he fled the country in 1688. Predictably, he lost it.

# HAROLD II

## KILLED 14 OCTOBER 1066   AGED *c.* 46

### *Waltham Abbey, Essex. Now lost*

Two lances penetrated Harold's body; one eye was pierced by an arrow; and a sword had smashed into his head. Ivo of Ponthieu, arriving when Harold was already dead, slashed into his thigh, almost severing it. Such was the savage death of the last Saxon king.

Harold's body was so mangled during the Battle of Hastings that afterwards no one, not even his mother Gytha or his nephew Haakon, could pick out his remains from the jumbled corpses. The one hope of identification lay with Harold's mistress, Edith of the Swan Neck. She was taken to the battlefield and with her own hands she undid the chain-mail armour on his chest, and recognised a tattoo on his skin.

Despite Gytha's pleas, William the Conqueror refused to give Harold a proper burial, so his body was simply placed, wrapped in royal purple, under a rough cairn of stones on the cliffs at Hastings.

Many years later his body was reburied in Waltham Abbey in Essex, and given a tomb of plain grey marble. But his remains were destined to be swept away and lost for ever when Henry VIII destroyed the monasteries.

Perhaps it ought to be added that a recent researcher has made a claim that Harold's body is buried in Holy Trinity Church, Bosham, on the Sussex coast. Experts disagree. But visitors to this little village church can see a gravestone marking the burial spot of King Canute's little eight-year-old daughter, who was drowned in the nearby mill stream. Her bones were uncovered and examined in 1865 and have now been given a new memorial stone marked by a striking black raven, emblem of the marauding Danes.

# WILLIAM I (THE CONQUEROR)

## DIED 9 SEPTEMBER 1087   AGED *c.* 60

### *Abbey of St Stephen, Caen, Normandy*

When William married Matilda, it was totally against the Pope's wishes because they were distant cousins. As a result, they were both excommunicated. Eventually, the Pope pardoned them, on condition that as a penance each of them should build an abbey. Accordingly, two abbeys were built in Caen in Normandy. Matilda built the Abbaye aux Dames, where she still lies buried. William built the Abbaye aux Hommes (the Abbey of St Stephen), where he was buried.

The story of the Conqueror's death is quite macabre. He died in Rouen, and, after the nobles attending him had left the room, the household servants plundered the whole apartment, even stripping the dead king of his clothes. It was left to one loyal supporter to convey William to Caen for burial.

Then, at the service in St Stephen's Abbey, proceedings were interrupted twice: once because a fire broke out and everyone scattered to help put it out; and then, quite astonishingly, because the original owner of the land on which William had built the abbey came forward to claim that the land had never been paid for! William's son, the future King Henry I, had to fork out 60 shillings there and then, and promise to pay the rest as soon as he could.

Unfortunately, the Huguenots destroyed William's sarcophagus in the sixteenth century, and at the time of the French Revolution almost all the Conqueror's bones were thrown into the River Orne and lost. A thigh-bone, however, is believed to have remained, and this was solemnly reburied under a new tombstone in front of the altar in the Abbaye aux Hommes as recently as 1987.

# WILLIAM II (RUFUS)
## MURDERED (?) 2 AUGUST 1100    AGED 44
### Winchester Cathedral, Hampshire

No one will ever know exactly what happened in the New Forest on that August day in 1100. Purkiss the charcoal-burner took the corpse to Winchester Cathedral, and the monks received it grudgingly and with horror.

For many years it was believed that the tomb between the choir stalls of Winchester Cathedral contained the bones of Rufus, but now it is thought that this is the tomb of Henry of Blois, Bishop of Winchester and brother of King Stephen. Rufus's bones are more likely to be mingled with those of the Saxon kings and bishops in the cathedral's 'Mortuary Chests'.

Writing in 1643, a cleric described how the Parliamentarian soldiers 'threw down the Chests, wherein were deposited the bones of . . . William Rufus, Queen Emma, of Hardecanutus . . .'. This was a period of crass destruction. The soldiers smashed the cathedral windows – 'which they could not reach with their Swords, Muskets, or Rests, . . .' – 'by throwing at them the bones of Kings, Queenes, Bishops, Confessors and Saints'. So, Rufus's bones came in handy for this wanton seventeenth-century vandalism.

# HENRY I

## DIED 1 DECEMBER 1135   AGED 67

*Reading Abbey, Berkshire. Now lost*

It took Henry a week to die of ptomaine poisoning after eating a huge dish of slimy, eel-like creatures called lampreys, ignoring his doctor's advice not to eat them. Lampreys were an expensive delicacy in medieval times and the city of Gloucester presented a lamprey-pie to the sovereign every Christmas, as a token of loyalty. Henry loved them.

Lampreys, however, have poisonous filaments in the back, which must be removed before cooking. Perhaps the cooks did not do their job properly. At all events, Henry seems to have known that he was dying, and during the week following the fatal meal he had time to organise his own funeral in his beloved Reading Abbey. He had laid the foundation stone himself fifteen years before.

The site of his burial-place is still marked there today with a cross, but of course the abbey itself was mostly destroyed in the reign of Henry VIII.

# STEPHEN

## DIED 25 OCTOBER 1154   AGED 57

*Faversham Abbey, Kent. Now lost*

Stephen died in Dover Castle and the following year his body was buried in the abbey at Faversham, Kent, which he had founded a few years earlier. At the time of the Dissolution of the monasteries his tomb was destroyed and his bones were thrown into the nearby river. The church of St Mary of Charity, Faversham, is claimed to be his final resting-place. This, however, is open to speculation.

# HENRY II

## DIED 6 JULY 1189   AGED 55

*Fontevrault Abbey, France*

As he lay dying of a cerebral haemorrhage, Henry had been forced to sign a humiliating treaty by his son, the future Richard I, who had just conquered him in battle. He asked for a list of Richard's supporters to be read out to him, for he had promised to pardon them. His anguish was complete when the name at the top of the list turned out to be that of his youngest son, John. He realised he had no one left to trust.

'Now let all things go as they will, for I care no more for myself nor for anything in the world,' he murmured. His last words reveal his misery: 'Shame, shame on a conquered King!'

An old chronicle tells that when Richard came to view his father's corpse which was lying in state, blood flowed from the old king's nostrils, 'as if his spirit were angered at Richard's approach'. Henry died in the castle at Chinon, France, and is buried in Fontevrault Abbey, a few miles south of Saumur.

# RICHARD I (THE LIONHEART)
## DIED 6 APRIL 1199   AGED 41
### *Fontevrault Abbey, France*

Richard died of a gangrenous arrow-wound in his shoulder. He too is buried in Fontevrault Abbey, as are both his parents and Isabella of Angoulême, wife of King John. This abbey had been founded in 1099, and was rather unusual, being a monastic society of both monks and nuns. It was rich, and its abbesses were subject only to the Pope. The impressive tombs and carved effigies have survived well. The Order of Fontevrault was abolished after the French Revolution and the abbey itself turned into a state prison during the time of Napoleon.

Although Richard's body is in Fontevrault, he asked that his heart should be buried in Rouen Cathedral. This was rediscovered in 1838, and placed within a silver box which was contained within a lead box. It was noted at the time that it was 'reduced to the semblance of a dry, reddish leaf'.

# JOHN
## DIED 18/19 OCTOBER 1216   AGED 49
### *Worcester Cathedral*

The story goes that when King John boasted that he would soon raise the price of a half-penny loaf to twenty shillings, a monk decided to poison him. The monk sought absolution beforehand, and then prepared poisoned peaches for the king. One version of the tale says that when he was presented with the dish, John asked the monk to eat some first. With great courage the monk did so, leaving the room immediately so that he would not die in front of the king.

John was granted his wish to be buried in Worcester Cathedral, near his favourite saint, Wulfstan. His effigy there is beautifully preserved.

When his tomb was opened up in 1797 his body was found to be wrapped in a monk's cowl and robes of crimson damask. Having been inspected, John's remains were duly put back again, but not before one of his thumb-bones had been nefariously taken.

However, the person who took the bone must have had a crisis of conscience, for it was returned shortly afterwards. It seemed hardly worth disinterring John again to put the thumb back on, so for many years this grisly object was on view, mounted in gold, in a nearby case. Sad to say, even this has now somehow disappeared. So the hand that once put the seal to Magna Carta is mutilated for ever.

# HENRY III

## DIED 16 NOVEMBER 1272   AGED 65

### *Westminster Abbey*

Henry III completely rebuilt Westminster Abbey, and so much of what we see there today was his own personal gift to posterity. It is only fitting therefore that he should be buried in this place, after dying peacefully in his sleep.

Henry had given Edward the Confessor a magnificent new tomb, and Henry's own remains, royally robed, were placed in the Confessor's original coffin for burial near the saint he had so much venerated. Such a resting-place would have pleased him deeply.

The Knights-Templar undertook the funeral arrangements, and it was at their expense that his sumptuous monument was erected, adorned with precious stones from the Holy Land, brought back by his son, Edward I, for that purpose.

In fact, Henry was the first king after Edward the Confessor to be buried in Westminster Abbey. Such was its magnificence after his rebuilding that afterwards most English kings were buried there right up to the time of

George III, when St George's Chapel, Windsor, became the preferred place of burial.

Although Henry III's body is in Westminster Abbey, his heart was cut out and now lies in Fontevrault Abbey, France, with his Angevin ancestors.

# EDWARD I

## DIED 7 JULY 1307    AGED 68

### Westminster Abbey

Edward died of dysentery and bowel haemorrhage. He never fulfilled his ambition to conquer the Scots, so on his deathbed he asked his son, Edward II, to boil the flesh off his bones, wrap them up, and carry them at the head of his army as a kind of talisman. That way he would be sure of success.

However, he was never boiled, and his bones still lie in Westminster Abbey, quite close to the shrine of Edward the Confessor, after whom he was named. Needless to say, the Scots were never conquered.

Someone in the sixteenth century carved the inscription on his tomb which we can see today: '*Edward primus Scottorum malleus hic est. Pactum serva*' – 'Edward I, hammer of the Scots, is here. Keep the agreement'.

Edward was noted for his long legs; his nickname was 'Longshanks'.

# EDWARD II

## MURDERED 21 SEPTEMBER 1327    AGED 43

### Gloucester Cathedral

The homosexual Edward II was murdered by having a red-hot poker thrust up his anus. Probably this unspeakably cruel assassination was a deliberate way of making the royal corpse, when on display, appear to have no wound.

After he was killed in Berkeley Castle, Gloucestershire, his body was taken to Gloucester Cathedral for burial. His tomb immediately became an object of pilgrimage, and the cathedral amassed great riches from the thousands of pilgrims and sight-seers who came to visit it. Edward's tomb is one of the finest in England.

# EDWARD III
## DIED 21 JUNE 1377   AGED 65
### *Westminster Abbey*

Edward III died in his palace at Sheen, allegedly from gonorrhoea contracted from his mistress, Alice Perrers. (Sheen Palace was later pulled down by Richard II and rebuilt by Henry VII as Richmond Palace.)

Edward was said to have a face like a god, and certainly his tomb in Westminster Abbey has a magnificently noble bronze effigy. Also still on view in Westminster Abbey Museum is his death-mask, made of plaster and linen.

The French historian Jean Froissart, who was a friend of Edward III and a frequent guest at his court, wrote a vivid account of Edward's death.

Shameful to relate, during the whole time that he was bed-ridden, King Edward had been attended by that infamous whore Alice Perrers, who always reminded him of things of the flesh. . . .

When she realised that he had lost the power of speech and that his eyes had dulled, and that the natural warmth had left his body, quickly that shameless doxy dragged the rings from his fingers and left.

# RICHARD II
## DIED (PROBABLY MURDERED) EARLY FEBRUARY 1400
## AGED 33
### *Westminster Abbey*

No one knows how Richard II died. Shakespeare's account of his murder by 'Sir Pierce of Exton' is pure guess-work. However, disappear he did. And when the French King insisted on knowing what had happened to him (after all, he was naturally curious to know whether or not his daughter Isabella was now a widow), the reply came back that Richard had died a natural death in Pontefract Castle.

Rumours were rife. Some said he had been murdered; others said that he was still alive. A poster even appeared on the door of St Paul's to say that Richard would soon be coming back to reclaim his throne from the usurper King Henry IV. It was all very mysterious and embarrassing.

Eventually, to get rid of all these rumours, Henry IV ordered Richard's body to be brought through London in a public procession from Pontefract

Castle to Langley Priory, in Hertfordshire, where he was to be privately buried in the cloister. An astonishing sight was now produced. Richard's dead body, dressed in royal robes, with a crown on his head and a sceptre in his hand, was drawn on a bier with an escort of knights and friars bearing lighted torches, all the way from Pontefract in Yorkshire to Cheapside in London. There, it was exhibited for everyone to see. Richard's body was then taken for burial at Langley Priory, where it lay for over fourteen years.

Then, in 1413, King Henry V decided that Richard deserved a better resting-place, so he ordered Richard's remains to be brought to Westminster Abbey, to be buried in the tomb which Richard himself had prepared.

In the eighteenth century holes appeared in the side of his tomb and a mischievous schoolboy pulled out Richard's jawbone. One of the boy's companions, named Andrews, fought him for it, and the jawbone stayed with the Andrews family for 130 years. They kept it on a writing desk. It wasn't put back until 1906.

# HENRY IV
## DIED 20 MARCH 1413    AGED 46
### Canterbury Cathedral

After suffering greatly from eczema and epilepsy, Henry IV finally succumbed to a seizure. A fortune-teller had once told him that he would die in Jerusalem. Although he never actually got to the Holy Land, the prophecy was fulfilled in a curious way. Henry was taken ill while he was praying at the shrine of Edward the Confessor. He was carried into a nearby room that was hung with tapestries depicting events in the history of Jerusalem. The room was named the 'Jerusalem Chamber', and there he died. (Visitors to Westminster Abbey may be interested to know that this 'Jerusalem Chamber' is alongside the Abbey bookshop just outside the east front.)

Henry, the usurper, suffered badly from his guilty conscience, having ousted Richard II from the throne. Perhaps it was this feeling of 'blood-guiltiness' that prevented him from asking to be buried among the other kings in Westminster Abbey. Or perhaps he wanted St Thomas Becket to intercede for him on the Day of Judgement. At any rate, he arranged a burial for himself in the Becket Chapel in Canterbury Cathedral, near the tomb of the Black Prince, and here he has a splendid tomb.

A story was put about that when the royal corpse was being taken by boat to Faversham, on its way to Canterbury, the superstitious sailors were so terrified by a sudden storm that they threw the body into the sea. Later, so it was said, they substituted another corpse in its place.

To test the truth of this, Henry IV's wooden coffin was opened in 1832 and it was found that there was another air-tight leaden coffin inside. And when they opened this, a spine-tingling sight was revealed: the face of the king was in a state of complete preservation, with a thick beard 'of a deep russet colour'. Apparently the Royal Usurper had one front tooth missing, which had probably been lost during his lifetime. Exposed now to the air, the facial features quickly disintegrated.

# HENRY V

## DIED 31 AUGUST 1422    AGED 35

### Westminster Abbey

Henry V died of dysentery in the Château of Vincennes, on the outskirts of Paris, so his body faced a journey of several weeks before it could be buried as he wished, in Westminster Abbey. The only practical way to deal with the problem therefore was to dismember him, and boil the flesh from off his bones. The water in which they were boiled was put in a French cemetery, and the cleaned-off bones were then brought back to England in a lead coffin.

Catherine, his young widow, not yet twenty-one, was grief-stricken. She paid for a beautiful silver statue to put over Henry's tomb in Westminster Abbey but this disappeared at the time of the Dissolution of the monasteries. Today, Henry has a new one made of polyester resin.

# HENRY VI

## MURDERED 21 MAY 1471    AGED 49

### St George's Chapel, Windsor

Henry VI dearly wished to be buried right next to Edward the Confessor and even as a young man he had the exact spot marked out on the stone floor.

It seems certain that he was murdered in the Tower of London, but the precise details will probably never be known. All that is certain is that the decisive Battle of Tewkesbury took place on 4 May 1471, and that King Henry rather conveniently 'died' in prison a few days later, on 21 May.

Henry's successor, Edward IV, felt it necessary to prove that he was really dead, otherwise perhaps people would have spread rumours that he was planning to return. Therefore, the corpse was borne bare-faced 'that every man might see it' on its bier to a funeral service in Old St Paul's. To everyone's horror, in the middle of the service, the corpse began to bleed. And it kept on bleeding. Clearly it was trying to get a message across – 'a dread token of the manner of his death,' so it was believed.

It would have been embarrassing to bury Henry in a prominent place such as Westminster Abbey, so Edward IV had him bundled off to be buried in the relatively obscure abbey at Chertsey, in Surrey. Thirteen years later, however, Richard III ordered the body to be disinterred and brought to St George's Chapel, Windsor, where it still lies.

Miracles began to occur around Henry's tomb, and it soon became a place of pilgrimage. The original octagonal iron money box can still be seen beside the tomb, with the royal initial H, and twenty coin slits for pilgrims' offerings.

Henry VI might well have had an even more imposing resting-place, for it was the intention of Henry VII, his nephew, to have Henry VI canonised and buried yet again in his specially built new chapel in Westminster Abbey – the 'Chapel of King Henry VII' at the far east end of the abbey, with the wonderfully beautiful vaulted roof. The Pope agreed. The building plans went ahead. However, Henry VII died before either the building or the canonisation could take place. Then, of course, came the Reformation and the subsequent break with Rome so Henry VI just failed to make sainthood after all.

# EDWARD IV

## DIED 9 APRIL 1483   AGED 40

### St George's Chapel, Windsor

Edward IV was responsible for rebuilding St George's Chapel, Windsor, and creating the lovely place we know today. In fact, he was prompted partly by jealousy, because he wanted to outdo Eton Chapel, which had been built by Henry VI. It was inevitable, then, that his remains should lie in the place that he had just created.

Edward died of pneumonia or perhaps typhoid, aged forty, his health having been undermined by all sorts of imaginable excesses. As his death was not expected, there were rumours of foul play. Therefore, to allay suspicion, his disembowelled and embalmed body was put on public exhibition for ten whole days, naked to the waist, in the Chapel of Westminster Palace. Thousands of people filed past the corpse, making quite sure that he really was dead.

Then the king's body was taken to Westminster Abbey for a Requiem Mass, after which, followed by a vast procession, it was carried slowly on its way to Windsor for burial in the newly built St George's Chapel.

Edward IV was the first monarch to be buried in the new chapel, needing an outsize oaken coffin to contain his vast frame. It has always been claimed that he was England's tallest king, at 6 foot 4 inches (193 cm).

# EDWARD V

## MURDERED (?) 3 SEPTEMBER 1483   AGED 12

### Resting-place unknown

No one knows what became of the 'Princes in the Tower'. They were brought to the Tower of London on the death of their father, Edward IV, and then simply disappeared.

Bones were discovered in 1674 during some work on a stairway in the Tower of London. An eyewitness wrote that 'they were small bones, of lads in their teens and there were pieces of rag and velvet about them'. Charles II had these bones buried in an urn in Westminster Abbey. This is to be found in the north aisle of the Chapel of Henry VII, on the east wall, just a few feet away from the combined tomb of Queen Mary I and Queen Elizabeth I. It is easy to miss it, especially as the inscription is in Latin. Of course, no one could prove beyond doubt that these were really the remains of the young princes, but most people assumed so.

The bones were examined in 1933, but the results could only be guesswork. And they were examined yet again in 1987, and an article appeared in *The Times* on 21 May, which stated that the bones were indeed almost certainly those of the princes. Immediately on the publication of that article, however, a chorus of disbelieving letters appeared, and there was a call for carbon-dating. Nowadays DNA tests might prove something, but the discussion, it seems, will go on for ever.

# RICHARD III
## KILLED 22 AUGUST 1485  AGED 33
### *Grey Friars' Abbey, Leicester. Now lost*

Thrown over a horse, Richard's naked body was brought back to Leicester after the Battle of Bosworth and exposed to public view for three days in the Grey Friars' Abbey and then buried in an unmarked grave there.

On Bow Bridge in Leicester there is a tablet declaring that Richard's spur struck a large stone on that bridge as he passed over it on the way to Bosworth, and that on the way back, lying dead on the packhorse, Richard's head was dashed and broken on the selfsame stone. The event had been prophesied by a 'wise woman'.

When the Grey Friars' Abbey was destroyed in the time of Henry VIII, Richard's bones are said to have been thrown into the River Soar. However, recent research has suggested that his bones may lie under a car park in Leicester. The fact is, no one knows.

# HENRY VII
## DIED 21 APRIL 1509  AGED 52
### *Westminster Abbey*

In contrast to Richard III, Henry VII, the victor at Bosworth, has one of the finest tombs of any English king. Not only is the tomb itself a magnificent piece of work, by the Italian Renaissance sculptor Torrigiano, but the chapel in which it stands, ordered by Henry himself, is one of the greatest masterpieces of architecture in England. It was his son, Henry VIII, who supervised the tomb and the completion of this magnificent Henry VII's Chapel in Westminster Abbey.

The death-mask of Henry VII is one of the finest to be seen, and is on view in the Undercroft Museum in Westminster Abbey. It is astonishingly lifelike, and when it was carefully examined in 1950 it was noticed that one of the eyebrows shows how the grease used in taking the mould has clotted the hair. This would suggest that it is a genuine mask, and not just a made-up face.

# HENRY VIII
## DIED 28 JANUARY 1547   AGED 55
### St George's Chapel, Windsor

When Henry died, possibly of syphilis, he was a mass of rotten flesh. He died at Whitehall and his huge carcass was put into a lead coffin and taken in procession through the streets of London and reached Syon House at twilight. It was put down in Syon Chapel, and there a horrific event took place. According to a contemporary account:

> . . . the leaden coffin being cleft by the shaking of the carriage, the pavement of the church was wetted with Henry's blood. In the morning came plumbers to solder the coffin, under whose feet was seen a dog creeping and licking up the King's blood.

The story gained wide circulation and people remembered Friar Peto's denunciation of the king from the pulpit of Greenwich Church four years previously, in which the bold friar compared Henry with Ahab, and told him to his face 'that the dogs would, in like manner, lick his blood'.

Henry was buried in St George's Chapel, Windsor, and had a large marble sarcophagus built over the burial spot. Today, however, Henry's burial place is marked only by a small memorial plaque on the floor. His sarcophagus had to be moved in the eighteenth century when King George III ordered a new enlarged vault to be made under the floor of the chapel, large enough to contain forty-eight coffins.

Oddly enough, Henry VIII's sarcophagus was never put back in its rightful place, but was commandeered in the next century and is now the tomb of Vice-Admiral the Viscount Nelson in the crypt of St Paul's in London.

It has recently come to light that in 1813 a workman in the vault stole one of Henry VIII's finger bones and subsequently used it to make a knife-handle. It can only be assumed that this gruesome artefact still exists somewhere.

# EDWARD VI

## DIED 6 JULY 1553    AGED 15

### *Westminster Abbey*

Edward VI was only fifteen when he died of consumption aggravated by an attack of the measles. He had been completely dominated by his guardian, the Duke of Northumberland, who was plotting desperately to put his daughter-in-law Lady Jane Grey on the throne. In the last stages of the plot, everything hinged on the timing of the young king's death. Northumberland dismissed the king's doctors and brought in a female quack, who gave the king arsenic to stop his haemorrhages and prolong his wretched life for a few more days.

The problem came when Edward actually did die. Northumberland had the corpse disembowelled and put in its coffin with the utmost speed, lest the poisoning should become suspected. One of the Duke's own sons is reported as having said that his father did not dare let Edward lie in state, and had 'buried him privately in a paddock adjoining the Palace, and substituted in his place, to be seen by the people, a young man not very unlike him, whom they had murdered'.

This scenario is not proven, but certainly the manipulation of Edward's death was a very shady business. It is just possible that the bones under the altar in Henry VII's Chapel in Westminster Abbey are not quite what one would expect.

# LADY JANE GREY

## EXECUTED 12 FEBRUARY 1554    AGED 16

### *The Tower of London*

Jane paid the ultimate price for other people's treason. The story of her execution is painful to contemplate: we can but admire her awesome courage. The British Museum still holds her small prayer-book, from which she read as she walked to the scaffold.

As she knelt, blindfolded, she stretched out to where she thought the execution block was, and at first could not find it, having misjudged the distance. 'Where is it? Where is it?' she called out in distress. And a spectator had to climb up to guide her towards it. The executioner was exceptionally tall and burly: one blow was enough.

The French Ambassador who witnessed the event remarked that he was 'amazed at the great effusion of blood, the body being so small'. Everyone must have been appalled at the sight, and the body lay on the scaffold for some hours, half naked, before it was finally removed for burial.

The Nine Days Queen was buried a few yards away, in the Chapel of St Peter ad Vincula, in the Tower of London.

# MARY I AND ELIZABETH I
## DIED 17 NOVEMBER 1558   AGED 42
## DIED 24 MARCH 1603   AGED 69
### Westminster Abbey

These two queens, half-sisters, and with such contrasting characters and religious beliefs, lie together in what looks at first to be one tomb in Westminster Abbey.

Mary, of course, was buried first, and lies underneath. She died during an influenza epidemic. Her embalmed body was in fact buried as a king, because there was no precedent for a ruling queen's funeral. Accordingly, and rather oddly, a helmet, sword and body-armour were carried before her corpse, on the way to Westminster Abbey. Hers was the last Catholic funeral to be held in the Abbey, celebrated in Latin.

Her successor, Elizabeth, was at the funeral, and heard Bishop White of Winchester give the funeral sermon also in Latin, a language which she understood as clearly as English. The tactless bishop, praising the late Queen Mary, said in Latin: 'Our late sovereign hath left a sister, a lady of great worth, behind her, whom we are bound to obey, for a living dog is better than a dead lion.' Elizabeth was so enraged at this that she had the bishop arrested on the spot, even as he left the pulpit.

There followed an amazing scene, in which the bishop threatened to excommunicate the new queen. But Elizabeth diplomatically pardoned him: she evidently didn't want to stir up even more religious trouble.

Elizabeth's monument lies on top of Mary's, as one might expect. The face of her effigy lying there is an exact portrait, taken from her death-mask.

She took a couple of weeks or more to die from infected tonsils, at times refusing to take nourishment or even to go to bed. Her courtiers were nonplussed as she slid in and out of consciousness, and they pressed her as far as they dared to make some sort of sign to tell them who her successor should be.

At times Elizabeth's old spirit returned. When Secretary Cecil told her that 'to content the people she *must* go to bed' she smiled at him with regal pride: 'Little man, little man! The word *must* is not to be used to princes!'

But she knew she was dying, and in her last hours she was desperately reluctant to let the Archbishop of Canterbury leave her bedside. She needed his prayers.

The inscription on the double grave is poignant, especially when one considers the turbulent days in which they both lived. A translation reads:

> Consorts both in throne and grave, here rest
> we two sisters, Elizabeth and Mary, in the
> hope of one Resurrection.

# JAMES I

## DIED 27 MARCH 1625    AGED 59

### *Westminster Abbey*

James I, the 'wisest fool in Christendom', died following a stroke, complicated by dysentery. There followed the most extraordinarily elaborate funeral ever known in England. After his death, James's body lay in state in Somerset House for a month, while Inigo Jones created a gigantic hearse with four caryatides at the corners, made of 'playster of Paris', but looking like white marble.

The sum of £50,000 was lavished on the funeral arrangements – an enormous amount of money in those days. Black cloth was provided for nine thousand people who were all required to file past the coffin. Although the hearse set off from Denmark House at about ten in the morning, there were so many people involved that the service in Westminster Abbey couldn't get started until five in the afternoon.

Despite all this, there is no monument in the Abbey for James I. Indeed, it is a curious fact that none of the Stuarts has a monument erected over them, except Mary, Queen of Scots, who of course was never Queen of England.

# CHARLES I

## EXECUTED 30 JANUARY 1649   AGED 48

### *St George's Chapel, Windsor*

The execution of Charles I took place just outside the Banqueting Hall in Whitehall. It was a cold January day and the king took the precaution of wearing two shirts so that he shouldn't be seen to shiver, and thus be accused of being a coward.

According to someone who saw the event the king lay fully stretched out on his stomach with his head on the block. After the execution the head was lifted up and held by the hair 'and thus shown to the people'. A bystander said that the crowd made 'such a groan . . . as I never heard before, and desire I may never hear again'.

Charles had wanted to be buried in Westminster Abbey near his father, but this wish was not granted. He was taken to St George's Chapel, Windsor, and laid in the royal vault not far from Henry VIII, Jane Seymour and Edward IV. The body was embalmed and the head was stitched back on to it by Thomas Fairfax's surgeon.

At the Restoration, Parliament gave Charles II £70,000 to pay for a royal monument, but when it was announced that the body of Charles I could not be found, no one thought to ask for the money back. It was not until 1813 that a coffin was found, and the Royal Physician Sir Henry Halford was asked to investigate the contents. Sure enough, it held the body and severed head of Charles I. Secretly, Sir Henry stole the piece of vertebra where the executioner's axe had fallen, took it home, and had it set in gold for use as a salt-cellar.

Decades later Queen Victoria heard about it. She was definitely not amused, and ordered its instant return to its proper place in the vault of St George's. It was duly returned in 1888, in a wooden casket encased in oak and lead, which now rests on top of Charles's coffin.

# OLIVER CROMWELL

## DIED 3 SEPTEMBER 1658   AGED 59

### *Westminster Abbey. Now lost*

Oliver Cromwell was given a magnificent funeral in Westminster Abbey, but when the monarchy was restored in 1660 Charles II gave his approval to Parliament's decision to dig up his corpse. The order was for the remains of Cromwell, Ireton, and Bradshaw to be taken up and dragged on hurdles to Tyburn 'there to be hanged in their coffins for some time with their faces turned towards Whitehall, and then buried under the gallows'.

All this was done. The vault in Westminster Abbey was opened in the presence of the Speaker of the House of Commons. The body was dragged to Tyburn, and Cromwell and his two confederates were hanged on the gallows until sunset. At sunset they were cut down and decapitated and their heads were stuck on poles over the top of Westminster Hall, with Cromwell's in the middle. The bodies were quartered. A local tradition claims that the mutilated remains of all three men were interred in Red Lion Square, Holborn.

As for Cromwell's head, it stayed on the pike over Westminster Hall for twenty-five years, and then it blew down in a gale. A passing soldier picked it up and took it home in his cloak and hid it up a chimney, confessing the deed to his wife only on his deathbed.

The wife sold it to the Russell family of Cambridge, and Samuel Russell earned himself an honest shilling or two exhibiting it in Covent Garden, finally selling it to someone called Cox for £118. Cox, in turn, sold it to three men, and the niece of one of these sold it to a Mr Wilkinson, and the head remained in the Wilkinson family for several generations.

The last Wilkinson to own Cromwell's head died at a ripe old age in 1992, but he had been increasingly uneasy at possessing it. He had it most carefully examined by a leading anthropologist, who pronounced it a 'moral certainty' to be that of Cromwell. Having had it rejected by Westminster Abbey, by St Paul's Cathedral and by the then Home Secretary ('Rab' Butler), it was finally offered to, and accepted by Sidney Sussex College, Cambridge, where Oliver had studied in his youth. Visitors to the college may see an elegant plaque in the College Chapel, noting the fact that Oliver Cromwell's head has its final resting-place nearby.

# RICHARD CROMWELL
## DIED 1712    AGED 86
### *Hursley Parish Church, Hampshire*

Richard Cromwell died at a ripe old age and is buried in the little village church at Hursley, about 6 miles from Winchester, Hampshire. No one knows exactly where his burial site is, except that he lies somewhere under

All Saints' Church. The fact is that when John Keble, the famous high-church Victorian hymn-writer, was vicar of Hursley, he rebuilt this church in 1848 out of the profits he made from his popular collection of poems, *The Christian Year*. Keble was so strongly anti-Puritan that he flatly refused to have anything to do with the Cromwells in his newly rebuilt church. It was only in 1993 that a plaque was put up in the church in memory of Richard Cromwell.

So Richard Cromwell's remains are in Hursley church, together with his wife and eight of his children. Today there is no direct descendant of either Oliver or Richard Cromwell.

# CHARLES II
## DIED 6 FEBRUARY 1685   AGED 54
### *Westminster Abbey*

Charles II was only fifty-four when he died, of uraemia caused by gouty kidneys, very unexpectedly, after an orgy. John Evelyn, the diarist, gives a vivid account of the situation:

> I can never forget the inexpressible luxury and prophanenesse, gaming and all dissoluteness and as it were total forgetfullnesse of God (it being Sunday evening) which this day se'nnight I was witnesse of, the King sitting and toying with his concubines, Portsmouth, Cleveland, and Mazarine, etc., a French boy singing love songs, in that glorious gallery, whilst about 20 of the greate courtiers and other dissolute persons were at Basset round a large table, a bank of at least 2000 in gold before them, upon which two gentlemen who were with me made reflexions with astonishment. Six days after was all in the dust!

The king died in public, surrounded by five bishops, twenty-five peers, Privy Councillors, foreign ambassadors, six doctors, the queen, his brother, and ten ladies-in-waiting.

When he knew for certain that he was dying, Charles asked for the crowds to be hustled out and then, with great secrecy, Father Huddleston, a priest who had saved the king's life after the Battle of Worcester, entered from behind an arras. He first admitted Charles into the Catholic Church, received the king's final penance, and finally administered the last rites. The priest disappeared, and the crowds were let back in.

On Wednesday 6 February 1685 the king died, and he was buried at midnight on 14 February in Westminster Abbey. It was a mysterious burial.

The suddenness of his death led to many rumours that he had been poisoned. Quite reputable courtiers, including the Duchess of Portsmouth, one of Charles's own mistresses, went on record as believing this. But of course it could never be proved.

# JAMES II

## DIED 16 SEPTEMBER 1701 IN EXILE    AGED 67

### St Germain-en-Laye, France

James II, ousted from the throne by his daughter Mary and her husband William of Orange, lived in exile until his death from a brain haemorrhage in the Château of St Germain-en-Laye, near Versailles, France. The Château had previous Stuart connections because Mary, Queen of Scots (who had also previously been Queen of France), had lived there between the ages of six and sixteen. Louis XIV had been born there.

James was laid in the former Church of the English Benedictines in the Rue St-Jacques, Paris. (This is now No. 269 Rue St-Jacques, a music, dance and drama school.) He was not buried, but simply put in one of the side chapels. His daughter Queen Anne made no effort to give her father a proper tomb. However, lights were kept burning round his coffin right up to the time of the French Revolution.

The final chapter in James's extraordinary story came when the revolutionaries broke into the church, and prised open his coffin. To their astonishment, his corpse was entire, in an amazing state of preservation. Immediately, all those who were bent on destruction were filled with superstitious awe and their mood changed completely. The municipal authorities then stepped in, took charge of the remains, and James's corpse was put on public exhibition, with many thousands of citizens paying for the privilege of viewing it.

Miracles were said to have happened, and eventually Robespierre gave orders for the body to be buried. However, his instructions were ignored and the body was still being kept above ground when the allies arrived in Paris. When George IV heard about it, he ordered the corpse to be taken to its final resting-place in the parish church of St Germain-en-Laye. So, in 1824, after a solemn funeral procession from Paris to St Germain-en-Laye, James was at last given a funeral of royal splendour. The Stuart saga was over.

# WILLIAM III AND MARY II
## DIED 8 MARCH 1702   AGED 51
## DIED 28 DECEMBER 1694   AGED 32
### *Westminster Abbey*

Mary died with great dignity, realising that the disease she had contracted, smallpox, was fatal. She spent her final hours carefully going through all her papers, and forbade her sister Anne to visit her, lest she too should catch the infection and die.

'Dutch William', none too affectionate or faithful to Mary during her lifetime, was overcome with grief and gave her a magnificent funeral in Westminster Abbey, which was the first ever attended by both houses of parliament. At her lying-in-state in Whitehall there were 300 glass chandeliers, each with 100 candles. Thousands of yards of black cloth were distributed among would-be mourners, and 200 poor old women were given black gowns so that they could join the funeral procession.

After her death William ruled alone for eight years, and then he was thrown from his horse while riding to Hampton Court, sustaining a broken collar-bone. His horse had stumbled on a molehill. He went on to the palace, where the bone was set, but then he insisted on riding back to Kensington Palace, despite the fall. Pneumonia set in, and he died just over a fortnight later.

William's funeral, also in Westminster Abbey, cost far less than Mary's. Very few people mourned his death, and those who wished to see the return of the Old Pretender would frequently raise their glasses to the 'little gentleman in black velvet' (i.e. the mole who had provided the convenient stumbling-place for William's horse).

William lies next to Charles II in the Abbey vaults. He has no monument.

# ANNE
## DIED 1 AUGUST 1714   AGED 49
### *Westminster Abbey*

It has been reported that Anne's body became so fat with dropsy that her coffin had to be completely square. She had appalling health problems, not helped by her notorious gluttony. She died of cerebral haemorrhage.

Anne also lies in Westminster Abbey, but there is no memorial of any kind. The only reminder of Queen Anne in the Abbey is the wax figure in

Undercroft Museum there. Oddly and inexplicably, the remains of all her sixteen tiny babies were put into the huge tomb of Mary Queen of Scots, where they still lie, together with the bones of her sole surviving child, the pathetic little Duke of Gloucester, who died aged eleven.

# GEORGE I

## DIED 28 MAY (?) 1727    AGED 67

### *Herrenhausen, Hanover, Germany*

George I much preferred to be in Germany rather than in England, so perhaps it's just as well that his remains are now resting in his palace of Herrenhausen in Hanover.

He was superstitious and implicitly believed a fortune-teller who told him that he would not live more than a year after the death of his wife, Sophia Dorothea. When she did die, in November 1726, he left her unburied for six months, and then eventually decided to travel to Hanover to make the funeral arrangements. On his last departure for Germany, he took leave of his son and daughter-in-law, saying that he would never see them again.

True enough, George I had a stroke in his coach as he was approaching Osnabruck, and he died when he got there, in the very room in which he had been born, sixty-seven years before. His first burial place was in a church called the Leineschlosskirche in Hanover, and then after the Second World War his remains were reburied in the Herrenhausen Palace there.

# GEORGE II

## DIED 25 OCTOBER 1760    AGED 77

### *Westminster Abbey*

George II died while sitting on a loo in Kensington Palace. He suffered a heart attack. His queen, Caroline of Ansbach, had died twenty-three years previously. The king's wishes were that when he died the sides of the queen's coffin should be opened, and a side of his own should not be closed, so that his remains and those of Caroline should mingle in death. This was done.

Their remains are in one huge stone sarcophagus, which stands in the vault of Henry VII's Chapel. A century after George's funeral the planks removed from the two coffins were found resting up against a nearby wall.

George II and Caroline were the last English monarchs to be buried in Westminster Abbey. Since then, all monarchs except Victoria and Edward VIII have been buried in St George's Chapel, Windsor.

# GEORGE III

## DIED 29 JANUARY 1820    AGED 81

### *St George's Chapel, Windsor*

For the last ten years of his life George III cut a pathetic figure before he died of senile decay. A contemporary who saw him in his padded chamber at Windsor wrote:

> His hair was as white as snow, whilst his long beard flowed in a silvery shower to his waist. He was apparently quite happy, living in a world of dreams, singing snatches of old songs and talking to himself. He was, moreover, always gentle, but did not recognise even his own children.

In such a sad state George was given a very quiet funeral, but as it was he who had ordered a new enlarged vault to be made at St George's Chapel, it was fitting that he should be the first monarch to be buried there.

# GEORGE IV

## DIED 26 JUNE 1830    AGED 67

### *St George's Chapel, Windsor*

George IV became a grotesque mountain of flesh as a result of his greedy lifestyle. His sister Mary remarked that he was 'enormous, like a feather bed'. He finally died of a ruptured blood vessel in the stomach, and cirrhosis of the liver. A few days earlier, the Duke of Wellington saw him eat a typical breakfast of two pigeons, three steaks, three-quarters of a bottle of wine, a glass of champagne, two glasses of port, and a glass of brandy. Decades of gluttony speeded him to an unmourned grave.

Sir Wathen Waller, the king's physician, was with him in his final moments and afterwards wrote that 'he took my hand in his and I felt him instantly press it harder than usual and he looked at me with an eager eye and exclaimed, "My dear boy, this is Death!"'.

George knew his end was near and had asked that he should be buried 'with whatever ornaments might be upon my person at the time of death'. It was the Duke of Wellington who noted that he was wearing a black ribbon round his neck, carrying a small locket. That locket is still with his remains in Windsor's vault. It contains a miniature portrait of the only woman George really loved – Mrs Fitzherbert.

# WILLIAM IV
## DIED 20 JUNE 1837   AGED 71
### St George's Chapel, Windsor

William IV loathed Queen Victoria's mother, Victoria of Saxe-Coburg, who would have become Regent if he had died before the young princess was eighteen. He swore that he hoped to God his life might be spared till the princess came of age. Luckily for Victoria, his wish was granted. He survived for just a month after her eighteenth birthday, before succumbing to pneumonia and cirrhosis of the liver.

Another of William's wishes was that he might live to see another anniversary of Waterloo. 'I know that I am going,' he said to his doctors, 'but I should like to see another anniversary of Waterloo. Try if you cannot tinker me up to last over that date.' That wish was also granted. Two days later he was dead.

William's wife Adelaide survived for another twelve years, and was laid to rest beside him in St George's Chapel, Windsor.

# VICTORIA
## DIED 22 JANUARY 1901   AGED 81
### Royal Mausoleum, Frogmore, Windsor

After the death of her beloved Prince Albert in 1861 Victoria spent the last forty years of her life as a recluse. She was overwhelmed with grief and for years she slept with his nightclothes in her arms. Little wonder that when she died, of senile decay, she had no desire at all to be buried in Westminster Abbey or St George's. She simply had to lie next to Albert, who had been laid to rest in the Royal Mausoleum, Frogmore, near Windsor Castle.

She had previously given meticulously detailed instructions that a considerable number of items should be placed in her coffin: Albert's dressing-gown, a plaster cast of Albert's hand, rings, bracelets, lockets, photographs, handkerchieves, etc. All these were laid underneath her. She herself was wearing white, with her wedding veil over her face.

Finally, again according to her own private instructions, a photograph of John Brown and a case containing some of his hair were put in her left hand, which was then discreetly covered with flowers.

After an impressive funeral service in St George's, the funeral procession bore her off to Frogmore. She was ready to rejoin Albert.

The Royal Mausoleum is only rarely open to visitors, but those who are fortunate enough to have the opportunity to do so will see two beautiful recumbent effigies of the royal couple, carved in white marble. Albert is depicted as the young man he was when he died. As for Victoria, she had her own effigy carved at the same time – so that it is with a shock of surprise that we see her – youthful as ever – forever turning towards her beloved Albert in love.

# EDWARD VII
## DIED 6 MAY 1910   AGED 69
### St George's Chapel, Windsor

Edward VII enjoyed immense popularity. He died of heart failure, and it is estimated that a quarter of a million people filed past his body as he lay in state in Westminster Hall. His cousin, the Emperor William, 'Kaiser Bill', prayed beside the catafalque on which he rested.

In the funeral procession which moved through the streets of London from Westminster Hall to Paddington station, Edward's coffin was borne on a gun-carriage followed in strict precedence first by his fox-terrier Caesar, and then by the Kaiser, eight European kings and scores of other royals from all over the world. Edward, a strict observer of protocol, would have enjoyed the spectacle.

Edward and his queen, Alexandra, are buried to the south side of the high altar in St George's Chapel, Windsor, and visitors can enjoy their splendid monumental effigies. At Edward's feet is a carving of the little dog Caesar.

# GEORGE V

## DIED 20 JANUARY 1936    AGED 71

### *St George's Chapel, Windsor*

In his last months George V, suffering from a bronchial infection, had tried to restore his health in the seaside town of Bognor in Sussex, and the citizens were so proud of this that they sought to give dignity to their town's name by adding 'Regis' to it.

As the king's health steadily declined, a deputation from the town anxiously waited his decision. Being pestered on his deathbed was the last straw. Rumour has it that the last words uttered by the king were 'Bugger Bognor'. Readers of the *Daily Express*, however, were told that his last words had been 'How is the Empire?' To which Stanley Baldwin replied, 'All is well, Sire'. And the king smiled.

This story of the king's last words has now become a part of British folklore. But what is perhaps less well known is the way in which the king died. It is now on record that the king's physician actually injected a lethal dose of morphine and cocaine into the dying sovereign, partly to alleviate his suffering, and partly to speed up the process of dying. It was felt that it would be far more appropriate for the announcement of the king's death to appear in the morning papers, including *The Times*, than to be relegated to the less prestigious evening papers. This act of euthanasia was, of course, kept a close secret for many years.

The king died in Sandringham and was brought to St George's Chapel, Windsor. Marble effigies of George V and Queen Mary present remarkably lifelike memorials to these two dignified figures.

# EDWARD VIII

## DIED 28 MAY 1972    AGED 77

### *Royal Burial Ground, Frogmore, Windsor*

Choosing love and marriage to Mrs Simpson rather than duty and kingship, Edward lived a restless life, mostly in a kind of self-imposed exile, finally dying in his home in the Bois de Boulogne on the outskirts of Paris. He died of cancer of the throat shortly after a final visit by Queen Elizabeth, to whom he had always been 'Uncle David'.

It must have been a poignant moment, and of course there is no record of what passed between them. Apparently, the British Ambassador in Paris gave firm instructions to the duke's physician that the ex-king could die before the queen's visit, or indeed afterwards: but in no circumstances must Edward die during it. In fact, he managed to survive for another eight days.

His body was flown back to England and he was given a quiet burial in the Royal Burial Ground, Frogmore, in Windsor Home Park, near his great-grandparents Victoria and Albert.

# GEORGE VI

## DIED 1952   AGED 57

### St George's Chapel, Windsor

The people of Great Britain hardly knew just how ill George VI was. When he died the connection between smoking and lung cancer was only just beginning to be recognised, so his death from this disease came with surprise and shock.

He survived two major operations, and one of his cancerous lungs was removed. Special clothes were made, with a battery-operated heated waistcoat to keep him warm. The end, however, came suddenly and unexpectedly after a happy day spent shooting hares on his Sandringham estate. He died peacefully in his sleep.

His burial place is not in the royal vault with the other kings and queens. His body lies under a black ledger stone in a new, specially made Memorial Chapel built on to the north choir aisle of St George's Chapel, Windsor. This new King George VI Memorial Chapel was dedicated in 1969, seventeen years after the king's death.

On her death fifty years later on 30 March 2002, George's widow, Queen Elizabeth the Queen Mother, was laid to rest beside him within this same chapel.

# ROYAL MISTRESSES
# AND BASTARDS

❦ ❦

Records concerning the love lives of England's kings are understandably incomplete. Names of royal mistresses are not always documented or even known; some of those that have been preserved for posterity are listed below, and some of the stories told in this chapter. Although scarce, the evidence that does exist seems to suggest overwhelmingly that throughout history monogamous kings have been extremely rare. The Saxon King Edwy, perhaps, provides a suitable starting point for a closer look into the amorous affairs of some of England's monarchs.

## FAMOUS MISTRESSES OF ENGLISH KINGS

Harold II    Edith of the Swan Neck
Henry II    'Fair Rosamund'
Edward III    Alice Perrers
Edward IV    Elizabeth Shore, Elizabeth Lucy
Henry VIII    Lady Anne Hastings, Jane Popicourt, Elizabeth Blount, Mary
            Boleyn, Madge Shelton
Charles II    Lucy Walter, Barbara Palmer, Hortense Mancini, Louise de
            Keroualle, Nell Gwyn, and many more
James II    Godotha Price, Lady Elizabeth Denham, Arabella Churchill
            (by whom he had five illegitimate children), Catherine Sedley
George I    Sophia von Kilmansegg ('The Elephant'), Ermengarda
            Melusina von Schulenburg ('The Maypole')
George II    Henrietta Howard, Amelia Sophia von Walmoden
George IV    Mary Robinson ('Perdita'), Maria Fitzherbert, and many
            more
William IV    Dorothy Jordan (by whom he had ten illegitimate children)
Edward VII    Lillie Langtry, Mrs Keppel, and many more

## EDWY THE FAIR

### c. 940–959   REIGNED 955–959

Edwy was only fifteen when he came to the throne in 955. However, his sexual precocity was such that immediately after his coronation in Kingston upon Thames he left the royal banquet to have sex with a lady friend and her daughter, 'wallowing between the two of them in evil fashion, as if in a vile sty'.

Dunstan found the three of them enjoying themselves, gave the young king a sound rebuke, thrust the crown back on his head and dragged him back to the coronation feast, where he was given another telling-off by Archbishop Odo. Later, poor Dunstan had to pay for being a spoilsport, as Edwy quite naturally exiled him.

## EDGAR THE PEACEFUL

### c. 944–975   REIGNED 959–975

Edgar's mistress, round about the year 961, was a nun called Wulfryth, by whom he had a bastard daughter, St Edith of Wilton. Wulfryth was a novice of Wilton Abbey, and ultimately became the abbess, despite the fact that she had borne this illegitimate daughter. Edith died at the age of twenty-three, and miracles at her tomb ensured that she became a cult figure.

Edith's legitimate half-brother was King Edward, Saint and Martyr. Perhaps it is worth remarking that King Edgar, therefore, fathered two saints: one legitimate and another a bastard. This must surely be a record.

## CANUTE

### c. 992–1035   REIGNED 1016–1035

It has been said that, among the Vikings, 'monogamy had not as yet a firm hold'. He therefore enjoyed two queens simultaneously. The first one was Elfgifu of Northampton. He may not have actually married her, so perhaps she can be counted as a mistress.

Elfgifu, however, was sent into Denmark, where she was treated as queen. Meanwhile, Canute married Emma, the widow of his predecessor, Ethelred the Unready, and she became his queen in England. The arrangement worked quite well, and Canute's sons by both queens succeeded him on the English throne.

# HAROLD II
## *c.* 1020–1066   REIGNED JAN.–OCT. 1066

Harold II, who was defeated at Hastings, lived for more than twenty years with Edith of the Swan Neck, without being married to her. They had three or four sons and two daughters. One of these daughters became a nun at Wilton and the other married Vladimir II, Prince of Novgorod and Kiev.

It was only as a political convenience, a few months before he was killed at Hastings, that Harold married his 'proper' wife, Aldgyth, but Edith was his life-partner. At the time of Harold's death at Hastings Aldgyth was pregnant, and gave birth to a son shortly after.

# WILLIAM I (THE CONQUEROR)
## 1027/8–1087   REIGNED 1066–1087

Surprisingly for those times, William the Conqueror, although a bastard himself, was a faithful husband, devoted to his tiny wife Matilda, by whom he had four sons and six daughters. He was renowned for his fidelity and it was noted that he was severe on priests who took mistresses.

# WILLIAM II (RUFUS)
## 1056–1100   REIGNED 1087–1100

No wife, no mistresses, and probably no bastards – he was homosexual.

Anselm, the Archbishop of Canterbury, preached against Rufus's sexual habits and then had to flee to Europe to escape from the king's wrath.

# HENRY I
## 1068–1135   REIGNED 1100–1135

Henry I, third son of William the Conqueror, holds the record among English kings for the greatest number of illegitimate children. He had at least twenty-five bastards by about a dozen women. (The number varies in different accounts, but nine sons and sixteen daughters are certainties.) The fact is, no one could keep up with his lusty ways.

He was kind to all his children and provided for them generously. One bastard daughter became Queen of Scotland on marrying Alexander I, King of the Scots; another married Rotrou, Count of Perche; another married Conan III, Duke of Brittany. Robert, one of his bastard sons, became Earl of Gloucester, and another, Rainald, became Earl of Cornwall.

It was a tragic irony for Henry I that his only legitimate sons, William and Richard, were drowned in the 'White Ship' disaster, thus leaving England with no proper male heir.

## STEPHEN
### *c.* 1097–1154   REIGNED 1135–1154

Stephen fathered at least five bastards, one of whom, Gervase, became Abbot of Westminster.

## HENRY II
### 1133–1189   REIGNED 1154–1189

Henry II bedded whores and concubines everywhere. There are no conclusive statistics, but at least twelve bastards are on record, and there must have been many more. He acknowledged a fair number of them and gave them honourable positions. Geoffrey Plantagenet, for example, became Archbishop of York, and William Longespée, Earl of Salisbury, has a magnificent tomb in Salisbury Cathedral. Their mother was a woman called Ykenai, described by the Archdeacon of Oxford as 'a base-born common harlot who stooped to all uncleanliness' – but this may have been slightly unfair, as she was probably a knight's daughter. Then there was Nesta, another knight's daughter, who gave birth to Morgan, later to become Provost of Beverley and Bishop-Elect of Durham. There were other children, too, by unknown mothers.

Certainly the most scandalous of all Henry's affairs was with Alys, daughter of King Louis VII of France. She had been brought to England to become the bride of Henry's son Richard (the future 'Lionheart'), and was living under Henry's care – still a teenager aged about fifteen when Henry started this relationship. In all, Alys bore Henry four children, but they all died young and their existence was somewhat hushed up. Little wonder that Richard was reluctant to marry Alys, and turned instead, with his mother's active encouragement, to an alternative bride.

But Henry's most famous mistress was Rosamund Clifford, the 'Fair Rosamund', who was about sixteen when he first fell in love with her, after he had been married to Eleanor of Aquitaine for twenty-one years. This love affair became the subject of countless romantic stories and poems for centuries afterwards, all more or less at variance with one another and with the probable truth. According to these legends Henry seems to have kept Rosamund in some sort of hideaway or 'bower' made for her in the grounds of Woodstock, where Blenheim Palace stands today. Legend has it that Eleanor managed to track Rosamund down by following a silken thread through a maze. Legend also has it that when she got there Eleanor tried to kill Rosamund, offering her a choice between either drinking a goblet of poison or committing suicide with a dagger.

Contrary to rumours, legends and assertions by nineteenth-century historians, Rosamund does not seem to have given Henry any children. He was deeply distressed when she died after only three years of liaison with him. He gave generous sums of money to the nunnery at Godstow in Oxfordshire, where she was buried and for a while the nuns there treated her as a saint, decorating her tomb with rich silks, lamps and expensive candles.

After Henry's death, Hugh, Bishop of Lincoln, visited Godstow and was horrified to find all this flummery. 'She was a harlot' he declared, and ordered her to be dug up and buried elsewhere.

Curiously, there were rumours that the good bishop himself was an illegitimate son of Henry by yet another unknown mother. . . .

## RICHARD I (THE LIONHEART)
### 1157–1199   REIGNED 1189–1199

Richard the Lionheart had at least two bastard sons. It is thought by some that he was homosexual or bisexual, and it is alleged that one of his principal gay partners was Philip Augustus, King of France. One of Henry II's clerks wrote that they ate at the same table, fed from the same plate, and 'at night the bed did not separate them'.

Of course it's impossible at this distance in time to prove such allegations, but it is on record that in 1195 a hermit, meeting Richard on one of his hunting excursions in Normandy, accosted him with a warning to 'abstain from illicit acts, for if you do not, God will punish you in fitting manner.' Significantly, the hermit told him to 'remember the destruction of Sodom!'

## JOHN
### 1167–1216   REIGNED 1199–1216

John was notoriously lecherous and lost the support of many of his barons for raping their wives and daughters. He had at least twelve bastards by a variety of mothers. One of his sons became known as Richard Fitzjohn of Dover, and was created Baron of Chilham, Kent. Another, named Oliver, was killed at the siege of Damietta and is buried in Westminster Abbey.

One story concerning John's lusty habits tells how once, when he wanted to have sex with the wife of Baron de Vesci, the baron cunningly managed to smuggle a prostitute into the king's bedchamber instead. The next day John boasted to de Vesci how good the night had been. But the baron immediately confessed to the deception. He had to flee for his life.

# HENRY III
## 1207–1272   REIGNED 1216–1272

Henry III was a model of devotion, piety and monogamy. He was a faithful husband to his wife, Eleanor of Provence, by whom he had nine children, five of whom died young.

# EDWARD I
## 1239–1307   REIGNED 1272–1307

Despite his deep love for his wife, Queen Eleanor of Castile, in whose memory he built the 'Eleanor Crosses', and by whom he had sixteen children, Edward I still found time to produce at least one bastard son.

# EDWARD II
## 1284–1327   REIGNED 1307–1327

Edward II was by far the most overtly homosexual of all English kings, showering gifts, honours and kisses upon his gay partner, Piers Gaveston. 'I do not remember to have heard that one man so loved another' wrote one commentator.

Edward did marry, but the marriage was obviously just a piece of political manoeuvring. Even at the wedding banquet Edward paid far more attention to Gaveston than to his wife, Isabella, and then afterwards he gave all Isabella's best jewels and wedding presents to him. She was enraged and disgusted, and wanted to go back home to France.

Eventually, the barons could stand it no longer and beheaded Gaveston on Blacklow Hill, just outside Warwick. The head and bleeding corpse lay on the ground for several days until some cobblers found them and sewed them back together. For two and a half years Piers Gaveston's embalmed body lay unburied in Oxford, and then it was interred in Kings Langley Priory Church.

For a while after Gaveston's death Edward and his queen Isabella lived in relative harmony and she gave birth to their first child, the future King Edward III. But then Edward began to shower gifts and rewards on two other favourites, Hugh Despenser and his father, also called Hugh. It was at this time that Isabella's patience, if any, finally snapped, and from then on she plotted first in secret and then openly, to get rid of the husband she had come to loathe.

Homosexual relations between Edward and the Despensers cannot be proved, but Isabella herself wrote that 'someone has become between my husband and myself . . . and I shall assume the robes of widowhood and mourning until I am revenged'.

Revenged she was, for their deaths were even more horrific than that of Gaveston. The elder Despenser in Bristol and the younger in Hereford were each hanged high up and their genitals cut off 'because of unnatural practices with the king'. They were then disembowelled and forced to watch as their entrails were burnt in front of them.

# EDWARD III
## 1312–1377   REIGNED 1327–1377

Edward III had three bastards by his mistress Alice Perrers. He may have had yet another son by an unknown mother.

Even before the death of his wife, Queen Philippa of Hainault, there was scandal at court as the old king fell in love with Alice Perrers, one of her ladies-in-waiting. He would have been about fifty-four at the time, and had been married to Philippa for thirty-eight years. The royal accounts record that in 1366 he gave Alice Perrers two tuns of wine. It is reasonable to assume that it was for good services rendered.

Philippa died in 1369, and after this, as the old king gradually became more and more senile, so his gifts to Alice became more and more extravagant. He gave her the manor of Wendover, much of his late wife's jewellery, and settled a useful annuity on her.

She is said to have struggled to get the rings off his fingers just after he died, before rigor mortis set in. Other rumours were that she used witchcraft to gain influence over him, and that she infected him with gonorrhoea.

# RICHARD II
## 1367–1400   REIGNED 1377–1399

Richard II and his first wife, Anne of Bohemia, were both fifteen when they married. At her death, childless, thirteen years later, Richard was so upset that he ordered Sheen Palace, where she died, to be destroyed.

Two years after Anne's death Richard married again, to Isabella of Valois, who was a child of seven at the time. Richard had no children and is said to have been homosexual.

Two of Richard's allegedly gay court favourites were Michael de le Pole and Robert de Vere. Richard created de Vere Marquis of Dublin in 1385 and Duke of Dublin the following year. When de Vere, aged only thirty, was killed in Flanders during a boar-hunt, Richard was so grieved that he had his friend dug up from his foreign grave and reburied with a magnificent funeral service at Earl's Colne, Essex. Such was Richard's grief that he ordered the coffin to be opened up so that 'he might look upon the face and clasp the fingers.' Richard was an odd king.

# HENRY IV
## 1367–1413   REIGNED 1399–1413

Henry IV was married twice. His first wife was Mary de Bohun, who died five years before Henry seized the throne. Mary never knew that her husband and son would be kings. After he became king Henry married again, to Joan of Navarre.

Henry had seven children by Mary, none by Joan, and appears to have been a faithful husband to each of them.

# HENRY V
## 1387–1422   REIGNED 1413–1422

Henry V married only once, to Catherine of Valois. The courtship scene in Shakespeare's *Henry V* gives a dramatic account of their first meeting.

The couple had only one son, the ill-fated Henry VI, and poor Catherine was widowed when he was only nine months old.

Henry V seems to have been a faithful husband during a short marriage of just over two years. However, he is reported to have sown his wild oats, having 'fervently followed the service of Venus as well as of Mars'. However, the names of his early mistresses are not recorded.

# HENRY VI

## 1421–1471   REIGNED 1422–1461 AND 1470–1471

Henry VI was far too monkish to be led astray by any wicked woman. He married Margaret of Anjou, the 'She-Wolf of France', and they had only one child, Edward, who was killed at the Battle of Tewkesbury before he could succeed to the throne.

Henry's attitude to sex can be judged by an incident one Christmas when some topless dancers were brought in to entertain him, and 'to entice his youthful mind'. It was reported that Henry was 'not unaware of the devilish wile, and very angrily averted his eyes'. 'Fy, fy, for shame, forsoothe ye be to blame!' he said, and fled.

It was truthfully written of him that he 'eschewed all licentiousness in word or deed'.

# EDWARD IV

## 1442–1483   REIGNED 1461–1470 AND 1471–1483

Edward IV fell madly in love with the beautiful blonde widow, Elizabeth Woodville, and married her secretly in a Northamptonshire village. It was the first time an English king had ever married a commoner and it was something of an embarrassment a few months later when Edward, urged by parliament to consider marriage, had to confess that in fact he already had a wife. They had ten children, including the future Edward V. Their eldest daughter, Elizabeth of York, later married Henry VII.

But quite apart from this prolific legitimate family, Edward also had a large number of mistresses, including Elizabeth Shore, the wife of a London grocer, and Elizabeth Lucy, by whom he had a bastard son, Arthur Plantagenet, and a daughter, Elizabeth. There was also another daughter, Grace, by an unknown mother.

An Italian at the court of Edward IV wrote that 'he was licentious in the extreme. . . . He pursued with no discrimination the married and unmarried, the noble and lowly'.

Sir Thomas More also described Edward's lustful ways and commented that Elizabeth Shore was the king's favourite mistress, observing: 'The merriest was this Shore's wife, in whom the king therefore took special pleasure. For many he had, but her he loved.'

# RICHARD III

## 1452–1485   REIGNED 1483–1485

When he usurped the throne, Richard III did his best to vilify his predecessor, Edward IV, and naturally enough one of his chief targets of hatred was Elizabeth Shore. He accused her of witchcraft and had her taken before the Bishop of London's court as a common harlot. She was made to do penance by walking through the streets of London barefoot, while wearing a white sheet and carrying a lighted taper. She was then cast into Ludgate prison and had to forfeit all she possessed. Nevertheless, she must have had powers of survival, as she didn't die until 1527, and had the joy of seeing her persecutor, Richard, killed at Bosworth.

Richard himself had no cause to take a high moral tone with her, for he had had at least seven bastard children, one of whom, John of Gloucester, he appointed Captain of Calais. Richard and his wife, Anne of Warwick, had one son, Edward, Prince of Wales, who died aged eleven.

# HENRY VII

## 1457–1509   REIGNED 1485–1509

Henry VII seems to have been a good and faithful husband to Elizabeth of York. They were good parents, loving their children dearly. They were devastated at the death of Arthur, heir to the throne, who died aged sixteen, and they shared their grief together. All told, Henry and Elizabeth had eight children, but the last three died young, and Elizabeth herself died shortly after giving birth to their eighth and last child.

Henry deeply mourned Elizabeth when she died, and lived miserably for the remaining six years of his life. It may come as a surprise that Henry did in fact have a bastard son, by a woman from Brittany. His name was Roland de Velville and he grew up to be Constable of Beaumaris Castle in Anglesey.

# HENRY VIII

## 1491–1547   REIGNED 1509–1547

It's a measure of the chauvinist double standards of his time that Henry VIII beheaded two of his wives for infidelity, yet he himself had several mistresses, and at least four bastards by various mothers.

His first affair was with a Lady Anne Hastings, the younger sister of one of Catherine of Aragon's ladies-in-waiting. Catherine was pregnant when she heard about this, and there was a right royal rumpus about it. Henry's next bed-sharer was a somewhat low-born Frenchwoman who had been a French tutor to his sisters. Her name was Jane Popicourt. Neither of these two affairs resulted in any children, but the next mistress he took, Elizabeth Blount, gave Henry just what he would have dearly liked from Catherine – a healthy bouncing boy.

The little bastard was called Henry FitzRoy. He was born in 1519 and died aged seventeen in 1536: thus he was born after Mary Tudor, but before Edward VI and Elizabeth. Had he lived, he may well have been an embarrassingly active claimant for the throne. Henry VIII made a great fuss of his illegitimate son, and when he was only six he was created Duke of Richmond and Surrey, and Lord High Admiral. In fact, so much was lavished on him that Queen Catherine tried to complain that he was given much more honour and attention than was given to their legitimate daughter, Mary Tudor.

Henry's next mistress, for a while, was Mary Boleyn, sister of Anne Boleyn. She doesn't appear very often in the history books, but she did bear Henry another bastard son, in 1525.

All the world knows that Anne Boleyn came next, being known about court as 'The Concubine', but as she made a stand for marriage, she can hardly be called a mistress. Henry and Anne Boleyn were secretly married on 25 January 1533 and Anne gave birth to Elizabeth on the following 7 September. It was a near thing.

There were rumours, too, about another liaison, with a girl called Madge Shelton, during Anne Boleyn's pregnancy. We have to accept that Henry VIII was no saint.

# EDWARD VI AND MARY I
## EDWARD: 1537–1553   REIGNED 1547–1553
## MARY: 1516–1558   REIGNED 1553–1558

Edward was too young and Mary was too pious for frivolity of any kind.

However, Mary's husband, Philip of Spain, had an eye for the ladies and Mary noted with displeasure that Philip was far more interested in her half-sister Elizabeth than in herself. At least one other lady attracted him while he was in England, a young noblewoman called Lady Dacre, but she had the presence of mind to beat him off.

# ELIZABETH I
## 1533–1603   REIGNED 1558–1603

As the 'Virgin Queen', Elizabeth I was almost professionally committed to chastity. It was a part of her policy to keep people guessing. However, she was a (perhaps willing) victim of sexual advances by Lord Thomas Seymour, who once wrote to her crudely asking if 'her great buttocks were grown any less or no'. Caught in a compromising situation with him (she was fourteen at the time) she was quickly packed off to Cheshunt for a rigorous educational programme under the famous teacher Roger Ascham. He found her a brilliant pupil. Elizabeth commented about Thomas Seymour that he was 'a man of great wit, but little judgement'. His Lordship was later beheaded.

There is little doubt that of all her admirers Elizabeth had genuine affection for Robert Dudley, Earl of Leicester, but it's unlikely that they ever made physical love. Poignantly, after Dudley's early death from cancer, only weeks after the defeat of the Spanish Armada, Elizabeth shut herself away for days in her private chamber, refusing to speak to anyone. For the rest of her life she had a little box by her bedside, containing a letter she had received from him in his final days. She inscribed it: 'His last letter.'

When her later admirer, the Earl of Essex returned to England after conducting a disastrous military campaign in Ireland, he presumed too much on the old queen's fondness for him. He strode into her bedroom unannounced, to tell her all about it. Elizabeth had no make-up on, and was loosely dressed in her night-clothes. Nobody had ever seen her quite like this before, and she was furious. Essex was sent to the Tower of London, and beheaded.

# JAMES I
## 1566–1625   REIGNED IN ENGLAND 1603–1625

Although married, James was quite openly homosexual, publicly slavering kisses upon his favourites. Two of his courtiers stood out among all the others. The first was the young Scotsman Robert Carr, whom James made Viscount Rochester and then Earl of Somerset; but Robert lost favour when suspected of murder.

The second favourite was George Villiers, whom James first met when the young man was twenty-two. George was to have an almost mesmerising effect on the 47-year-old king. James said that George reminded him of a painting he had once seen of St Stephen, so his pet-name for him was 'Steenie'.

One of the young George's letters to James finished: 'So, craving your blessing, I kiss your dirty hands and end, your Majesty's most humble Slave and Dogge, Steenie.'

As for James, one of his letters to Steenie read: 'I care for nothing so I may once have you in my arms again. God grant it! God grant it! God grant it! Amen, amen, amen.'

James quickly made Steenie a knight; then a Knight of the Garter; then Viscount Villiers and Baron Whaddon; a year later he created him Marquis of Buckingham; then Lord High Admiral; and finally, in 1623, the grand title of Duke of Buckingham was bestowed on him.

When James gave Steenie his earldom he told an incredulous gathering of Lords of the Council:

I, James, am neither God nor angel, but a man like any other . . . I love the Earl of Buckingham more than anyone else and more than you who are here assembled. I wish to speak in my own behalf and not to have it thought a defect, for Jesus Christ did the same, and therefore I cannot be blamed. Christ had his John, and I have my George.

Unsurprisingly, James had no bastards.

# CHARLES I
## 1600–1649   REIGNED 1625–1649

Exquisite in taste and behaviour, Charles I was an exemplary husband and father. In the last months of his life, however, while a prisoner in Carisbrooke Castle on the Isle of Wight from 1647 to 1648, Charles developed a tender and clandestine relationship with a young lady called Jane Whorwood.

From his prison, Charles wrote to Jane at least sixteen times, signing himself 'your most loving Charles' and he met her secretly on several occasions. He told a go-between: 'Tell Jane Whorwood that her Platonic Way doth much spoil the taste of my mind.' Apparently, he told Jane he would tell his wife Henrietta Maria about her. But he never did. And in his last letter to Jane he said she had given him 'great contentment'.

# CHARLES II

## 1630–1685   REIGNED 1660–1685

It's quite impossible to list all the mistresses of Charles II: his appetite for women was insatiable. He was without inhibition and quite impervious to criticism. His well-known nickname, 'Old Rowley', derived from an old goat of that name, tethered on the green at Whitehall and noted for its energy and lasciviousness.

All told, Charles had at least sixteen known bastards – nine sons and seven daughters. He was very proud of them, treated them well and gave them dukedoms and grand titles. In fact he created six of his sons dukes, and, generations later, the late Diana, Princess of Wales, was descended from the families of two of them (the Duke of Grafton and the Duke of Richmond). The British aristocracy owes a debt of gratitude to Charles for much of its existence.

Some of the women who bore Charles's children were created duchesses, but there were many more besides. There was Margaret de Carteret of Jersey, for example, by whom Charles had what was probably his first love-child, James, who became a Jesuit and died in his early twenties. Charles himself was only sixteen at the time of James's birth. Then among his many other lesser-known mistresses there were Hortense Mancini, Duchess of Mazarin; Eleanor Needham (Lady Byron); Margaret Hughes, an actress; Winifred Wells; Mary Knight; Jane Roberts, a clergyman's daughter; and Mary ('Moll') Davies, who bore Charles a daughter named Mary Tudor, later to became the Countess of Derwentwater.

More famous than these, however, were a bevy of beauties who bore Charles his large illegitimate family. The first of these was Lucy Walter, a Welsh girl whom he met in The Hague in 1648. John Evelyn, the diarist, described her as 'a brown, beautiful, bold, but insipid creature.' Poor Lucy died before Charles became king, so she was never ennobled. However, it was their son James who was to become the Duke of Monmouth, and who tried to claim the throne when his father died.

Then there was Elizabeth Killigrew, sister of his brother's chaplain, who later married Viscount Shannon. In 1650 she bore Charles's first daughter, Charlotte FitzRoy, who later became the Countess of Yarmouth.

Katherine Pegge, daughter of a Derbyshire squire, produced three of Charles's children: Charles FitzCharles, who was ennobled as Earl of Plymouth; Katherine, who became a nun in France; and (perhaps) another unnamed daughter who is thought to have died young.

However, perhaps Charles's most spectacularly promiscuous mistress was Barbara Villiers, wife of Roger Palmer, Earl of Castlemaine. She was later created Duchess of Cleveland. Apart from children sired by other fathers, she gave Charles no fewer than *six* bastards: Anne FitzRoy, later to become Countess of Sussex; Charles FitzRoy, Duke of Southampton and Cleveland; Henry FitzRoy, Duke of Grafton; Charlotte FitzRoy, later Countess of Lichfield; George FitzRoy, Duke of Northumberland; and Barbara, who later became a prioress in France.

To record such relentless philandering becomes somewhat tedious, and it comes as a relief that Frances Stuart (known as 'La Belle Stuart') firmly resisted Charles's persistent approaches. She must be the only woman in history to be famous for *not* being a mistress. However, she did achieve lasting fame of another sort, for perhaps without realising it we see a picture of her every time we look at the figure of Britannia on our coins, for she was the original model for this. Samuel Pepys wrote of 'Mrs Stewart's face . . . and a pretty thing it is that the King should choose her face to represent Britannia by.'

Two more of Charles's mistresses must be mentioned. Firstly Louise de Kéroualle, a beautiful Breton girl who was a lady-in-waiting to his sister Minette. Louise had in face been sent to England by Louis XIV as a spy. He told her to try to become the king's mistress, which she did with conspicuous success, being created Duchess of Portsmouth. Charles's nickname for her was 'Fubbs' because of her chubby cheeks, and a ship of the Royal Navy was named after her. A Greenwich pub still exists called the Fubbs Yacht. Louise produced a son for Charles, named Charles Lennox, who was created Duke of Richmond – one of whose descendants was to be Diana, Princess of Wales.

Lastly, perhaps the most famous mistress of all was Nell Gwyn, a young, lively comic actress at Drury Lane Theatre. Once, Nell's carriage was being stoned in a London street by people thinking Charles's unpopular Catholic mistress, Louise de Kéroualle, was the occupant. Nell's dramatic instinct came to her rescue. She thrust her head out of the coach window and shouted: 'Don't hurt me, good people! I'm the *Protestant* whore!'.

One of Nell Gwyn's two sons by Charles II became Duke of St Albans, and Nell herself was to have been made Countess of Greenwich, but alas, Charles died too soon for this to happen. Nell died soon after, and was buried in St Martin-in-the-Fields, in Trafalgar Square.

Once, someone asked Charles how many women he'd had. Charles thought for a moment and then said thirty-nine. He explained that the number of Articles of the Anglican faith was the right total for the Head of the Church of England.

Charles's poor wife, Catherine of Braganza, had to put up with a lot, and on his deathbed he begged her forgiveness. They had had no children.

# JAMES II

## 1633–1701   REIGNED 1685–1688

James II was just as lecherous as his brother Charles, though perhaps his affairs are less notorious. He was married twice, and upset both of his wives by producing several bastards as well as his legitimate children.

James married his first wife, Anne Hyde, because he had made her pregnant, and his brother Charles insisted that he kept his promise to wed her. Poor Anne Hyde had a number of children who did not survive, but she did manage to produce two future Queens of England – Mary II and Anne.

During his marriage to Anne Hyde, James's sexual appetite was voracious, and it is said that some of his nobleman friends had to keep their wives from court, simply to protect them from him. Among his mistresses at this time were Godotha Price, Lady Elizabeth Denham (wife of the poet Sir John Denham), and the most celebrated of all, Arabella Churchill, sister of John Churchill, who later became the 1st Duke of Marlborough.

Arabella Churchill presented James with at least four bastards: Henrietta FitzJames, later to become Lady Waldegrave; James FitzJames, Duke of Berwick; Henry FitzJames, Duke of Albemarle; and Arabella, who became a nun in France. After Arabella Churchill, James then fell in love with Catherine Sedley, Countess of Dorchester, who bore him a daughter, Katherine Darnley in 1679, and a son, James Darnley in 1684.

James was crowned king in 1685, by which time he had married again, this time to Mary of Modena, whose legitimate son by James was the famous 'warming-pan' baby, who later grew up to become the Jacobite 'Old Pretender'. But Mary was determined to stop James's lechery with other women, and threatened to become a nun unless he stopped his perpetual sex with other women.

After James had been deposed and was forced to flee to France in 1688, he seemed to turn over a new leaf and began to repent of his former lifestyle. He became more and more religious, spending his time among priests and men of religion. He told his heir: 'I abhor and detest myself for having lived . . . so many years in almost a perpetual course of sin.'

# WILLIAM III

## 1650–1702   REIGNED 1689–1702

William's mistress was one of his wife's childhood friends, Elizabeth Villiers. She was no beauty and her nickname at court was 'Squinting Betty'.

William's wife, Mary, was quite well aware of this liaison, which gave her much distress, particularly as she knew that she herself was unable to have children.

William is also thought by some to have been homosexual. The Bishop of Salisbury, Gilbert Burnet, referred to this supposed dark secret, writing that William 'had no vice but of one sort, in which he was very cautious and secret'. Later, the bishop told a friend that this was 'too notorious for a faithful historian to pass over in silence'. One of the two gay partners he is believed to have enjoyed was Hans Willem Bentinck, whom he had known since his teenage days. Bentinck landed in England with William in 1688 and was quickly made Earl of Portland. Later in life, a younger man, Arnoud Van Keppel, enjoyed the king's favour and William created him Earl of Albemarle.

William was secretive and undemonstrative. However, when his young wife and co-monarch Mary II died, William wore a lock of her hair and her wedding ring next to his heart for the rest of his life. On her deathbed Mary had written to him begging him to discard Elizabeth Villiers. William told the Archbishop of Canterbury: 'I must mend my life.' And he never saw Elizabeth again in public.

# ANNE
## 1665–1714   REIGNED 1702–1714

Although Anne became pregnant eighteen times by her husband Prince George, thirteen of these pregnancies resulted in stillbirths or miscarriages, four babies lived only briefly, and the surviving child, the Duke of Gloucester, lived to the age of eleven.

Anne had no bastard offspring, but rumour was strong that she enjoyed a lesbian relationship with the wife of the Duke of Marlborough, Sarah Churchill. They had 'secret' names for each other: Sarah was 'Mrs Freeman' and Anne herself was 'Mrs Morley'. Their intimacy was intense for several years, but then broke up as the domineering 'Mrs Freeman' became more and more demanding.

Their relationship began to cool after Anne established another possible lesbian relationship, this time with a lady of the bedchamber called Abigail Hill. Sarah Churchill became jealous and openly accused Anne of having 'no inclination for any but of one's own sex', and circulated a scurrilous poem which began:

When as Queen Anne of great Renown
Great Britain's Scepter Sway'd,
Besides the Church, she dearly lov'd
A dirty Chamber-maid.
O! Abigail that was her Name,
She stich'd and starched full well,
But how she pierced this Royal Heart,
No mortal Man can tell.

It ended:

Her Secretary she was not
Because she could not write
But had the Conduct and the Care
Of some dark Deeds at Night.

# GEORGE I

## 1660–1727   REIGNED 1714–1727

When George I came to England he had already locked up his wife, Princess Sophia Dorothea, for good, in the castle at Ahlden, Germany. Apart from a daily walk in the afternoon, she never left her prison, and certainly never came to England. The reason for this punishment was alleged infidelity. Meanwhile, George provided himself with two mistresses and brought them with him to London. As with Henry VIII, his own infidelity never seemed to have struck him as anything but normal. The two mistresses were an odd pair. One was large and fat; the other was tall and thin.

The fat one, Sophia von Kilmansegg, was a vast mountain of flesh. Horace Walpole wrote of 'her enormous figure, the fierce black eyes, large and rolling between two lofty arched eyebrows, two acres of cheeks spread with crimson, an ocean of neck that overflowed and was not distinguished from the lower part of her body'. George soon created her Countess of Darlington, and she became popularly known in court circles as 'The Elephant'.

The tall thin one, whose name was Ermengarda Melusina von Schulenburg, quickly gained the nickname of 'The Maypole'. George created her Duchess of Munster and also Duchess of Kendal. She was, in fact, his preferred mistress, by whom he had two daughters. Melusina and her children provided the king with a stable family background, and Sir Robert Walpole's comment about her was not only that her intellect was 'mean and contemptible' but also that she was 'in effect, as much Queen of England as any ever was'.

Towards the end of his reign George had another affair, with Anne Brent, a young daughter of the Countess of Macclesfield. She had such black hair and dark skin that her nickname was 'The Sultana'.

George never publicly acknowledged his bastard daughters, although he was extremely fond of them.

# GEORGE II

## 1683–1760   REIGNED 1727–1760

It's said that George II's wife, Queen Caroline of Ansbach, chose his mistresses for him, making sure that they were uglier than herself. Whether they really were uglier is a matter of opinion. However, his main mistress for almost a decade was Mrs Henrietta Howard, wife of Charles Howard, the younger son of the Earl of Suffolk. George would visit her regularly every night promptly at nine o'clock, and when after several years she felt she'd had enough, he gave her a pension of £2,000 a year.

George followed this liaison by a short affair with Lady Deloraine, but then in 1735 he met Amelia Sophia von Walmoden in Hanover and was completely captivated by her. Astonishingly, George described his infatuation for Walmoden in letters he wrote to his wife: 'I know you will love Madame Walmoden', he declared, 'because she loves me.'

The extent of Madame Walmoden's love for George was demonstrated in 1736, when she produced a baby son by him: John Louis, Count Walmoden-Gimborn. He died in 1811.

Queen Caroline died of cancer in 1737. On her deathbed she begged George to marry again. But George comforted her, weeping with emotion: 'No, no,' he said, 'I'll just have mistresses.' After the queen's death, Madame Walmoden came to live permanently with George. She divorced her husband and George made her Duchess of Yarmouth.

And when George himself died, hundreds of locks of women's hair were discovered among his personal belongings.

# GEORGE III

## 1738–1820   REIGNED 1760–1820

George III was only twenty-three when he married Charlotte, his queen. However. there had already been two other women in his life – Hannah and Sarah.

A mystery surrounds the first of these, a Quakeress called Hannah Lightfoot. Indeed George is said to have gone through two forms of marriage with Hannah and the couple had no fewer than three children. Of course the affair was hushed up, but a story has emerged, increasingly and intriguingly well documented. Apparently the first of these marriages, a somewhat irregular one, took place at Kew Chapel on 17 April 1759, and the second, which took place a month later at their secret home in London, was according to the rites of the Church of England.

From this marriage two sons were born, the elder of whom – who was, of course, arguably the heir to the throne – was sent as a young man to the Cape of Good Hope and lived for the rest of his life in South Africa under the name of George Rex. He died in 1839 and is buried at Knysna, about 160 miles west of Port Elizabeth, where his grave can still be seen today. He had children, but in his will, so we are told, he went to great lengths to emphasise that they were all illegitimate, and that he had steadfastly refused to marry their mother. (Somewhat urgently, as George Rex had left England, the parting words to him from his father, King George, had been: 'You must never marry. There must be no legitimate heirs!'). Today, the results of all this are that there are many people claiming to be George III's descendants living in South Africa.

If the George-and Hannah episode is to be taken seriously, there was also a daughter who died aged three, and also another son, whose great-great-great-great-great grandson is now living in Southampton. But this gentleman is understandably reluctant to be drawn into discussing his illustrious ancestry.

The second of George III's loves was the beautiful Lady Sarah Lennox, to whom he proposed marriage through an intermediary. The next time he met her he asked what she thought about his proposal. 'Tell me,' he begged, 'for my happiness depends on it.'

'Nothing, Sir,' came the reply, upon which the king abruptly left, muttering 'Nothing will come of nothing.'

Almost immediately afterwards he married Charlotte Sophia of Mecklenburg-Strelitz. The observant Robert Walpole watched George carefully during the marriage service, and reported afterwards that when a reference was made to Abraham and Sarah, George blushed scarlet. It was a revealing moment.

However, George became an exemplary husband, and Queen Charlotte presented him with no fewer than fifteen children. He was never unfaithful to her.

# GEORGE IV
## 1762–1830   REIGNED 1820–1830

It would be impossible to determine who had more mistresses, Charles II or George IV, but quite possibly George IV holds the record for royal licentiousness. The most famous mistresses were the actresses Mary Robinson, his 'Perdita', and of course Mrs Fitzherbert, whom he secretly married. But there were dozens of others. It would be tedious to enumerate them all.

Unlike Charles II, however, George had very few bastards. Two illegitimate children were privately acknowledged, and it is possible that he had four other children, but they were never given prominence or titles. It was a great misfortune that his one and only legitimate child, by his wife Caroline, died during her birth.

Of all his many mistresses, the woman he most constantly loved was Maria Fitzherbert, and when he died he ensured that he would be buried with her miniature portrait hung around his neck.

# WILLIAM IV
## 1765–1837   REIGNED 1830–1837

William, Duke of Clarence, brother of George IV, never really expected to become king, and certainly did not want to. However, as time went on, it became more and more apparent that he was likely to succeed, so his love-life had to be re-arranged.

For years William had had a very happy relationship with a successful and attractive actress, Mrs Dorothy Jordan. They lived in Bushey and had eleven healthy children, who were given the surname Fitz-Clarence, though malicious gossip-mongers called them 'les Bâtards'. One of these, George, became the Earl of Munster.

When it seemed inevitable that he would have to become king, William sent out invitations of marriage to royal and ducal palaces all over Europe. At length, it was Princess Adelaide of Saxe-Meiningen who agreed to marry him. It was hardly a love-match, but she proved to be an excellent consort. Their two baby daughters, however, both died within months of their birth.

William and Dorothy had already parted company well before Adelaide arrived in England. It is sad to record that Dorothy had to escape to France to avoid her creditors. She died in poverty in 1816, her bed-linen being sold off to pay for her funeral.

# VICTORIA
### 1819–1901   REIGNED 1837–1901

It may have been the memory of all those wicked uncles of hers that prompted Victoria to make her famous promise on coming to the throne: 'I will be good.' At any rate her court, with Albert, was a model of morality. However, even Victoria herself did not remain untouched by gossip.

For about ten years Victoria had as her attendant a Scotsman by the name of John Brown, a man who in the eyes of the queen could do no wrong. He actually called her 'wumman' and told her brusquely to change her dress if he didn't like it – and she would meekly obey him. Rumour was rife that they had married; some said that the queen had gone insane and that Brown was her keeper; others said that she had turned to spiritualism and that he was her medium.

In 1979 Dr Mitchell MacDonald, then curator of the Museum of Scottish Tartans, Perthshire, was interviewed about his many years of research on Queen Victoria and John Brown. He stated his belief that there was genuine evidence that their relationship was far from platonic – and he even referred to a deathbed confession made by a minister who is said to have officiated at a marriage ceremony between the Queen and Brown. Further to this, MacDonald claimed that a child was born to them, who lived in Paris until the age of ninety, returning from time to time to visit Balmoral.

MacDonald, who generously donated a kilt and matching bloomers given by Victoria to John Brown to the Museum of Scottish Tartans, also mentioned an episode in which a lady-in-waiting saw Brown emerging one night at 4 a.m. from the Queen's bedroom at Balmoral. The lady-in-waiting promptly handed in her resignation, but Victoria refused to accept it, asking the servant to take her word that what she had seen had been totally proper.

Who will ever know what truth lies in all this? The fact remains, however, that for a while, John Brown seemed to mesmerise Victoria, and at his death she asked Lord Tennyson to write a memorial epitaph for him. Victoria herself was buried with a photograph of Brown in her hand.

At her death, her son and successor Edward VII went about her rooms personally smashing up all the little statues of John Brown he could find.

# EDWARD VII

## 1841–1910   REIGNED 1901–1910

Edward VII's loves were many: Sarah Bernhardt, Miss Chamberlayne, Lady Warwick, Mrs Agnes Keyser, Mrs Cornwallis-West, Mrs Luke Wheeler, and many, many more. On one occasion, a bold young dancer at the Moulin Rouge greeted him as an old friend. 'Ullo, Wales', she is reported to have called out. 'Est-ce que tu va payer mon champagne?' Whereupon the prince did indeed pay for it.

Two mistresses stand out above all of the others. The first was Lillie Langtry, 'the Jersey Lily', whom Edward first met in 1877. She was the daughter of the Dean of Jersey, and was already married. Wherever she went Lillie attracted crowds because of her vivacious beauty and her well-known affair with the prince. Eventually, with the prince's support and encouragement, she went on the stage and became a rich and successful actress.

Edward bought a house for her in Bournemouth, a love-nest where he could visit her in relative privacy. Today it is a popular hotel and restaurant, Langtry Manor Hotel, and visitors may still see the small hatch that she had cut high in a wall so that Edward could view the guests before coming down for dinner.

The other mistress who remained close to Edward literally to his dying day was Mrs George Keppel. This was the same Keppel family that had been ennobled by William III two centuries earlier. As Edward lay dying, his wife Queen Alexandra led many of his friends in to see him and bid farewell. Such was her tolerance and understanding that Mrs Keppel was among those she invited. Alexandra's life cannot have been an easy one, and this final gesture showed an extraordinary degree of patience.

Two illegitimate children may have been born, fathered by Edward: one to Lady Susan Vane-Tempest, née Pelham-Clifton, in 1871 or 1872; and another may have been the mother of the art collector, Edward James. She left her son a bundle of over a hundred letters from the king. But facts are elusive. Victorian and Edwardian England maintained decorous silence on these matters.

# GEORGE V
## 1865–1936   REIGNED 1910–1936

George V was a pillar of rectitude. Nevertheless, for seventeen years he had to bear the indignity of a curious rumour that he had been married secretly in Malta to the daughter of an English Admiral and that he had had three children by her. He was still the Duke of York at the time. His supposed wife was allegedly living in Plymouth.

The news broke in April 1893, just before he became engaged to 'May' – the future Queen Mary. Unbelievably, the *Star* newspaper in London printed what purported to be an account of this marriage on 3 May, the very day he announced his engagement to her.

The rumour hung around until the time he had become king, and in 1910 a republican newspaper, *The Liberator*, published a scurrilous article, 'Sanctified Bigamy', and sent a copy to every Member of Parliament. 'Our very Christian King and Defender of the Faith has a plurality of wives just like any Mohammedan Sultan,' it said, 'and they are sanctified by the Anglican Church.'

The article went on to say that the king had 'foully abandoned his true wife and entered into a sham and shameful marriage with a daughter of the Duke of Teck'.

In its next issue *The Liberator* asked which wife would be accompanying King George on his forthcoming visit to India. By that time George had had enough. He sued the author, E.F. Mylius, for libel, scotched the nasty little rumour once and for all, and Mylius was given a twelve-month jail sentence.

# EDWARD VIII
## 1894–1972   REIGNED 20 JAN.–10 DEC. 1936

It is well known that Edward, as Prince of Wales, enjoyed an energetic life of philandering. Two of his special affairs were with Thelma, Lady Furness, and with Mrs Dudley Ward. All liaisons were abruptly broken off, however, when Mrs Wallis Simpson entered his life. From that moment he was completely ruled by her. But there is an intriguing post-script to the life of Edward as Prince of Wales.

An Australian half-Aboriginal woman, Barbara Chisholm, is so convinced that she is the granddaughter of Edward VIII that she is offering to take DNA tests to prove it. The story was widely rumoured in Australia, and finally hit the headlines in Britain in 1996. According to all the evidence, Edward enjoyed a brief visit by an Australian girl, Mollee [sic] Little, on board the battle cruiser HMS *Renown* during his world tour in 1920. It was a one-night stand, or more correctly a one-afternoon stand, according to the diaries of the late Lord Louis Mountbatten, who accompanied the prince on this tour.

Nine months later, Mollee gave birth to a son, Tony, who died aged sixty-six in 1987, outliving his alleged father by fifteen years. Barbara Chisholm claims to be Tony's own illegitimate daughter by an Aboriginal servant named May.

According to *The Times*, Tony Chisholm bore an 'uncanny resemblance' to the Duke of Windsor, and was nicknamed 'The Duke' by his Australian friends. Furthermore, Tony visited the Duke and Duchess of Windsor when they were living in Paris, and also entertained the Duke of Edinburgh, who visited him once during a royal tour.

Barbara Chisholm, who is quite convinced she is Edward VIII's granddaughter, is a social worker living in Darwin. She is an energetic and happy mother of nine and proud of her nineteen grandchildren.

If Barbara's claim is true, she and her growing family carry traces of genes descended in one way or another from every British royal dynasty: Hanoverian, Stuart, Tudor, Plantagenet, Saxon; back to Alfred the Great and beyond . . .

# APPENDIX

⪻ ⪼

## THE SUCCESSION OF
## THE ENGLISH MONARCHY

The lineage chart on the following two pages covers twelve centuries and thirty-eight generations of English monarchs.

Note that the Danish kings – Sweyn Forkbeard, Canute, Harold Harefoot and Hardecanute – entered into the genealogy of the British royal family with King George V, whose mother, Queen Alexandra, was the daughter of King Christian IX of Denmark, a distant descendant of Sweyn Forkbeard and King Canute. Also, Charles, Prince of Wales (and Princes William and Harry), can claim descent from Sweyn Forkbeard and King Canute through the lineage of Charles's father, Philip, Duke of Edinburgh. Thus all future monarchs will be able to add this Danish descent.

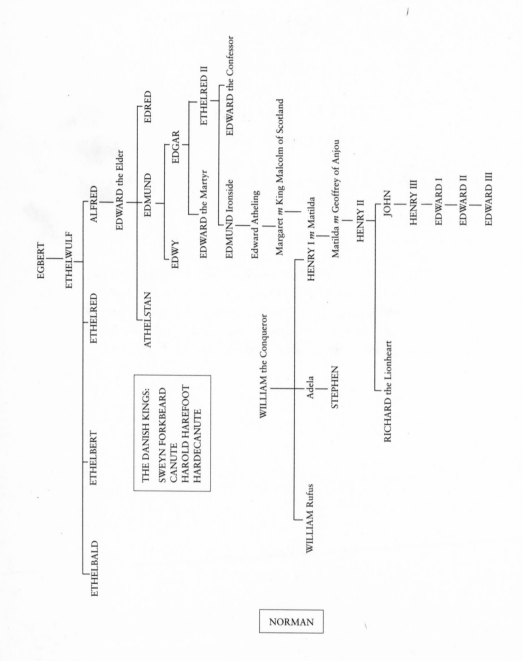

SAXON

PLANTAGENET

NORMAN

EGBERT

ETHELWULF

ETHELBALD

ETHELBERT

ETHELRED

ALFRED

EDWARD the Elder

ATHELSTAN

EDMUND

EDRED

EDWY

EDGAR

EDWARD the Martyr

ETHELRED II

EDMUND Ironside

EDWARD the Confessor

Edward Atheling

Margaret *m* King Malcolm of Scotland

HENRY I *m* Matilda

Matilda *m* Geoffrey of Anjou

HENRY II

JOHN

HENRY III

EDWARD I

EDWARD II

EDWARD III

RICHARD the Lionheart

WILLIAM the Conqueror

Adela

STEPHEN

WILLIAM Rufus

THE DANISH KINGS:
SWEYN FORKBEARD
CANUTE
HAROLD HAREFOOT
HARDECANUTE

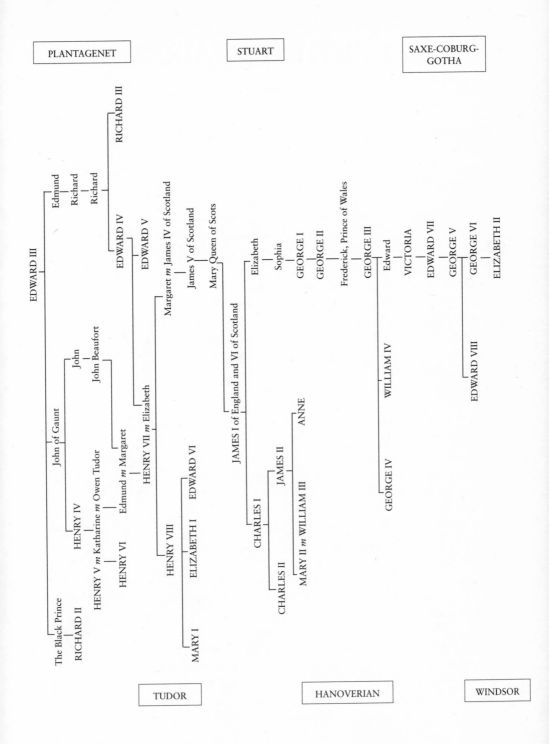

PLANTAGENET

STUART

SAXE-COBURG-GOTHA

EDWARD III

The Black Prince

RICHARD II

John of Gaunt

Edmund

HENRY IV

John

Richard

HENRY V *m* Katharine *m* Owen Tudor

John Beaufort

Richard

RICHARD III

HENRY VI

Edmund *m* Margaret

EDWARD IV

EDWARD V

HENRY VII *m* Elizabeth

Margaret *m* James IV of Scotland

James V of Scotland

Mary Queen of Scots

HENRY VIII

MARY I

ELIZABETH I

EDWARD VI

JAMES I of England and VI of Scotland

CHARLES I

CHARLES II

JAMES II

MARY II *m* WILLIAM III

ANNE

Elizabeth

Sophia

GEORGE I

GEORGE II

Frederick, Prince of Wales

GEORGE III

GEORGE IV

WILLIAM IV

Edward

VICTORIA

EDWARD VII

GEORGE V

EDWARD VIII

GEORGE VI

ELIZABETH II

TUDOR

HANOVERIAN

WINDSOR

# FURTHER READING

For anyone wishing to read more about any single monarch, possibly the best start is the series 'The Life and Times of . . .' under the general editorship of Antonia Fraser and published by Weidenfeld & Nicolson and Book Club Associates in 1972. Each book is by a different specialist historian and deals with just one monarch.

Ashdown, Dulcie M., *Royal Paramours*, Robert Hale, 1979

Brewer, Clifford, T.D., F.R.C.S., *The Death of Kings*, Abson Books, London, 2000

Brooke, Christopher, *The Saxon and Norman Kings*, Fontana, 1967

Bryant, Arthur, *King Charles II*, Longmans, 1931

Chapman, Hester W., *Lady Jane Grey*, Pan Books, 1972

Davey, Richard, *The Pageant of London*, Methuen, 1906

Fisher, Graham and Heather, *Monarchy and the Royal Family*, Robert Hale, 1979

Fraser, Antonia, *The Six Wives of Henry VIII*, Weidenfeld & Nicolson, 1992

Fulford, Roger, *Hanover to Windsor*, Fontana, 1966

Harvey, John, *The Plantagenets*, Fontana, 1970

Hilliam, David, *Monarchs, Murders and Mistresses*, Sutton, Stroud, 2000

——, *Crown, Orb and Sceptre*, Sutton, Stroud, 2001

Jones, Michael K., *Bosworth 1485, Psychology of a Battle*, Tempus, 2002

Kenyon, J.P., *The Stuarts*, Fontana, 1966

Lacey, Robert, *Majesty*, Hutchinson, 1977

Lofts, Norah, *Queens of Britain*, Hodder & Stoughton, 1977

Longford, Elizabeth (ed.), *The Oxford Book of Royal Anecdotes*, OUP, 1991

Morris, Christopher, *The Tudors*, Fontana, 1966

Oman, Sir Charles, *A History of England Before the Norman Conquest*, Methuen, 1924

Palmer, Alan and Veronica, *Royal England*, Methuen, 1983

Plumb, J.H., *The First Four Georges*, Fontana, 1966

Savage, Anne (trans.), *The Anglo-Saxon Chronicles*, Tiger Books International, 1995

Sitwell, Major General H.D.W., *The Crown Jewels and other Regalia in the Tower of London*, Dropmore Press, 1953

Stanley, Arthur, *Historical Memorials of Westminster Abbey*, John Murray, London, 1867

Strickland, Agnes, *Lives of the Queens of England*, G. Bell & Sons, 1911

Van der Kiste, John, *Queen Victoria's Children*, Sutton, Stroud, 1986

Wedgwood, C.V., *The Trial of Charles I*, William Collins, 1964

Weir, Alison, Elizabeth the Queen, Jonathan Cape, London, 1998

——, *Eleanor of Aquitaine*, Jonathan Cape, London, 1999

——, *Britain's Royal Families*, Pimlico, London, 2002

Windsor, H.R.H., the Duke of, *A King's Story*, Cassell, 1951

# INDEX